FORGOTTEN MUSICIANS

Forgotten Musicians

BY
PAUL NETTL

GREENWOOD PRESS, PUBLISHERS
NEW YORK

CONTENTS

v

FOREWORD

It is the aim of this book to recapture the memory of a number of musicians who have fallen into oblivion today. The first part is not only devoted to discussions of "forgotten" musicians, such as the old Jewish minstrels, but to certain individual musicians as well.

The second part may serve as source reading for the musician, the student of music, and the musicologist. While Dittersdorf's autobiography has been translated into English, the others are so presented here for the first time. Furthermore, this book marks the first appearance of Benda's autobiography in a modern edition in any language.

I am indebted to Professor Willi Kahl, from whose book, *Selbstbiographien deutscher Musiker*, I took the text for the autobiography of Quantz. This was particularly feasible since Professor Kahl presents the text in facsimile.

Others to whom I am indebted are Mr. Paul Mueller, who was responsible for the English translation of the Quantz autobiography, and also very helpful in reading the proofs and writing the index. I am also very grateful for the help of Mr. Walter Sorell and Mrs. Margaret Busch.

P. N.

PART ONE

CHAPTER ONE

HOW AUGUSTIN CHEATED THE PLAGUE WHILE JOHANN HEINRICH SCHMELZER SUCCUMBED

WE generally think of "the great Viennese classical school" as a highlight in the evolution of world music. The line of development can be followed from Gluck, Haydn and Mozart to Beethoven, thence traced to Schubert, Brahms and Bruckner, to Hugo Wolf and Gustav Mahler from whom it leads directly to our modern composers, Arnold Schoenberg and Alban Berg. But the great planets in the universe of music have their accompanying satellites. These lesser musicians often have special significance of their own. Some of them, on the other hand, owe their place in the history of music solely to the existence of those few musical giants.

Vienna could always boast of a popular art in addition to its "great art"; an art of the petit bourgeois next to that borne by the aristocrats and spiritual nobility. It is only natural that these two artistic trends became closely interwoven. Beethoven liked to imitate the fiddlers of the Vienna suburbs in his German dances. Schubert drew many a fine inspiration from the "Atzenburg" wine-fiddlers, and Brahms envied Johann Strauss his ideas—the ideas of the "musikalischesten Schaedel" (the most musical head) of Vienna.

The music of the Viennese classicists was born out of folk music, the tunes and dances which were sung and danced to in the Viennese suburbs Hernals and Alsergrund and in the villages along the Danube, in the Vienna Woods and in the mountains of Upper-Austria and Styria. For centuries Vienna had been the city of song and dance. Back in 1548, the musician and poet Wolfgang Schmeltzl wrote the following verses in the style of Hans Sachs:

> "Ich lob diss Ort fuer ander Land!
> Hie seind viel Saenger, saytenspiel,
> Allerlei gesellschaft, frewden viel.
> Mehr Musicos and Instrument
> Findt man gwisslich an khainem end,"

which praise "this place", namely Vienna, for its many singers and fiddlers, its many people and pleasures.

But how many of the singers of Viennese songs and dances are still known to us? It is true that the abovementioned Schmeltzl has acquainted us with a collection of quodlibets containing a total of over 370 melodic fragments ("Guter, seltzamer, und kunstreicher teutscher Gesang"), which gives us an idea of the types of songs and tunes sung in Vienna at that time (1544). But, on the whole, the composers' names as well as those of their interpreters have sunk into oblivion. From time to time we learn about the names and fates of these early singers from old tales and legends.

We know, for example, about the "Liebe Augustin", this legend-adorned figure of the well-known folk song which still enjoys world-wide popularity. He was a typical Viennese minstrel, wandering from house to house with his bagpipe, begging for alms, eking out a pitiful existence; however, he never lost his good humor. It is said that in 1679, the year in which the murderous plague raged in Vienna, Augustin was rescued from the "plague pit" (the common grave of all the plague-stricken victims who succumbed to the black death). Two old books claim this rescue as historical fact. The best known source is P. Fuhrmann's "Alt-und Neues Wien" (1739). This work is based on the writings of a Silesian law student, Joh. Konst. Feigius ("Wunderbahrer Adlers-Schwung") and also on the plague ordinances of the year 1679 which had been drawn up by Sorbait and Managetta, two Viennese doctors. Peter Fuhrmann tells how "someone by the name of Augustin, a bagpipe player" who had been found lying "in a state of advanced inebriation" somewhere between the Imperial castle and St. Ulrich and who had been picked up by the "Siechknechte", was loaded on a wagon and had then been thrown into the plague pit. He awoke next morning and wanted to climb out. His attempts remained fruitless, because the pit was quite deep and so he "cursingly" tramped around on the corpses

3

"until, at last, the 'Siechknechte' came at daybreak with their load of plague victims and helped him out; it seems that this night's lodging did not harm him in the very least."

The aforementioned Peter Fuhrmann also presents us with a list wherein he catalogues the professions of the victims claimed by the plague. A similar list can be found in "Merks Wien!", the work of Abraham a Santa Clara, that famous court chaplain, who filled his church, attracting thousands of people with his popular and often coarsely humorous sermons which, in their severity, did not spare even the most high-born aristocracy. He makes mention of the most noteworthy plague casualties; among them, however, no musician is included.

It seems that such common fiddlers, harpists, and itinerant bagpipe players as our Augustin were not worthy of being mentioned and mourned for, as were the respected and honored clergymen and townspeople, the university professors and the members of the aristocracy. The distinguished court musicians fled with the royal household and escaped the scourge of pestilence. But not for long were they safe from the plague which soon reached Prague where they had sought refuge.

What actually is the deeper meaning of the Augustin legend? It is nothing other than the ancient concept of the power of music. Orpheus with his lyre wins over the Gods of the underworld and succeeds, through his singing, in seeing his beloved again.

4

Tamino defies all dangers with his magic flute and finally wins his Pamina. This religious faith in the magical power of musical sounds, a belief so deeply rooted in the soul of man, had again taken shape, perhaps for the last time, in the legend of Augustin, that character of crass reality, of an age of death, despair and destruction.

> "O, du lieber Augustin
> Alles ist hin!"
> (O, my dear Augustin,
> everything's lost!)

In the Managetta-Sorbait plague ordinance, the Augustin story differs in a few details. It tells of a bagpipe player who had fallen asleep in a tavern and, mistaken as a plague victim, had been thrown into the plague pit on top of all the uncovered corpses. When Augustin awoke, he felt the dead bodies around him, but, believing them to be his boon companions, he took out his pipes and started to play a tune, which scared to death the corpse-bearers, who had meanwhile arrived with "a fresh load".

The intermarriage of city music and rustic elements finds expression in the musical passages of his bagpipe song; we can find these passages not only in contemporary manuscripts, but also in the "Dictionaire de Musique", published by Rousseau, where they appear almost note for note under the name of "Kuhreigen". "Der liebe Augustin" had, in fact brought his melody from the mountain country and we can be fairly sure that it proved no novelty to the cityfolk. This air had been handed down from generation to generation for centuries. We also find written evidence in several Viennese manuscripts of Augustin's days—songs and dance tunes which are quite similar to his famous song. There must have been many others like this drunkard who, as he, were neither inclined nor interested in noting down the favorite songs of the Viennese.

We speak symbolically of the "Liebe Augustin" as having brought the yodel and bagpipe tunes from the country to the city. At the same time, Schmelzer was reputedly the first to stylize this musical language of the Viennese Bierfiedler (beerfiddlers) and Baenkelsaenger (streetsingers) adapting it for court consumption and making it an integral part of music as an art. He was also the first to record on paper the genuine Viennese dancing tunes.

Schmelzer was born in 1623. His father was a soldier in the service of the emperor and had fought against the rebels in the battle "am weissen Berg" (1620). He was a typical soldier of the Thirty Years War and finally gave his life in line of duty. It might well be that from the hundreds of military songs and marches brought home by this soldier that his son received his strong inclination toward the popular music of the people. With regard to the boy's early education we conjecture that he may have become the pupil of some court musician—possibly Giovanni Samsoni—when no older than 10 or 12. During his boyhood he also sang as choir boy in the court chapel and, after his voice changed, he was "apprenticed to" the violinist Burkhart Kugler. The "master musician" received 30 fl. for the training of young musicians. This tuition was paid by the court and included room and board unless the pupil happened to be a guest at the royal dinner table.

Schmelzer married at an early age. His wife bore him six children. Andreas Anton the first born, followed in his father's footsteps as composer of dance music for the court. After Kaiser Ferdinand III's death, the emperor's successor also took over the court orchestra and with it Schmelzer, the Imperial court musician. Leopold loved to take along his "Kapelle" on his travels. In 1665, on a journey to Innsbruck, Schmelzer and some of his colleagues accompanied the emperor. His Majesty reported good-humoredly how much he had enjoyed himself at an opera performance which had been staged in his honor, while the royal party was enjoying an opulent dinner. At that time, M. A. Cesti, the famous Venetian, was Kapellmeister at Innsbruck. It was there that Schmelzer made his acquaintance and when Cesti was later called on contract to Vienna, Schmelzer, who in the meantime had been advanced to the official post of dance composer, wrote a vast number of ballets for Cesti's operas.

Schmelzer's fame as violinist soon spread over all of Germany and before long over the whole of Europe. As far back as 1660, he was labeled the "most famous and almost the most distinguished violinist in all of

Europe" by Joh. Joachim Mueller in the latter's "Reise-Diarium bey Kayserlicher Belehnung des Chur und fuerstl. Hauses Sachsen". No other violinist had ever before resorted to "such high regions on the finger-board" as did he in the fast passages of his sonatas composed in 1664. This "Sonate unarum fidium seu a violino solo" was preceded by two other works: "Duodena selectarum Sonatarum" (1659, six of them for two violins, three for violin and viola da gamba), and "Sacroprofanus concentus musicus fidium aliorumque instrumentorum" (1662), a collection of one movement orchestral canzones in the style of Gabrieli, an orchestral form which enjoyed widespread popularity in Vienna until late into the 18th century.

In 1671 Schmelzer was promoted to the post of Imperial Vice-Kapellmeister. It had been his duty ever since 1665 to furnish the appropriate music for all operas performed at the court and also for all the manifold court festivities, such as "Wirtschaften", "Landschaften", "Schaefereien", peasant weddings, contests, and sleigh rides; in short, whenever dance or instrumental music was needed, it was Schmelzer who wrote the music demanded by the occasion.

The majority of these dance tunes has been preserved in the so-called Particello (for upper voice and bass) in two voluminous manuscripts at the Vienna Nationalbibliothek, while they, in orchestrated form are to be found in the Kremsier archives. In those days, Karl Liechtenstein-Kastelkorn was "Fuerstbischof" of

Olmuetz, but he spent most of the summer months at his castle in Kremsier which he had built for himself. He had a special liking for Schmelzer's dance tunes. This bishop (1664-1669) was the prototype of a highly cultured Austrian aristocrat. He had studied in Innsbruck as well as Ingolstadt and lived in Salzburg before he assumed his episcopal duties.

He had a strong predilection for splendorous court festivities and both Olmuetz and Kremsier became the scene of many a sumptuous peasant wedding or "Wirtschaft". The Moravian dignitaries were among the steady guests at these extravaganzas at which no cost was spared. The dance music needed for these festive occasions was commissioned from our friend Schmelzer in Vienna with whom the bishop entered into an amusing correspondence which often struck a "somewhat gossipy" note. On one occasion, the bishop sent Schmelzer a jar of drippings as a sign of appreciation and gratitude; Schmelzer returned the kindness with a present of Vienna "Faschingskrapfen" (the world famous Viennese jelly doughnuts). One can deduce from mutual relations such as these that the high aristocracy deemed Schmelzer worthy of social intercourse.

In 1665 Schmelzer's wife passed away and, after remaining a widower for a few years, he remarried in 1668. In this new marriage Schmelzer became the father of five more children. As fate would have it, it was Schmelzer who did all the work at the Hofkapelle, while others reaped his deserved glory. The two men who got the better of him were the Italian Kapellmeister Felice Sances and Antonio Bertali. In those days, only foreign-born musicians were held in high esteem; the prejudice against homebred talent reached such proportions that it took two years of careful premeditation on the emperor's part, before he decided to make Schmelzer Vice-Kapellmeister. Finally, in the year 1671 the promotion came through. Let us look at the position of an "official Kapellmeister" and see exactly what duties it embraced. He was the consultant on musical matters to both the "Obersthofmeister" (head steward) and the emperor. It was his responsibility to give his opinion when it came to considering the applicants for musical positions; in this connection it was not sufficient to merely evaluate their artistic qualifications, but in addition also their financial and social position, their ambition, conduct, allegiance to the throne, etc. He was also in charge, to a certain extent at least, of the financial accounts of the Kapelle. Frequently it was he who had to make the honorary contributions to visiting musicians upon whom the emperor wanted to bestow a special honor.

The Kapellmeister often had a difficult time with the hot-headed and undisciplined musicians of the orchestra and quite frequently he had to settle the quarrels that arose. The understandable jealousy between Italian and German musicians which had grown into a traditional rivalry as early as then, and which persists to some extent in our day, often resulted in violent arguments and even physical violence. In such cases the Kapellmeister had to intervene. In this respect, one should keep in mind the dilemma of the poor Kapellmeister who was truly between the devil and the deep blue sea. On the one hand he was the confidant of the court, attempting to safeguard the court finances which were usually in a pitiful state; on the other, he had to protect the interests of his colleagues. In addition to all this, the Kapellmeister acted as the official court composer. He had to attend to the church music and to the opera scores as well as supply the ballet music for the opera written by the Italian head-Kapellmeister. Last but not least, he played the solo violin part at the intimate chamber music performances. One can well imagine then, how overburdened such a court musician must have been!

It had long been the custom at the Vienna court that the Italian court Kapellmeister also acted as chief court composer. It was he who was supposed to compose the music for operas. The writing of the entr'acte ballet music, however, was delegated to the lower-ranking ballet composers. Thus it was Wolfgang Ebner (1612-1665) who supplied the ballets for the operas of Bertali, who was Hof-Kapellmeister and chief court composer and who reigned over the musical activities at the time when Schmelzer joined the court. Schmelzer succeeded Ebner as ballet composer, writing a wealth of mostly short dances in the then "popular" style. He wrote these dances for all the operas of Cesti, the famous representative of Venetian opera, as well as for all of Ant. Draghi's (1635-1700) operas.

The arrival of the Emperor's bride, the Spanish princess Margarita, on January 24, 1667, occasioned the world famous performance of the "Balletto à cavallo" (Equestrian Ballet) at the Vienna Burghof. The vocal parts were composed by Bertali, while Schmelzer supplied the instrumental sections of the ballet, consisting of a Courante, a Giga, an Allemande and a Saraband. Shortly thereafter a performance of another equestrian ballet took place—"La Germania esultante". Again Cesti and Schmelzer collaborated, subdividing the composer's tasks in the same manner as before.

Glancing over Schmelzer's many dance tunes, we are invariably struck by their popular melodies. In addition to the Allemandes, Courantes and Gigues we come across a new type of Viennese or Austrian dance, filled with alpine elements and yodel phrases which remind one of the "Laendler" and waltzes by Lanner and Johann Strauss. Schmelzer was obviously the first one to capture the alpine folklore in his "Viennese arias". These dances stand in crass contrast to the stiffly graceful gavottes and minuets. What a vivid picture to imagine the counts and earls swinging the ladies, their skirts swirling, to the sound of these popular dance tunes. After all, was it not a prerogative of the aristocracy on such events to cast aside the formal Spanish ceremonial and assume the roles of the unsophisticated peasantry? And were not Schmelzer's dances just the thing for that purpose?

In 1679, Kapellmeister Sances died, and the situation was such that no one but Schmelzer could have become his successor. Schmelzer's relationship with Emperor Leopold had grown to be so cordial, his repute so high that truly no one else might have been considered for the job. However, he was not to enjoy his new post for long.

It is in this connection that Schmelzer's fate ran opposite to that of the "Liebe Augustin", the musical vagabond. It was in those days that the murderous plague broke out, felling, as is historically authenticated, thousands upon thousands of Viennese, but miraculously sparing that legendary street musician. The Imperial court and its retinue left Vienna and fled to Bohemia. They took up temporary residence at the Hradschin in Prague and led an easy life. But the "Black Death" rode fast, without stopping at the gates of the Bohemian capital. The emperor found himself compelled to transfer his quarters to Brandeis on the Elbe, about 30 miles outside of Prague. A severe quarantine was put into effect; all schools were closed and the Imperial residence remained in a state of complete segregation from the outer world. In spite of that state of affairs, or possibly just because of it, the exiled court indulged in festivities.

With the special purpose of cheering up the royal party, a burlesque opera ("Scherzo dramatico") was performed. Draghi supplied the music for "La Pati-

enza di Socrate con due moglie", a comic opera
which was the first work of its kind to be performed
in Bohemia. Through sheer coincidence its dance
tunes composed by Schmelzer have been preserved.
We are not sure whether this ballet music which was
performed in Prague in 1680, was part of this comic
opera; it might also have been the incidental music
for some carnival festivity—in which the royal party
indulged, while the plague raged on the "Kleinseite"
and the Prague "Alstadt" . . .

Schmelzer did not return from Prague to Vienna.
Undoubtedly, he fell victim to the ravages of the
plague. He was a man who never forgot the light
and humorous side of his existence and occupation
over the more serious aspects of life and art. He had
made quite a name for himself and the abundance
of his compositions had netted him a tidy sum. Among
the pieces of property listed in his legacy we find a
house and a vineyard as well as a multitude of gold
and silver household utensils and medals. It appears
that one of his main sources of income stems from a
goodly amount of fine Austrian wine. I call attention
to this fact because it seems to bear out a close relationship to the special nature of Schmelzer's muse.
Schmelzer, the man as well as his Vienna, are mirrored in his genuinely Austrian folk dances with
their alpine "Laendler" melodies and pounding rhythms, so deeply rooted in the Styrian and Tyrolese
alps and in the valleys of Upper-and-Lower-Austria.

Until recently, Weber's "Invitation to the Dance"

and possibly Joh. Sebastian Bach's "Laendler-styled" overture to his Peasant cantata were looked upon as being the first representatives of the waltz form. It was Schmelzer though who had taken the popular alpine melodies based on the triad and had introduced them into the realm of "art" music. I have elaborated on this subject in my work about the dance music of Vienna during the latter 17th century and also in my book, "The Story of Dance Music". In these works I have designated Schmelzer as the first Viennese dance composer, the "Johann Strauss of the Baroque". His name is not one to be omitted in the ranks of "forgotten musicians".

It is not without premeditation that I have put the name of the "Liebe Augustin" next to Schmelzer's, strange bedfellows indeed, in one and the same chapter. The former—a wretched musician of whose life we know only his name and fate's strange amnesty allowing him to "return from the dead" in the plague pit; the other—his contemporary—caught in the merciless grip of pestilence in his attempt to seek refuge with the fleeing Austrian court. Both these men were fiddlers and each a devotee of popular music. One of them a pathetic scraper, the other a great artist on the violin. And yet both drew their inspiration from the same source—the wealth of Austrian folk music. The familiar Augustin tune, which he probably played on the pipes every day, found its way, in a slightly modified version, into the dances of Schmelzer, the true founder of the "Viennese School".

Their rich vigorous melodiousness continues to live in the symphonies of Haydn and Mozart, in the dances of Franz Schubert and in those of the great Waltz King, Johann Strauss.

CHAPTER TWO

HEINRICH FRANZ BIBER,
A GREAT AUSTRIAN VIOLINIST
OF THE BAROQUE

HE was the son of a simple guncharger in the service of Count Liechtenstein-Kastelkorn whose estate and beautiful baroque castle were situated in the vicinity of Reichenberg, near the little town of Wartenberg in northern Bohemia. There he was born on August 12, 1644. It is highly probable that his father too had been a "musical servant", as was often the case in Bohemia during the 17th and 18th centuries, since the Bohemian and Austrian nobility of that time were in the habit of only employing such valets, hunters, grooms, footmen and lackeys as could carry a part in the orchestra or who knew how to blow a merry trumpet call for the chase.

There lived in the little town of Wartenberg a musician who was somewhat of a drunkard. His name was Weigant Knoefel, a member of a Silesian or Bohemian musician's dynasty. I believe that it was this Knoefel who became little Heinrich Franz' first music teacher. The boy may have taken to the road afterwards. His travels probably took him to Vienna, Prague, and Styria, because he reputedly entered the service of "the younger princes of Eggenberg in Styria" according to historical sources.

At the age of 22 he was a mature musician and violin virtuoso as well as composer and Kapellmeister in the service of Fuerstbischof (bishop of princely rank) Karl Liechtenstein-Kastelkorn in Olmuetz, Moravia. His duties consisted of composing orchestral masses, litanies, and church sonatas in addition to various chamber works for church performances. He was also obligated to function as the violin soloist whenever his talents were needed. The Fuerstbischof, however, was not exclusively interested in church music. In his Olmuetz castle and in his summer residence Kremsier chamber music was frequently performed; on nice evenings, the magnificent parks with their bizarre statues of Biblical and Greek mythological origin resounded with the delicate suites and ballet music of the time. Quite often a scaffold was erected over the pond of the park and a complete stage set upon it. This became the scene of the "divertimento" (a short drama performance) which took place on the occasion of the Emperor's birthday or the bishop's name-day. Usually three or four persons dramatized a humorous incident which had occurred on the estate. Sometimes a short opera of mythological or historical subject matter composed by Biber was presented instead.

The sonorous orchestral sonatas for string, brass, or woodwind instruments resounded from all sections of the park. These sonatas, composed for several parts and modelled after the festive sonatas of the Venetian Gabrieli, sounded like enchanted echoes. In the same way that baroque taste was dissatisfied with trees, bushes and flowers as they grew in the fields and forests and consequently insisted on symmetrical arrangements in artistic gardens, so the music of the period too had to be fraught with meaningful and stylistic effects—the ingenious and artistic echoes in the orchestra.

Many of Biber's charming open-air compositions have been preserved for posterity.

Once Biber performed one of his works, a serenade containing a Gavotte, Allemande, Saraband, Chaconne and a Retirade. Suddenly in the middle of the Chaconne, the voice of the night-watchman was heard in the familiar call (stylized by Wagner in his "Meistersinger"), while the artistically composed Chaconne continued with a pizzicato accompaniment played by the violins.

These baroque princes really knew how to enjoy life to the fullest in spite of being bishops or archbishops—or perhaps just because of it!

The Fuerstbischof himself conducted the grand masses which Biber delivered to him. The bishop laid stress upon having the musical parts of the service well regulated and he was a pious priest who austerely guarded the salvation of his flock. This, however, did not diminish his concern about putting up a grand front in secular matters. At carnival time he sponsored great balls, masquerades, peasant weddings, sleigh rides and other festivities. Again it was Biber who was commissioned to compose all the appropriate allemandes, courantes, sarabands and gigues, the trezze, canarii, passe-pieds, minuets, branles, gavottes and Viennese arias demanded by the occasion. The majority of these dances has been preserved for modern times.

Biber's day must have been a busy one as can be concluded from the great wealth of compositions which he turned out. He performed his own violin sonatas, conducted the orchestra and wrote all the church music; it is not at all unlikely that in addition to his musical duties, Biber was called upon to perform diplomatic missions at the court. The bishop was at that time carrying on the aforementioned correspondence with Johann Heinrich Schmelzer. In one of his letters to the Viennese Kapellmeister, the bishop wrote that Biber left Olmuetz with one "ejusdem qualitatis et conditionis insalutato hospite", meaning that he had taken "French leave". Presumably Biber had found the demand put upon him too trying and the bishop's pay was probably not any too satisfactory either!

One can well imagine the bishop's indignation at his Kapellmeister's conduct. In fact, the bishop issued a sort of warrant against him in which he instructed his deputy in the Tyrol (where Biber and his companion had fled) to seize the fugitive. At that time, Biber stayed with the violin maker Jacobus Stainer in Absam where he tried out the master's wonderful violins. When still in the service of the bishop, Biber had ordered for his master a whole set of violins from Stainer, well-known as the artistic German violin maker.

Making Absam his center of operation, Biber now attempted to secure a new position and he had little trouble finding one. His new employer was Max Gandolph, Archbishop of Salzburg. The life he led at his new position was typical of that of any musician of his day in the service of a nobleman. He became a duly installed court musician, much like Leopold Mozart who served at the same court some hundred years later. In 1672 he settled down, marrying Maria Weiss, the daughter of a Salzburg citizen and merchant. Biber enjoyed the highest esteem of his fellow citizens; he also won the favor of Archbishop Max Gandolph von Kuenburg as well as that of his successor, Count Johann Ernst von Thun, a member of a well-known noble Bohemian family, who assumed his office as archbishop in 1687.

In those times, Biber's reputation as a musician was uncontested. In the year 1683, the raging plague in Vienna caused Emperor Leopold I to take up temporary residence in Linz and in the cloister Lambach. During his sojourn, the emperor, himself an accomplished composer, invited Biber to perform for him and to play "violin soli". Biber's musical achievements later merited him a title of nobility. The official diploma issued in 1690, extols his qualities as follows: "Honesty, sincerity, good breeding, virtue and common sense, especially as applies to his music which he brought to the highest perfection... and his manifold artistic compositions have spread his fame widely."

Now let us ask: how was the financial situation of a recognized musician such as Biber? We gain insight into this subject through an act dating from the year 1700. He drew a monthly salary of sixty florins (approximately equivalent to $60....). In addition he received a daily ration of 2/4 Austrian wine (about one bottle) from the Archbishop's wine cellar and four "sembl" (rolls) equivalent to about 100 florins and 10 kronen; furthermore, 12 Klafter firewood (10 fl.) as well as free board. Altogether he received the equivalent of 852 fl. 10 kr. At that time, Biber was in charge of 35 musicians in addition to two kettledrummers, eight trumpeters and twelve to eighteen choir boys.

We have very little information about Biber's later years. We do know that he was bestowed with a variety of honors and granted all kinds of privileges which seem absurd and ridiculous to us today, but which undoubtedly meant a great deal to the artist of that time. We cannot help but feel a bit amazed when we glance through the text of his promotion dating from the year 1679 (which incidentally went in effect):

"In most gracious recognition of his faithful services, we hereby propitiously bestow upon our Vice-Kapellmeister and servant, the dear and faithful Heinrich Franz Biber, the honor of occupying the official rank immediately below that of our superintendents and judges of the superior court in Chiembsee, St. Peter and Numberg, who are not members of the council."

Biber's legacy also contained a number of chains of honor and other gifts. He died on May 3, 1704, and was buried the next day in the cemetery of St. Peter.

Biber was looked upon as one of the leading, if not *the* most outstanding German violinist of his time. His violin and orchestral sonatas were praised highly. Johann Mattheson, the critic and *Arbiter Musicae* of the epoch, mentions in his gallery of famous musicians (published in 1740 under the name of "Ehrenpforte"): "In the Emperor's patrimonial dominions as well as in France and Italy, his compositions have earned him the highest esteem wherever they were played."

A collection of Biber's violin sonatas were put into print and published in 1681 by Lohner in Nuremberg. Still a more famous collection of which only a handwritten copy is preserved, contains sonatas which depict the mysteries of Jesus and the Virgin Mary. It is an early document of a most peculiar kind of program music. To each sonata an etching is prefixed which is a graphic presentation of the particular Biblical scene which the composer portrayed in music. Here we see the true expression of the baroque spirit, very much in the vein of lyric poetry of that time, as exemplified in the songs and poems of the Jesuit Father Schnueffis, in which we find a wondrous intermarriage of pictures, music and poetry to form an impressive entity.

Biber resorted to the so-called "Scordatura" in his sonatas. This artistic device of the Baroque period called for an "out-of-tune" adjustment of the violin strings by one or more intervals. Through this process, strange and bizarre sounds could be produced. One is led to believe that the composer and his audience were not satisfied with the natural capacity of the violin and consequently aimed at creating artificial scales and unusual harmonies. Such idiosyncrasies may very well be likened to the unnatural voices of the castrati who were literally worshipped during the Baroque era.

Biber did not always play in the natural manner like the Italians Corelli, Veracini, Torelli, etc. Although he was quite fond of the loud tone on the E string, he preferred playing on several strings at once in a harmonic fashion to which the scordatura lent itself so well. His violins—mostly the product of the Tyrolean Stainer—had a low bridge, much lower than in the modern instruments, and his bow was never taut. This enabled him to produce mystic-harmonic effects, such as we no longer practice. Certain pieces, written in three voices, with bold runs, parallel progressions of sixths, thirds, and other polyphonic means, surely served as a model for Bach's famous sonatas. Biber's sonatas are filled with a certain mysticism which has given rise to all sorts of speculations.

We find in many of his sonatas a profoundly expressive art, making an interpretation stimulating, challenging, even exciting. The same may be said about his orchestral sonatas (preserved only in the handwritten original manuscript), among which the "Harmonia Romana" ranks highest, a work of expressive instrumental recitatives and abounding with bold virtuosity. The German musicologist Arnold Schering had already pointed out emphatically the esoteric - programmatic quality of the "Mystery Sonatas". The sixth sonata of this collection, the "Oelberg Sonata" is especially indicative of Biber's art which may not have been a unique phenomenon of his day, but which is certainly difficult to comprehend and to interpret for our modern generation.

In fact, it seems that, in this sonata, Biber superimposes musical phrases directly originating from the text of the Gospel of St. Matthew, namely the text: "Patermi, si possibile est, transeat a me calix iste." The continuation of the Biblical scene, the walking, falling down, the repeated prayers, the sleeping of the disciples, is expressively represented. We discover such programmatic tendencies also in the tenth sonata depicting the crucifixion of Christ, symbolized by dotted triplets, expressing the physical pain of the Saviour, whereas a following contemplative "aria" reminds us of the function of the chorale in the Passion. We meet this rare symbolism in the slow sections of the sonatas, a symbolism pointing directly to Bach.

In another sonata the resurrection is shown by the introduction of a hymn of resurrection. In another one, representing the emanation of the Holy Ghost, the atmosphere is symbolized by parallel runs of thirty-second notes. The last sonata, no. 16, is an addition by Biber, since there are only 15 mysteries. The engraving shows a guardian angel leading a child by the hand. It is a "Passacaglia" based on the descending tetrachord. Biber evidently had in mind the symbolization of this religious idea by introducing a "basso ostinato" which runs through the whole composition, indicating the permanent presence of the guardian angel. Just as the guardian angel, faith does not leave man,—so the ostinato continues throughout the piece.

There is a strong probability that in many instrumental compositions of the 17th century, in sonatas, symphonies, concertos composed for the church, certain religious ideas are expressed, according to the designation and time of the performance.

Biber wrote orchestral sonatas for the day of St. Joseph, St. Polycarp, the Holy Virgin, etc., and I believe that in writing these works the composer was impressed by ideas from the lives and activities of those Saints. This esoteric mysticism, however, seems to have disappeared in the later part of the 18th century, and with it also our ability to enjoy that music according to its designation.

The outstanding compositions of Biber should be

revived, and violinists should pay the greatest attention to the works of this great forgotten composer.

CHAPTER THREE

THE UNKNOWN JEWISH MINSTREL

IN his autobiography, Franz Benda (1709-1786), the excellent violinist and composer, tells of his father's occupation as fiddler in his native town of Alt-Benatek near Prague and also of the village band headed by Lebel, the blind old Jew. It is to this blind man that Benda owes "the fine tone which he took such great pains to develop", according to a short biographical sketch of his life. His autobiographical writings give testimony of his indebtedness to early musical impressions and to the village dances for his rhythmical precision and exactitude.

The Jewish musician typified by Lebel is a character who for centuries has been indigenous to Germany and especially to the Slavic countries. The following pages are dedicated to his memory.

Those Jews who have lived in the diaspora since the destruction of the Temple have tenaciously adhered to their religious tradition; in many respects, however, they have adopted the customs and ways of life of those people among whom they were forced to live. It is therefore quite understandable that their contribution to the "higher aspects of music" was inconsequential during the Middle Ages, since this type of music was a prerogative of the Church at that period. But as soon as music began to hold its own outside the churches, monasteries and *cantoria,* Jewish names make their appearance among the musicians.

One of the earliest representatives is the Jewish minstrel Suesskind von Trimberg, a German Minnesinger. An illustration in the famous "Manesse Liederhandschrift" shows him garbed in sumptuous Jewish costume. He has a long beard, and on his head we see a pointed hat. Next to his picture we find that of a bishop with mitre and crosier. The juxtaposition of these two pictures suggests an attempt at religious conversion which, in all likelihood, remained unsuccessful. On the other hand, the two pictures might signify an allusion to the Church patronage of Jews which was an exigency during the Middle Ages.

All we know about Suesskind's life is his year of birth, 1220, and his native village, Trimberg near Wuerzburg. His songs, though formally quite similar to those of other German Minnesingers, are nevertheless an unmistakable product of the Jewish spirit. Suesskind is not satisfied with attacking his enemies, the Jew baiters; he also takes up the cause of the poor and oppressed. It is understood that he felt little spiritual kinship for the romantic-Christian Minne ideals, nor for the idealization of the Virgin Mary. In its place he adheres to the traditional chanting of the **Psalms** and to the ideals of the 11th and 12th centuries of Hebrew poetry.

> "The purest female is the spirit of the man.
> She is his honor and his greatest pride.
> The beauty of his house would be of no avail,
> If the woman were not its soul inside.
> Together with his faithful wife, he may
> Thus spend his life in joy most happily,
> Her light will brighten every sombre day.
> I'll sing her praise as long as I shall be."

As is apparent from the picture in the "Manesse Liederhandschrift", Suesskind led the life of a minstrel wandering from castle to castle. One may well imagine the many humiliations and degradations that were heaped upon the wandering musician. Many of the Jewish readers will surely be able to sympathize with Suesskind's song:

> "I want to grow a beard,
> Long must it be, its hair quite gray.
> And then I'll go through life the way
> The Jews have always gone:
> Wrapped in a cape, billowy and long;
> Deep under the hat hiding my face;
> Meek and with a humble song;
> Bare of God's grace."

One of his poems gives evidence of Suesskind's role as "Lezim" (mockers)[1], those Jewish satirical comedians who, in the mask of fools, often spoke the truth in its unpleasant nakedness. These Lezim were invariably present at every Jewish family celebration.

---

[1]The author is aware that "Lezim" is a plural form. It is used here as a singular in keeping with general usage.

Suesskind once sang the following verses:

> "Jew, what are you singing?" I could hear him yell.
> Did he refer to me? How can I tell?
> "You daring singer," 'twas the voice again,
> "Do not forget, I am a mighty nobleman!"
> But words make Suesskind not afraid.
> His heart filled with contempt, he said:
> "Noble is he who does but noble deeds,
> His feelings are credentials of nobility.
> But I despise the showy cloak of aristocracy
> On which the shame of sin still bleeds.
> The chaff flies off, the golden wheat remains.
> Let's do away with noblemanish bluff!
> The man who nobly thinks is made of better stuff
> And gives us better fruits on higher planes.
> No matter where his cradle stood,
> Let only be his heartbeat good
> And let him plan his life as only virtue can
> And I shall honor him as nobleman."

Was Suesskind's music influenced in some respect by old Hebrew music? We have no way of knowing, since unfortunately none of it has been preserved.

* * *

Like distant lights in the night, the names of Jewish musicians emerge occasionally from the dark shadows of the Middle Ages. According to the historian of literature, Friedrich Wilhelm Arnold, it was supposedly a Jew, Woelffle von Locham, who deserves the credit for the authorship of the famous "Lochamer Liederbuch" (approximately 1450), one of the oldest monuments of German vocal polyphony. This book of songs bears a Hebrew dedication from Woelffle to his wife. In particular reference to this dedication, Arnold, in his thesis advances a strong argument in

31

favor of his contention. He claims that the author of this world famous dedication must undoubtedly have been a Jew, since at about 1450 only those of Jewish origin understood the Hebrew language. Even the philologist Reuchlin, who included Hebrew among his linguistic studies some fifty years later, had to learn this language from a Jew. Arnold's thesis was opposed by the philologist Johann Janssen who championed the friar Jodocus von Winshofen as the principal contributor to the book and only concedes that Jodocus may have drafted this book for a citizen of Nuremberg, *Woelflein* von Lochamer and his (possibly) Jewish wife Barbara. But—it can rightly be held against it—it is very unlikely that in those days a baptized Jewess would receive a Hebrew dedication. Arnold's thesis still stands as valid, having withstood the onslaught of many challenging arguments.

At the dawn of the Renaissance, Italy too produced a few Jewish musicians whose names remain shining lights in the history of music. In Germany, however, the Jewish minstrels led an obscure existence. They were called "Kahle Bierfiedler" and only asked to play at weddings and christenings. On such occasions they were forced to play through all of the night in order to make a bare living and, because of such "unfair" practices, they incurred the jealousy and hatred of their non-Jewish fellow musicians.

"A maximum of four musicians are to be permitted at any wedding.... Should any Lezim play longer, he will not be employed for one full year there-after,"—to quote from the "Juedische Denkwuerdig-keiten", 1717, of the Frankfurt citizen Schudt who also gives an explanation of the word "Lezim": "The Jews heap abuse upon such musicos as are rightfully called 'Mesaurim' (singers) by calling them 'Lezzanim' which means mockers. . . ."

He further explains that this expression was con-nected with the fact that the old true Hebraic music had been lost and that the new one was at best a poor imitation.

Let us see how these old "Lezim", these Jewish "Bierfiedler", actually played. In an old book about Jewish ceremonies (P. Ch. Kirchner's "Juedisches Ceremoniell", published in Nurmberg, 1734) we find an etching depicting a wedding procession which is headed by two fiddlers and one cellist. The Berlin Kupferstichkabinet (permanent etching exhibition) has as one of its pieces an etching entitled "An accur-ate presentation of a Jewish wedding" (at about 1700). Here again we find the same number and types of instruments. This is in fact the primitive orchestra-tion of the "Bauernkapelle" (peasant bands), com-mon during the 17th and 18th century. Mozart still designates two violins and bass for the peasant band in his "Don Giovanni". Let us also keep in mind that it is this very orchestration which is common in the trio sonatas of the 17th and 18th centuries and in the orchestral trios of the 18th century.

The Jewish bands in Bohemia, above all in Prague,

seem to have enjoyed particularly great fame. Going back as far as the 16th century we find reports about the excellence of these Jewish bands. In Wenzel Březan's biography of the Bohemian nobleman Peter Wok von Rosenberg there is mention of a Jewish band playing magnificently for the dance. These bands were an old institution in Bohemia. In the year 1641, the Archbishop of Prague granted permission to Jewish bands to play at Christian weddings and christenings. Ever since then there seems to have arisen a violent struggle between the Jewish and non-Jewish musicians. This fight must have laid heavy demands on the Bohemian governors judging by the wealth of official documents accumulated in the archives of the Czechoslovakian government. Public opinion seemed to have favored the Jews and it was of little avail that the gentile musicians turned against their hated competitors and announced in 1651 that the Jews "confused and obstructed all music, neglected to play in time and rhythm and mockingly robbed the noble art of music of its intrinsic value. Furthermore, they possess no composers of their own and consequently imitate Christian music in an abominable fashion...."

The aforementioned Schudt speaks in another part of his writings about a patriotic pageant (staged in Prague in 1716 in celebration of the birth of the Emperor's son). At this celebration a Jewish band consisting of 19 trumpets, 8 violins, 4 French horns and 4 kettle drums took part in the festivities. Also assisting was "an organ built by Rabbi Maier Mahler." Finally a German song ("Teutsch Lied", as Schudt called it) was sung by a certain Isaac Bass whose name, said Schudt, stems from the fact that "he sang the bass part and aspired to be a good bass."

Although we are told by Hebrew scholars that the Jewish name Bass (Basch) ought to be explained differently, we should not dismiss Schudt's interpretation entirely. Perusing the files of the Czecho-Slovakian Government Archives, I came across a roster listing the names of some 17th century Prague musicians. To mention a few:

Loebel Bass (bass)
Joachim Trebes (treble)
Loesser Zimbal (harpsichordist)
Loeb Klaffzimmer (harpsichordist)
Joachim Krummholz (lute player; Krummhals means curved neck in German)
Seelig Fiedler (fiddler)

It is a matter of fact that such names as Bass, Fiedler, and even Zimbalist occur frequently in Central Europe. They are professional names whose earliest bearers were musicians. The "Specification der juedischen Spielleute" mentions treble and bass singers and thus makes it clear that these musicians were not exclusively instrumentalists. We know very little about the musical pieces which were played and depend for all of our knowledge on a few but nevertheless significant documents. Idelsohn calls to attention the collection "Simchat Hannefeth", the first known collection of Hebraic-Ashkenazic chants printed (words and music) in Fuerth in 1727. The poems are Jewish-German and were written by a certain Elchonon-Henle Kirchhain. The music is believed to have been composed by professional musicians. These melodies are quite like the German songs and dances of the 17th and 18th centuries and a few of them call to mind the operas and cantatas of Ant. Caldara and the dance tunes of J. H. Schmelzer, while others draw upon 16th century folk tunes. Some of the tunes are reminiscent of the songs found in Valentin Rathgeber's "Augsburger Tafelkonfekt", an anthology published in 1733. But we also find certain songs which remind us somehow of the old oriental tradition of Judaism.

The constant contact between Germans, Poles and Hungarians had eventually brought about an Eastern influence. Does not the well-known chant sung on "Shavuoth" bear a certain resemblance to a still popular and well known Hungarian dance?

An analysis of the melody sung at the New-Moon festival brings to light its decided oriental origin.

We may assume that the Jewish minstrels also embellished those song and dance tunes, which they had taken over from the Christian world, with all kinds of chromatic passing tones. They presumably employed these passing tones to an excessive degree—in the so-called gypsy scale—imitating the traditionally familiar synagogue chants. They also resorted to strange rhythmical patterns and in particular to rubato-tempi, devices so customarily used in oriental music. This makes understandable the reproach voiced by the gentile musicians that their Jewish competitors "neglected to play in time or rhythm" and that they violated the laws of music. This also explains why a few of the "Judentaenze" (Jewish dances) handed down by Christian musicians are veritable caricatures.

Such is the case with the "Juden Tantz" which appeared in Hans Neusiedler's "Lautenbuch" in 1544: The chromatic intervals of the "Hurdy Gurdy Bass" and the almost atonal dissonances point to the style of the Jewish Bierfiedlers. The composer gives the naive direction: "To be played with vehemence and emphasis, otherwise it sounds bad." In other words, this "Beckmesseriade" was too much even for the composer! Yet this piece clearly indicates that sliding from note to note and an utter contempt for the rules of gentile music provided a guiding principle for the Jewish minstrels. Many other Jewish dance tunes dating from the 17th century are written in a minor key which was quite unusual for that era and hardly ever employed by Christian dance composers in Central Europe at that time.

No one ever investigated whether any connection existed between the anonymous Jewish musician of the 17th and 18th centuries and the celebrated 19th century musicians of Jewish descent.

In 1794 there is mention of a Jewish singer living in Prague by the name of Hartung, who sang Sarastro in Mozart's "Magic Flute". The Prague newspapers stressed the fact duly that a Jewish singer had performed in public for the first time. The emancipation of the Jews brought a number of Jewish Bohemian musicians into the limelight, and it is no sheer coincidence that Bohemia is the home of such a large number of Jewish musicians. It was there that the Lezim tradition was most alive. One of the first of these Jewish musicians was Ignaz Moscheles, born in Prague in 1794 whose musical talent was discovered in good time. Prague was also the birth place of the composer Josef Dessauer, born four years after Moscheles. The renowned pianist Joseph Fischhof, whose research on Beethoven yielded important material for a biography, was born in 1804 in the Moravian town of Butschowitz. Bruenn is the native town of the violinist Heinrich Wilhelm Ernst, born in 1814. Miska Hauser, another Jewish-Bohemian violinist came from Pressburg (born in 1822), while Joseph Joachim, the finest violinist of the Schumann-Mendelssohn period and one of the greatest of all time, hailed from Kittsee near Pressburg. One year after Joachim's birth, the violinist Ferdinand Laub saw the light of day in Prague. Julius Schulhoff, the pianist, also came from Prague where he was born in 1825. His grandson Erwin Schulhoff, pianist and ultra-modern composer, was killed by the Nazis in one of the Eastern concentration camps in 1941. The early days of the emancipation of the Jews in Bohemia produced a number of other outstanding pianists: Ignaz A. Tedesco (1817), Siegmund Goldschmidt (1825), Moritz Strakosch (1825) and Siegmund Lebert (Levy), born in

1822. This list is by no means complete, but even this limited selection makes apparent that an intimate connection must have existed between the unknown Jewish minstrels in Bohemia, the minstrels of the old Ghetto, and the numerous famous 19th century musicians of Bohemian-Jewish origin.

We do not know whether Maier Mahler, the rabbi from Prague who had built that precious organ, was related to Gustav Mahler, born in Kalischt near the Bohemian-Moravian border. Nor can we trace any definite connection between Efrem Zimbalist and that line of musicians who called themselves Klaffzimmer after their instruments. But it is very likely that certain ties exist between them.

In one case, at any rate, the relationship between the old Lezim and one of the most significant of Jewish composers is definitely established. I am speaking of Jacques Offenbach, the founder of the modern operetta, the creator of the "Tales of Hoffman," who, like no other composer, captured the spirit of the Second French Empire with his brilliant, witty, and melodiously sparkling music. The father of Jacques was none other than Isaac Juda Eberst, born in 1779 in the town of Offenbach. Jacques' grandfather, the Offenbach "Schutzjude" Juda Eberst was reputed to have held the position of private tutor at the home of Rothschild in Frankfurt. He possessed a beautiful tenor voice and taught music. His son, Jacques' father also was a musician. Pirazzi informs us that Isaac Eberst received his musical education from his first violin teacher, Moses Formstecher, who, in 1792, became a member of the Jewish congregation in Offenbach. This Moses Formstecher was the son of the Bohemian musician Abraham Wiener, a typical Jewish-Bohemian Lezim. Ever since his childhood days, Isaac Eberst had been very familiar with the synagogue chants, so when he took to the road in 1799, this brown-haired "Judenpursch" (Jewish chap), clad in a shabby grey beaver coat, became an itinerant synagogue musician, a wandering "Chassan", "Bocher" and "Lezim".

The ghettos of Frankfurt and Offenbach were a musical counterpart of those in Prague. Schudt, whom I have quoted before, tells of a royal visit from the famous Hessen-Darmstadt court to Count Isenburg's estate in Offenbach. For the occasion, the Frankfurt Chassan was called upon to sing, preceded by musical offerings from a Jewish band. In Frankfurt, too, as was the case in Prague, these Jewish musicians were persecuted and rejected by their gentile competitors, except that in Frankfurt less substantiative documentary evidence has remained in existence. But Schudt's remarks speak for themselves: "The Chassan or precentor lacked the faintest trace of any experience in the art of singing and he bleated and gesticulated as if he were beyond himself." The fiddlers also played in the Frankfurt "Tantzhaus" as well as for wedding celebrations: "Dancing, hopping and leaping gave the greatest pleasure to the younger set on such occasions."

The Lezim of the dance halls and the Chassanim of the synagogues comprised those anonymous Jewish composers on whom was based the musical tradition of the 19th century Jewish composers. It was not unusual for a bocher to walk eight to ten hours at a stretch in order to reach, often late at night, the house of a rabbi or that of some respected Jew of the "kille" (Jewish congregation). Sometimes he arrived at their door just in time for the festive welcome of the Sabbath. Overcoming his hunger and exhaustion, the poor musician unpacked his fiddle and played for them a hodge-podge of Jewish and German songs and dancing tunes. One minute he presented excerpts from a Paesiello opera, the next some phrases of an old German folk tune; even fragments of a Stamitz symphony memorized from a performance of the "Collegium Musicum" which he had been privileged to attend recently. All this he mingled together and possibly he also interspersed parts of the "Kaddisch" or "Aboda" or other synagogical chants, thus creating a peculiar "medley". Before long, such practices led to the incorporation of Stamitz or Mozart melodies into the chants of the synagogue!

Isaac Eberst, the father of Jacques Offenbach, was one of those wandering "music bochers". During one of his itineraries he stopped at Deutz (in about 1802), in the neighborhood of Cologne with a long established Jewish community. For many generations, the music "cultivated" in the town's taverns and dance halls had been in the hands of Jewish musicians, who, in 1778, were taken under the special protection of the Cologne "Kurfuerst". This nobleman had expressly prohibited that any out-of-town musicians should play at weddings "on their violins, dulcimers or basses". One of the members of the Deutz tavern band which usually consisted of three musicians (always among them one flutist and one violinist) was Jacques' father. He also tried his hand at composing; his operetta, "Der Schreiner in seiner Werkstatt" ("The Carpenter in his Workshop") was performed quite successfully at the christening festivities of Napoleon's son (the "King of Rome") on the 9th of June, 1811. We are indebted for much of this factual information to Julia Offenbach, the sister of the ingenious composer. She tells us about her grandfather, the itinerant musician from Offenbach, about his settling in Deutz and how he met his prospective wife, Marianne Rindskopf. A musical bocher like the Jew Eberst may have been very pleasant company, but he surely did not meet the requirements of an ideal son-in-law. Papa Rindskopf meditated for quite some time whether he should let his daughter become the wife of this fellow ("Juengl"). But Marianne was so in love with the "Offenbacher" and he himself felt quite ready to woo her seven long years, as did Jacob to win Rachel....

After the end of the War of Liberation, Juda Eberst could not stand the little town of Deutz any longer. Thus in 1816 he moved to Cologne and called himself Isaac Offenbach—in Deutz he had always been called "Offenbacher", the fellow from Offenbach. In Cologne he became music teacher and precentor in the synagogue. An old Cologne register lists him as "Guitar, flute, violin and voice teacher". He was especially popular as guitar teacher and, in 1833, he even published a "Guitarren-Schule" (method for the guitar).

Nevertheless, Offenbach did by no means rate as an esteemed musician in the city of Cologne. He was satisfied with his modest position as "Chassan". In this capacity he belonged to a certain group of "Chassans" who were responsible for the deterioration of synagogue music as a direct consequence of the emancipation of the Jews around the year 1800. Those were the days in which the rich merchant Israel Jacobson (1768-1828) undertook to reform Jewish education in Germany with the help of the reigning monarch, Jerome von Westphalen (Napoleon's brother). In the year 1810, Jacobson published a Jewish hymn book in the town of Cassel, a hymnal which contained Protestant music set to a correspondingly Protestant text. The printed music was read from the right to the left side of the page. The traditional reading of the "Pentateuch" or the "Prophets" which followed the traditional "Neginoth" was abandoned in the synagogues; instead a Protestant liturgy was introduced. In those days even bells were used in the Jewish temples. The chorales which were sung were Hebrew translations of texts by Paul Gerhardt set to such melodies as "O Haupt voll Blut und Wunden".

This was the result of the emancipation, this was the reaction to the old Ghetto tradition to which the Lezim, Chassans and Bochers of the 17th and 18th century belonged who performed their colorful medleys of popular operatic melodies and old Sephardic and Ashkenazic tunes. We read in "Caecilia" (1835), a periodical which took an interest in Jacobson's attempt at reform, one was content to have the psalms sung by a precentor who took the exalted poetry of the Bible and gurgled it off to some usually secular melody such as the minuet from "Don Giovanni" or the songs of the bridesmaids from "Der Freischuetz", all this for the pleasant diversion of the Christian members of the audience. These are the goings-on as they still exist in most of our synagogues. As a matter of fact, we find in Friedmann's "Der synagogale Gesang" (Berlin, 1908) a version of the Sabbath chant "L'chododi likras kallo" which contains to our great surprise one phrase out of Mozart's "Marriage of Figaro".

To come back to Isaac Eberst, it must be said that he was a versatile man, a man of letters in addition to being a musician. In 1839 he published an "Allgemeines Gebetbuch" (General Prayerbook) in German and Hebrew designed for young Jewish people, and one year previously he had published a translation of the "Hagadah". Those of my readers who are familiar with the works of Heine may recall the poet's beautiful words when he speaks of the Hagadah. In his "Rabbi von Bacharach" Heine relates how the head of the family and all his friends and relatives took their places at the table to listen to the recitation of the Agade, this book of adventures whose strange content Heine characterized as follows:

".... a strange mixture of legends of their forefathers, wondrous tales of Egypt, questions of theology, prayers and festival songs.... Mournfully merry, seriously gay, and mysteriously secret as some dark old legend is the character of this nocturnal festival, and the usual traditional singing intonation with which the Agade is read by the father, and now and then re-echoed in chorus by the hearers, at one time thrills the inmost soul as with a shudder, anon calms it as if it were a mother's lullaby, and anon startles it so suddenly into waking that even those Jews who have long fallen away from the faith of their fathers and run after strange joys and honours, are moved to their very hearts when by chance the old wellknown tones of the Passover songs ring in their ears."

Offenbach's transcription of the Hagadah also contains three of his compositions. The first is a musical setting of the 118th psalm: "O give thanks unto the Lord; for He is good," arranged for a four part men's choir with tenor solo, a work quite reminiscent of the glee club selections of those days. There is also a chorus for mixed choir: "Die Festgebraeuche sind vollbracht" (The festive rites have all been consummated) and finally the composition of the "lambkin" for solo voice with piano accompaniment (the latter composition appears erroneously under the name of

Jacques Offenbach in the modern editions of the Hagadah).

Anton Henseler upon whose writings ("Jakob Offenbach") most of my description of Isaac's life is based, informs us that the lambkin song is strongly influenced by the ballad, "Einst traeumte meiner sel'gen Base", from Weber's "Freischuetz". At any rate, Isaac Offenbach's compositions exercised a certain amount of influence on his son; thus we can recognize in Jacques' operetta "La nuit blanche" the end phrase of the lambkin song, while Isaac's melody for the 118th psalm is reborn in the second act finale of his son's operetta "Die Herzogin von Gerolstein" (The Duchess of Gerolstein). Moreover, the melodies in Jacques' "Die Seufzerbruecke" (The Bridge of Sighs), composed in 1860, can be traced to Isaac's transcription of "Traditionelle Melodien" (Traditional Melodies). The "Lezim" tradition then, the tradition of the old "Offenbacher", has left its clear imprint on the music of Jacques Offenbach, one of the greatest Jewish composers the world has ever known.

CHAPTER FOUR

THE PAGANINI OF THE
EIGHTEENTH CENTURY

"IT happened in the year 1803," so tells the noted musicologist Friedrich Rochlitz*. "It was during a late autumn day of that year that my servant entered to announce him: 'There is a gentleman to see you, sir. He refuses to give his name; he insists that you will recognize him.'"

"As soon as the man entered I was sure that I had never seen him before. Judging from his appearance he was in his late fifties. His figure was slightly bent; not from age it seemed, but rather from an inner humility and diffidence. His frame was squeezed into a shabby little jacket. He wore a dirty shirt, and the boots on his feet were a few sizes too large. Clutched in one hand, he held a hat devoid of any shape and at the point of disintegration. His unruly hair and

---

*Friedrich Rochlitz (1769-1842), friend of Goethe and Beethoven and editor of "Die Allgemeine Musikalische Zeitung" (1798-1818), the most influential musical periodical of the classical period, wrote about this incident in the second volume of his still entertaining work "Fuer Freunde der Tonkunst" (1825).

a week's growth of beard on his sallow emaciated face enhanced his unkempt appearance. He looked hungry, and his high cheekbones and forehead were flushed a reddish brown, suggesting the prolonged use of habit-forming drugs. His lively eyes never rested on one object for more than an instant. Even when he spoke to me his eyes shifted continuously, never looking me directly in the eye. He was one of those creatures who invariably evoke a feeling of repulsion mixed with compassion in those who cross his path. Facing me, the man began to speak in a hoarse and hollow tone: 'My name is Scheller, the famous Scheller—I am sure you must have heard of me—I believe that all the newspapers have written about me.'"

When the man had first entered, Rochlitz had taken him by mistake for another, but he realized his error when he caught sight of the violin case carried by the stranger. In a few moments the strange visitor held the instrument tucked under his chin ready to play. . . "He started his bow across the strings of the miserable looking violin. I wish I were able to describe his playing as faithfully as his appearance! First detached fingered chords, full and resonant, then smoothly tied arpeggios in cleverly modulated sequences, bold and brilliant but always clear and impeccably in tune, even the most difficult passages. After this initial warm-up he began a more coherent allegro passage, full of brilliance and evidence of his versatile virtuosity. A beautiful old German folk song followed which had inspired Goethe to write the serene and peaceful lyrics: "Da droben auf jenem Berge" ("Up there on that mountain"). Scheller played the simple tune in double stops to absolute perfection, often resorting to the most difficult positions to achieve the full inner voice harmonies. He played with so much spiritual depth and ardour that he himself—with his nerves being as weak as they were—was deeply moved and tears were trickling down his wrinkled face. The exposition of the melody was followed by four or five masterful variations and a lengthy, freely conceived cadenza executed to perfection, both artistically and technically. Resting momentarily on the concluding fermata, he went into a furious, almost savage presto, ending with a series of full and vehement chords, almost tearing the gut strings. His arms dropped slowly to his sides and he stooped over with mental and physical exhaustion. Like a defiant child he stood there, swallowing and conquering his tears with spasmodic motions of his head...."

We can imagine Hofrat Rochlitz' agitation, although he usually was a calm and self-possessed man. To form a clearer picture of this scene it may be worthwhile to dig up the theme and variations played by this unknown minstrel. It is an old 18th century folk tune which Karl Maria von Weber used as thematic material in his Flute Trio (op. 63, Berlin 1820). The same tune also appeared in Wilhelm Ehler's "Gesaenge mit Begleitung der Guitarre", published in the year 1804.

When the guest had finished playing, Rochlitz invited him to stay for a snack and soon the stranger became more talkative: "He was born in Bohemia, and had shown since early childhood prodigious talent and an unrestrainable propensity toward music. Even as a young boy, he joined and performed with the bands of roving musicians whenever he had the opportunity. During a tour of Prague he was favorably noticed in a Jesuit college. The Jesuit fathers had recognized his talent and had adopted him out of compassion in order to develop his talents, acquaint him with basic scientific knowledge as well as to guide him into an orderly way of life. But this life did not agree with the boy and he ran away to Vienna and joined another band of roving musicians. In this city he had the opportunity to listen to outstanding virtuosi and he attempted to equal their excellence with avid ambition and persistent diligence. And essentially, that had remained his way of life. As the years passed, his striving idealism gradually slackened and was eventually stifled by the way he lived. He became satisfied with exhibiting his previously acquired skill. In the ensuing years, he drifted all over Germany, France, Italy, and Switzerland. During his early travels, he listened to all the great violinists and was often encouraged to stay and study with them; however, he could never remain at any one place for any length of time. A few noblemen suggested that he remain in their service, but he soon moved on. I asked him whether he might consider giving a concert here. 'I

can no longer bear to show myself before all these
genteel people,' he retorted (and the expression he
used was uncivil). 'I wouldn't mind playing for a few
close friends and they might give me whatever it may
be worth to them'. . . .

"After talking and drinking his tenseness disappeared and his good mood, as he called it, came to
the surface. He began quoting epigrams: 'One God,
one Scheller—tears or laughter—always again'. I tried
to get rid of him, but this was impossible, especially
as I did not want to seem insistent. 'After the tears
comes laughter,' he said. Disregarding my impatience,
he seized his violin and began to play some musical
dramas (as I am inclined to call them). Never before
or after have I heard or seen anything similar presented with such admirable power of expression and
so unparalleled in its execution. The first was a short
masterpiece: An evening in an old Swabian town.
At least, that was the way he announced it. And to
each new episode he made—with a few words—his
comments which, though not nearly as descriptive as
his tone painting, nevertheless gave a fuller meaning
to his musical pictures. Not satisfied with a perfect
command of harmonies, he resorted to a variety of
strange but very functional gadgets in order to create
particular impressions and to achieve certain imitative effects. An old wooden snuff box was placed
on the instrument during certain parts of the composition. A key, which I supplied, served as a kind of
mute, producing a subdued nasal tone. He loosened

the hair of a second violin bow, so that the wooden part was free to dangle underneath the violin while the hair alone was drawn across the strings. The tone he produced in this manner was soft and delicate. It was wondrously moving when he applied this strange art of bowing to slowly and smoothly tied chords, somewhat in the style of a chorale. These were only a few of the many tricks he employed so skillfully. The plot of the picture he painted was somehow like this: The sun was setting. The old town gate was to be closed for the night and everybody on the outside came running to crowd through hurriedly. Now the last warning cry of the town sentry was heard and the creaking gate snapped shut followed by the grinding of the key in the old lock. The old officer of the guard shouted piercing words of command to his men. The key had to be handed over to the town magistrate and the small detachment marched off to the rhythmic beat of a drum. They disappeared around the next corner and the sounds of their steps on the cobblestones faded into the distance. Only an occasional sound was heard, carried gently by the evening breeze and the streets were hushed in silence. The warder of the tower trumpeted the evening chorale from the heights of his domain, then he closed the garret window, and the town fell asleep.

"Scheller seemed astonished that I did not break out laughing; but this episode affected my senses in quite a different manner. He was determined to go one step further. An excursion on the Rhine with an impending thunderstorm, he announced. The little boat was gliding along peacefully, the oars gently lapping the waves. The merry crowd was singing a folk song. Gusts of wind suddenly streaked, one after the other, across the darkening sky. An anxious atmosphere settled over the little party and the beats of the oars grew faster. The women were tripping around worriedly, while the men sneered. The sky became darker, the situation tenser. Thunder was rumbling overhead; the wind died down as suddenly as it had started, and even the men became somewhat concerned. And then the storm broke with full might. Bolts of lightning lit the angry sky, and claps of thunder accompanied the swift murmur of the rain. I do not know whether Scheller was aware of his expression, or whether he was simply carried away by his own narrative. At any rate, the picture he described was mirrored in his face—the black clouds, the grumbling thunder, the jagged streaks of lightning. Reflecting the latter, his face muscles twitched violently lending a horrifying ugliness to his aged features; a striking mirror image of his tone painting. The storm was now directly overhead, unleashing its full fury. The shrieks of the terrified women blended with the howling of the wind. The whipped-up waves crashed against the side of the little craft and the passengers were thrown about mercilessly. At the height of this turmoil the voice of the helmsman sounded over the raging storm: Land! land! land! and everyone chimed in joyfully. The landing was reached and the boat emptied quickly. An inn along the shore offered welcome refuge. A band played some lusty peasant dances, and soon everybody was dancing and rejoicing.

"I was downright impolite to him by not laughing out loud this time. Half-heartedly he listened to my words of praise; he was set, however, to outdo himself and all his previous efforts in a portrayal of a Bohemian peasant wedding with all the trimmings including a fight, etc."

While Rochlitz gave this picturesque account of his experience, he did not neglect to mention the repulsion he felt for Scheller's manner. This strange violinist was morally so debased that even in his speech and in his musical portraits the sexually vulgar elements of his debauched existence shone through. This was reason enough for Rochlitz to dismiss him rather brusquely.

In his story, Rochlitz did not do much more than sketch his impressions and feelings.

The planned concert never materialized. The keeper of the inn where Scheller had stayed reported that he had honestly paid for food and lodging and then left, despite the rain, on a foot journey to Schlackenwert near Carlsbad. "I have never seen him again and do not know what became of him."

We are in no better position than Hofrat Rochlitz when we attempt to trace the fate of this strange musician. The short biographical accounts found in the encyclopedia read as follows:

Scheller was born on May 16, 1759, in Schettal, a little town near Rakonitz in the province of Bohemia. There are accounts of performances in Prague, Vienna, and Mannheim where he played in the orchestra for two years (possibly in the position of concertmaster). He was reputed to have studied composition with the famous Abbé Vogler. After years of drifting from place to place he landed in Paris where he studied with Viotti for some time. In 1785 he accepted the position of concertmaster at the court of the Duke of Wuerttemberg in Montbeliard. Soon thereafter he began his aimless wanderings through all of Europe. Like a comet he appears and disappears mysteriously, displaying his circus tricks on the violin. The most enthusiastic report about this amazing individual comes from the encyclopedist Gerber who heard him perform in Sondershausen in the year 1794. Gerber expresses great amazement about Scheller's command of harmonics, double stop scales in thirds and octaves extending to the highest registers and particularly about his fantastic bowing technique: "His bowing of broken and running passages was so forceful that it may be likened in effect to a hailstorm drumming against a window pane."

Spohr had also heard him play and, in his autobiography, he makes mention of Scheller's pizzicato effect produced with his special fingernail technique. The composer Dittersdorf, too, includes Scheller in his autobiographical writings; he had heard him play in Vienna in 1786: "During my sojourn in Vienna

I chanced to meet seven violin virtuosi, all strangers in Vienna who had come to this city at their own risk and met there accidentally. The most outstanding ones were Jarnowich, Frenzel sen., and Scheller from the German Reich. The latter's excellence, which he showed off to the point of disgust, consisted of double stops and arpeggios in sequences, ill-modulated and against all rules of harmony and composition...."

All encyclopedias report 1803 as the year of Scheller's death. This, however, only marks the year during which we lose trace of him, the year of the Rochlitz incident. What became of this forerunner of Paganini? After a few more years he probably died a miserable death in some gutter or stable, and lies buried in a lonely pasture, his grave unmarked.

CHAPTER FIVE

FRANZ ABT, UNFORGOTTEN
SONG COMPOSER

ONE summer, some 80 years ago, America was visited by two musicians whose popularity was undisputed at that time. Franz Abt and Johann Strauss were here at almost the same time, and both owed their fame to the fact that their music appealed to the masses. While the melodies of the waltz king are today as alive as they were a century ago, Abt has been somewhat forgotten, although many an old singer of popular songs remembers well the hit tune "Wenn die Schwalben heimwaerts ziehen" (When the swallows come back home) which made the rounds of all the glee clubs and choral societies in their youth. With the possible exception of the "Blaue Donau", no choral selection has even reached such immense popularity with German and American choral societies as had this song by Franz Abt, a composer who, today, does not command the attention merited by a musician of his caliber.

Franz Abt was born in Eilenburg, in the province

of Saxony, on December 22, 1819. He was the son of a music-loving clergyman. At the age of 19 he published his first compositions after he had devoted time to music as a student in Leipzig. Young Abt moved in musical circles where he established lasting contacts with Lortzing, Mendelssohn and Schumann. He conducted a philharmonic chorus made up of students and soon embarked on his career as Kapellmeister of the theatre in Bernburg, after having married his youthful sweetheart Rosalie Neumann, the daughter of the innkeeper who ran "The Sign of the Three Swans" in Leipzig. Later he went to Switzerland to accept the position of Kapellmeister at the Akazientheater in Zurich where he cultivated popular choral singing. In 1844 he became director of the Harmonic Society, and from 1845 on he directed the concerts of the Allgemeine Musikgesellschaft. There he was a colleague of Richard Wagner, but real friendship never developed between these two diametrically different characters.

Abt's popularity in Zurich rose very rapidly and when he left Switzerland in 1852 he was given a tremendous send-off. Brunswick became his new home where he was offered the position of Hof-Kapellmeister, and there he remained until he retired. His last years he spent in Wiesbaden, devoting himself to his family and to his compositions until his death on March 31, 1885.

No other composer of his day enjoyed such widespread popularity. Abt had a remarkable gift of melody, the success of which rested on the esthetic law of "the apparently familiar"; this is why so many of his songs have become songs of the common people. In the houses of bourgeois Germany there was scarcely a piano or music stand on which his songs "Gute Nacht, du mein herziges Kind" (Good night, my dear child) and "Die stille Wasserrose" (The silent water lily) were not to be found.

The British Museum in London possesses a catalogue of the songs and choral selections of Abt. There are two folio volumes containing a total of 985 numbers. In fact, Abt—who wrote many of his songs to English texts—is relatively better known in England and America today than he is in his own country.

A personal friend of Abt, a certain Dr. Rost, published in a little, almost unknown volume, the letters which Abt wrote to his wife from America. They show that his visit, like that of Strauss, to the United States was an amazing success. Abt was honored in many cities by great torchlight processions; rarely has a German musician been feted like this in the New World. He visited New York, Philadelphia, Baltimore, Washington, Buffalo, Cincinnati, Louisville, Evansville and St. Louis. At the great *Saengerfest* in St. Louis, Carl Schurz greeted him personally.

On the 20th of May he wrote to his wife from New York: "Yesterday the delegate from the Boston Grand Music Festival was here. Just think what is going on! There are about twenty thousand singers and an orchestra of about three thousand men. The festival lasts six days and begins on the 17th of June. On each day my "Swallows" are to be sung in the following arrangement: the first verse by five thousand sopranos, the second verse by five thousand tenors and the third verse by twenty thousand voices in four parts, with full orchestra and organ."

One of Abt's letters written from Washington, D. C., May 8, 1872, does not only show how naive a musician he was, but also acquaints us with the prevailing musical conditions in America:

"Good morning, my dear Rosalie! Yesterday I had a lovely and interesting day which I cannot help describing to you a little. To be sure it is pretty hot, although it is only eight o'clock in the morning. I shall take a bath at once to cool me off, because there are bathing facilities here in the hotel. Yesterday my faithful companion, the lawyer Harte, a charming man, called for me in a magnificent open carriage (colored coachman). First we went to the White House, the dwelling of the President. Although it really wasn't a reception day, since there was a meeting of the Cabinet, I was taken before him in a reception room. He is a very serious man, this General Grant, President of the United States. He was very nice to me and assured me that he and his family would attend the concert. After we had seen all the magnificent rooms in which the Brussels carpets impressed me most, we went to another very interesting building, the Treasury, in which all the American money is piled up and from which it is sent into the world. I am hardly able to describe it. I was presented to Secretary of the Treasury Spinner, who personally led me into the main Treasury vault. I would have liked to keep the little package which he pressed into my hands and which contained bills of about two hundred thousand dollars. It was not heavier than a package of tea. It is interesting to go through the unbelievably large number of offices and rooms, all of them with the most beautiful carpets on the floor. In this Treasury there are, along with two thousand or more male secretaries and the like, also eight hundred female employees, pretty girls and women, all working hard. A special department of the Treasury is a department of architects, which I visited and where I met several German enthusiasts who have found wonderful positions there. I not only drove through this magnificent city, but after made some visits to the Capitol where Congress is assembled. I heard the meeting of the Senate and the House of Representatives, where there was a crowd of famous persons of whom one so often reads in the newspapers. I meandered through the entire edifice which is built of nothing but white marble, the largest building of this kind I have ever seen in my life. After some visits we dined at six o'clock in the evening and then I had to take care of the invitations of the various societies.

"First, I visited the choral society made up only of Americans who sing splendidly. They sang in English, do not speak any German at all, are without exception fine gentlemen, officials, bankers, etc. No society in Germany sings better than this one. Then for supper at the Arion, the German society; I was made an honorary member of this society and was given a magnificent bouquet which I would very much like to send you if we were not so far apart. In love, Franz."

The favorable testimony Abt gives for the American singing societies is all the more important as it is done so in an intimate family letter.

On the twentieth day of May Abt wrote from New York: "I was enthusiastically received in Philadelphia. There was a parade of about eight hundred torches on the first evening. This was followed by a welcoming speech by Langenhaus, brother of the notary here. I had fine private lodgings at Mr. Landenberger's house. You can read about all this in the papers. Reporters are always around you here. In Philadelphia there was almost too much going on to celebrate my presence. The concert in the great opera house was well attended. I haven't the final accounting yet. The expenses are always quite significant. Saturday morning at half past eight I came back from there to this place—the concert on Sunday here took place before a full house and was very brilliant. I don't know yet how high the expenses are. Of all the concerts up to now, a profit of three thousand dollars is perhaps left over. The great heat in Baltimore affected it very much. And there I liked it least so far. The main place is always New York. My trip will be somewhat changed, since I am not going to Chicago before July. This evening I'll depart for Buffalo where the concert is on Wednesday, the twenty-second, after which, next day, an excursion to Niagara Falls is supposed to take place and then on the twenty-fourth I am to come back here and stay for nine days which I shall use for work. I have many commissions from music dealers. Steinway put a piano in my room and I can relax a bit. On Wednesday, the twenty-ninth, I shall conduct "Tannhaeuser" or "Fidelio" here in the Grand Opera. For this, however, I won't be paid. The German opera here is financially in a bad condition and they would rather use me as an attraction. Then on the first of June there is the concert in the Arion, in its own headquarters which are somewhat smaller. They only hold 500 or 600 persons, but, since the expenses are very little there, certainly 500 or 600 dollars will be left over. Immediately thereafter I go to Cincinnati, Louisville, Evansville and from there to the great *Saengerfest* in St. Louis. This trip will be somewhat hard and hot. I hope it goes off well, too. The hardest, however, is then to come on the thirteenth of June, my trip from St. Louis to Boston. Fifty hours on the train in one stretch. But traveling in a train is always comfortable here. For the night there are Pullmans in which one has princely beds . . . On the twenty-seventh in Newark, a half hour by train from here. Nevertheless, one must not dream of the huge amounts as imagined in Germany. If these four concerts net perhaps three thousand dollars, then they are quite easily and comfortably earned. And this, my dear Sallerchen, you can take as gospel fact that six to eight thousand Thaler will be left over. I don't count on any more for the time being. If I had come in winter it might have been at least twice as much. In summer, however, the people dislike to go to concerts here just as much as they do in our country. . . ."

At the beginning of June Abt went back home again. One can imagine how overwhelming the impressions were which he received in America. It was a time of great successes and the days spent in America probably were the most adventurous in the life of this provincial musician who once was a glamorous figure.

CHAPTER SIX

JOHANN STAMITZ:
"ANOTHER SHAKESPEARE"

DURING his journey across the European continent, the 18th century English historian of music Burney happened to pass through Bohemia in his search for information pertaining to his work in music. He was particularly impressed by the little country's school system which afforded a musical education even to the youngest of children.

"In these common country schools a great genius appears now and then, as was the case at Teuchenbrod, the birthplace of the famous Stamitz. His father was cantor of the church in that town, and Stamitz, who was afterwards so eminent both as composer and performer, was brought up in the common school, among children of common talents, who lived and died unnoticed; but he, like another Shakespeare, broke through all difficulties and discouragements; and, as the eye of one pervaded all nature, the other, without quitting nature, pushed art further than any one had done before him; his genius was truly original, bold, and nervous; invention, fire, and contrast in the quick movements; a tender, graceful, and insinuating melody, in the slow; together with the ingenuity and richness of the accompaniments, characterize his productions; all replete with great effects, produced by an enthusiasm of genius, refined but not repressed by cultivation."

Burney visited Bohemia in the year 1772; writing later about his journey, he attributed the greatest significance to Stamitz by comparing him with Shakespeare. Undoubtedly, he considered him one of the greatest men of his time.

The fame Stamitz enjoyed was later eclipsed by his great classical successors, particularly by Haydn, Mozart, and Beethoven. For decades, he was totally forgotten; it was not until the 19th century musicologists exposed his true genius that Stamitz reaped his deserved claim to glory.

Johann Wenzel Anton Stamitz—often referred to as Staimitz or Steinmetz—was born in Deutschbrod (Teuchenbrod, as Burney calls it) on June 19, 1717, and died on March 27, 1757, in Mannheim where he was buried three days later.

His true nationality, whether Czech or German, is often disputed. It seems, however, quite trivial to argue this point. His true home, as that of so many others of his time, was in that certain "Austrian melting pot" in which the most different peoples became amalgamated into a typical Austrian mixtum compositum which finally became an entity in itself. The name Stamitz is very likely of Yugoslavian origin, because his grandfather who lived in Maribor, Yugoslavia, was named Martin Stamec. Martin left his native country to settle down in the Bohemian town of Pardubitz where he married Elisabeth Kuhey (or Kuley). They had a son, Anton Stamitz, the father of the composer. He married Rosine Boehm, the daughter of the Deutschbrod alderman Wilhelm Boehm who had been formerly a citizen of Prague. Rosine Boehm was most likely of German ancestry.

I have put special emphasis on the racial background in my attempt to show how little justification there is in labeling Stamitz as either Czech or German.

Young Johann Wenzel learned the fundamentals of music from his father who had been organist of the Dekanal church in Deutschbrod since 1710. We do not know where he received his higher education, but it is plainly evident from all sources and references that no famous musician ever had any part in his musical training. He may have learned as a roving minstrel depending on his own inventive genius, or he may have become indebted for his virtuoso violin playing to one of the countless Bohemian musicians, much like Franz Benda, who learned to play the violin from an obscure and blind Jewish fiddler.

However this may have been, we find Stamitz as an accomplished and successful violinist playing at the coronation of Emperor Charles VII, in Frankfurt on the Main in 1742. He also performed on the viola d'amore, the violoncello and the double bass.

His great success as soloist earned him a position as court musician in Mannheim with Karl Theodor von der Pfalz, who became *Kurfuerst* in 1743.

His sudden fame must have spread rapidly, because in the very same year Stamitz could dare decline an offer to join the court of the famous Duke Karl Eugen von Wuerttemberg.

On the 1st of July, 1744, Stamitz settled down; he was married to Maria Antonia Lueneborn the daughter of a Mannheim townsman. His musical career progressed in leaps and bounds. Already by 1745 he held the position of concertmaster and director of the *"engere Kammermusik"*. His many reforms were responsible for making the famous Mannheim orchestra the finest in the world. In 1747 Stamitz gained the able assistance of his compatriot Franz Xaver Richter (born in Holleschau, Moravia), and the new style inaugurated by Stamitz and his colleagues soon found its way to the musical centers of Paris and London. Around the middle of the century (1748, 1751, 1754) Stamitz' fame in Paris—where he was celebrated as composer and virtuoso—reached its climax.

He exercised an epoch-making influence on the Parisian world of music. As an example it may be interesting to note that it was his advice which induced de la Poplinière, the rich tax collector and supporter of a first rate orchestra, to add a horn section to the orchestra. The "concerts spirituels" conducted by LeGros included many performances of Stamitz' symphonies, and soon the "Symphonies d'Allemagne" became a familiar label in Paris with Stamitz' vivid, dynamic, and modern symphonies being featured. There is definite proof that Stamitz' symphonies were performed in Paris in 1754 and 1755. It was also in 1755, long before Mozart's time, that Stamitz employed clarinets in his orchestra. His school of composition gained widespread popularity. In France, Gossec and Schobert were influenced by his school; the Belgian composer Pierre van Maldere (1724-1768) and the Englishman, Earl of Kelly (1732-1781) also imitated his style.

Hugo Riemann, the German musicologist, attached the greatest significance to Stamitz. Riemann's catalogue of musical compositions by Stamitz lists: Ten trios for two violins and cello, fifty symphonies, twelve violin concerti, two solo violin sonatas in four movements, six violin solos with Basso Continuo ("Deux divertissements en duo pour un violon seul sans basse"), six violin solos with basso continuo which were listed by Breitkopf in 1766, but which have never been found, "Sei Sonate da camera", op. 4 and op. 6. The only remaining manuscripts are four trios, one "concerto per Cembalo, 2 violini, viola e basso" and one mass.

France, Holland, and England alike eagerly sought publication of his works.

Stamitz' father may be designated as founder of a dynasty of musicians. Johann's brother, Anton Thaddeus Stamitz (born 1721 in Deutschbrod, died 1768 in Altbunzlau near Prague) was also a musician of first rank. It is believed that Anton was active as a cellist in Mannheim, but in his later years he joined the priesthood. Johann Stamitz' two sons also became professional musicians. The elder, Karl, was born in Mannheim in 1746; he studied with his father's contemporary, Christian Cannabich and became a court musician at Mannheim. In 1770 he went to Paris, taking along with him Johann Anton, who was his younger brother. Karl performed on the viola and on the viola d'amore, giving successful performances in London (1776). He lived the life of a wandering minstrel. The success of Cagliostro and Casanova and other adventurous alchemists impressed him considerably; alchemy fascinated him and he never failed to take alchemical writings with him on his tours. He died in Jena in the year 1801. His younger brother Anton, a violinist, made Paris his permanent domicile where he became Rudolph Kreutzer's teacher. He is said to have died in 1820. Mozart was closely acquainted with both brothers, but he did not think very highly of either one. He met Karl in Paris in the year 1778 and characterized the nomadic and bohemian life of the great virtuoso with these words:

"Of the two Stamitz brothers only the younger one is here—the elder one (the real Hafeneder composer) is in London. They are a pair of miserable music scribblers and performers, drunkards and debauchees —they are not my kind of people. The one who is here in Paris has not even a decent suit to call his own."

The authenticated works of Karl Stamitz number among them seventy symphonies, several string quartettes, trio sonatas, violin duets, one concerto for viola, one piano concerto and two operas ("Der verliebte Vormund", Frankfurt, and "Dardanus", Petersburg). The younger brother, Anton, left thirteen symphonies, nine sets of string quartettes (six per set), trio sonatas, one violin concerto, three piano concertos, violin sonatas, string duets, etc.

* * *

During the forty short years of his life, Johann Stamitz had made tremendous strides in the art of music. His name is intimately tied to the reformed style which made its appearance around the middle of the eighteenth century, to the transition from the baroque to the classical school, from the polyphonic to the homophonic style of composition. The thematic material of earlier periods consisted mainly of one central melodic line easily combined in a horizontal manner with one or more different themes, while the new era ushered in a harmonically defined way of writing, symbolizing a distinct and clear-cut personality.

In previous times, the fugue or concerto began with the exposition of a strongly profiled principal theme, which, when taken up by other voices in imitative sequences, was soon engulfed in a contrapuntal maze. The new forms, based on the periodicity of folk tunes and dances, are penetrating and unique. The old fugue and concerto form is mono-thematic, the new form dualistic: a masculine, energetic theme is opposed to a feminine, reflective and more tender one. The two themes get involved in a dramatic struggle which takes place in the subsequent development along the principles of the sonata form.

In this regard, Stamitz—together with a few other contemporary masters (Sammartini, Pergolesi, etc.)—may be called a pioneer of classical music.

He had a pronounced personality as a composer. His fire, energy, and buoyancy, melodic penetration and impressiveness fascinated his contemporaries no less than his rhythmical verve and masterful orchestrations. Stamitz and his Mannheim colleagues developed peculiar tendencies which were later criticized as conventional mannerisms. To cite examples of these mannerisms: the "Mannheim sighs", the "Mannheim rockets" (the rocket-like melodic ascents from the lowest to the highest registers as can still be found in Beethoven's first F minor sonata and in the last movement of Mozart's G minor symphony), grand pauses, and the "Mannheim Crescendi" which produced a breathtaking effect on his contemporaries, especially when the climax culminated in a surprising piano instead of the expected fortissimo (dynamic fallacy).

The 18th century praised Stamitz to the skies. Joh. Ad. Hiller is quoted as saying (in 1768) that his name will remain sacred to all eternity. Gerber writes in his "Historisch-Biographisches Lexicon der Tonkuenstler" (1792) about Stamitz' divine genius which elevated him above all his contemporaries. Arteaga ("Le rivoluzioni del teatro musicale Italiano", 1783) calls him the Rubens of his time and celebrates him as the founder of a new style.

Soon, however, a reaction set in in regard to the appraisal of the master. The "Mannheim style" was deemed obsolete and affected. Leopold Mozart referred to it in one of his letters as ". . . der vermanirierte Mannheimer gout" (the super-stilted Mannheim taste).

While Stamitz himself was passionate and could be likened to the "Sturm und Drang" sensitiveness in the sense of Goethe's and Schiller's forceful genius ideal, his successors exhibited a trend toward the superficial-suave-gallant and sickly sweet style. The negative evaluation of the Mannheim style does not justly pertain to Stamitz, but rather to his two sons, to Anton Filtz, Georg Zarth, and his numerous imitators.

In France, Stamitz was considered a prophet. At about 1750 he was the accepted leading composer of "modern, German" orchestral music. The collection of Mannheim symphonies from the year 1755, "La Melodia Germanica", became the delight of the Parisian music circles. These "Symphonies d'Allemagne", were highly valued for their youthful vigor and German spirituality and served as a welcome and violent contrast to French traditionalism which was deemed out-of-date. It was Melchior Grimm, in his famous pamphlet, "Le Petit Prophète de Boehmisch Broda" (1753), who erected a monument to Stamitz. Grimm personifies Stamitz in the role of the imaginary character Franz Waldstroechel,[1] a student and violinist from Prague, whose young and fresh art is contrasted with the old and conventional operas of Lully. In this allegorical manifesto written in Biblical style, Grimm magically transplants this little minuet-fiddling musician from his garret in the Prague Ghetto to the French operatic stage where Waldstroechel shirks in disgust from the artificiality of the recitatives, the obsoleteness of the ballets and from the unrealistic staging. In reality, the opera-minded Grimm considered as the champion of the new style the composer Pergolesi, whose opera "Serva Padrona" caused such a commotion as to precipitate a veritable paper war between two Parisian factions: the buffoonists and the anti-buffoonists. At the same time, however, Grimm identifies the little Bohemian fiddler as the champion of a new and fresh kind of music which had crossed the Rhine and which had taken "tout Paris" by storm with its new dynamic rhythms and melodies.

---

[1]Grimm cites Boehmisch Brod as Waldstroechel's birthplace; he evidently confuses Boehmisch Brod, near Prague, with Deutschbrod, the town where Stamitz was born.

CHAPTER SEVEN

THE IRISH SINGER MICHAEL KELLY, A FRIEND OF MOZART

THE 18th century is the century of literary excesses. Goethe encouraged his contemporaries to write their autobiographies and Schiller speaks of the "tintenklexende Saeculum", the "ink-blot generation". The intellectual and witty set of that era could not bear the idea of blank paper; they availed themselves of every scrap of it, jotting down their experiences and adventures, no matter how banal or hackneyed. Indeed, never had man deemed himself so affirmedly the center of the universe as he presumed to be in the 18th century, the age of the overemphasized and exaggerated significance of individuality. Never before or since had letter writing been carried on so profusely, nor had its artistic aspect ever flourished to a greater extent than during Mozart's days.

The great memoir writers of that time were Goethe, Goldoni, Casanova, DaPonte, Madame de Staël. But the history of culture and music has also greatly benefited by the less scintillating minds who took it upon themselves to describe their adventures and encounters with the men and women of the theatre and music circles. Among these "supernumeraries" on the stage of history we meet Michael Kelly, the Irish singer, whose "Reminiscences" (London, 1826) has served as one of the most important sources of reference in the history of music of the later 18th century. His accounts are of such particularly great value, because he enjoyed the most intimate contact with Mozart and his circle in Vienna where Kelly was a court singer.

Kelly was born around Christmastide, 1762, in Dublin, as the son of Thomas Kelly, a wine merchant and dancing master. Even as a youngster, Michael exhibited a pronounced talent for music. His father was most anxious to provide a fine education for the boy. He had young Michael take piano lessons from masters, such as Morland (1770-1772) and Michael Arne (1777-1778), while such great singing teachers as Passerini, Peretti and St. Giorgio were entrusted with the cultivation of Michael's beautiful voice. It seems that St. Giorgio exercised a decided influence in shaping the fate of his pupil who, at the age of 15, was determined to make singing his career, although his father wanted him to take up medicine as a profession.

Kelly tells us about the following incident:

"I recollect once I saw Signor St. Giorgio enter a fruit shop; he proceeded to eat peaches and nectarines, and at last took a pineapple, and deliberately sliced and ate that. This completed my longing, and while my mouth watered, I asked myself why, if I assiduously studied music, I should not be able to earn money enough to lounge about in fruit-shops, and eat peaches and pineapples as well as Signor St. Giorgio."

Thus in Kelly's own words we find evidence that these contemplations were actually decisive in his final resolution to follow the career of a voice virtuoso. And what a strange reason it was indeed! At that time Kelly studied with Rauzzini, in all probability Matteo Rauzzini (1754-1791), brother of the famous singer Venanzio Rauzzini (1747-1810). Matteo settled down in Dublin and taught voice. It was also *he* who urged Kelly's parents to send the boy to Italy. Before Michael embarked on this distant journey, there was many an interesting experience in store for him right in his native city. First and foremost he was given the opportunity to perform publicly. He sang the part of the count in Piccini's opera "Buona figliuola" and also the heroic lead in Michael Arne's "Cymon", as well as some other operatic roles. Among the many famous musicians whose acquaintance he made I would like to mention only the oboist Johann Christian Fischer (1733-1800). Fischer was greatly admired by his contemporaries for his tone on the oboe. He was also well known to Mozart who was a severe critic of Fischer, but who nevertheless took it upon himself to compose "Twelve piano variations on a minuet by Fischer". In Kelly's own words, this minuet was considered "all the rage" at that time.

Fischer was also an intimate friend of the painter Gainsborough whose lovely daughter Mary became his wife. Gainsborough's beautiful portrait of his oboist friend is now one of the art treasures of Buckingham Palace. Fischer must have been a witty person judging from a charming anecdote told by Kelly which, incidentally, was later applied to other artists:

"Being very much pressed by a nobleman to sup with him after the opera, he declined the invitation, saying that he was very much fatigued, and made it a rule never to go out after the evening's performance. The noble lord would, however, take no denial and assured Fischer that he did not ask him professionally, but merely for the gratification of his society and conversation. Thus urged and encouraged, he went; he had not, however, been many minutes in the house of this consistent nobleman, before his lordship approached him, and said: 'I hope, Mr. Fischer, you have brought your oboe in your pocket.' 'No, my lord,' said Fischer, 'my oboe never sups.' He turned on his heel and instantly left the house, and no persuasion could ever induce him to return to it."

Kelly's journey to Naples took place during the American war: "The ship I was on board of, being a Swede, was under a neutral flag; yet, in the Bay of Biscay we were hailed by an American privateer. Our captain lay to, while a set of the greatest ragamuffins my eyes ever beheld, boarded us. They swore the vessel was under false colors, and proceeded to overhaul the Captain's papers, and seize everything they could lay hands on. A sturdy ruffian began to break open my piano-forte case with a hatchet which, when I saw, I manfully began to weep, and cry out: 'Oh! my dear piano-forte!' The cabin boy, who was about my own age, called out: 'For God's sake, don't cry, Master Kelly!' The chief mate of the privateer, who was quietly perusing some of our Captain's papers, on hearing these words, turned around and looking steadfastly at me, said: 'Is your name Kelly?' I answered: 'Yes.' 'Do you know anything of a Mr. Thomas Kelly, of Mary Street, Dublin?' he said. 'He is my father,' was my reply. The young man immediately started up, ran to me, clasped me in his arms, and with tears in his eyes, said: 'Don't you remember me? I am Jack Cunningham, who, when you were a little boy, nursed you and played with you?'"

This is the sort of adventure that could befall young musicians making sea voyages during the War of Independence!

* * *

Kelly made Naples his new home and studied with the singing master Finaroli, who was at that time director of the conservatory "La Madonna di Loreto". His most important teacher, however, was the famous castrato and contralto Giuseppe Aprile (1738-1814), also Cimarosa's teacher. It is Aprile to whom Kelly owes his career as a singer. Before long, he made appearances in several opera houses. He travelled to Sicily and spent some time in Rome, making the most interesting observations about persons and places wherever he went. Most naturally, his interest was directed in first line at opera; in this connection I would like to cite his humorous description of the manner in which the Romans criticized their vocalists:

"The numerous abbés were the severest of the critics; they would sit in the front of the pit, each bearing in one hand a lighted wax taper and in the other the score of the opera, and should an unfortunate singer make a mistake, the critical clerics would call out: 'Bravo, bestia!' (Bravo, you beast!)

"The composer of the opera used to preside at the piano-forte during the first three performances of his work, and a bad time he often had of it. Should any passage of his opera strike the audience as similar to the melody of another composer, the cry would arise: 'Bravo, il ladro!' (Bravo, you thief!) or: 'Bravo, Paisiello!' 'Bravo, Sacchini!'—if they considered the passage stolen from these masters."

The above cannot fail but call to mind the banquet scene from Mozart's "Don Giovanni" with the orchestra's rendition of melodies from operas which were currently in vogue. "Bravi! Cosa rara!" "Evvivano i Litiganti!" cries Leporello, the funny servant of Don Giovanni, thus greeting the popular excerpts from the works of Martini and Sarti. At the playing of the theme from "The Marriage of Figaro", he exclaims indignantly: "Questa poi la conosco pur troppo!" (I'm getting sick and tired of this!). Mozart parodies the goings-on in the Italian opera houses (on which Kelly comments) and, to some extent, he pokes a little fun at himself as well!

* * *

As I had mentioned before, the climax of Kelly's career was during his stay in Vienna—his engagement at the Imperial Opera house of Kaiser Joseph II and his friendship with Mozart.

After numerous adventures in Florence, Venice, Livorno and after a somewhat unsuccessful position in Graz, Kelly came to Vienna in 1783 with letters of recommendation from his patron, Count Orsini-Rosenberg. He went immediately after his arrival to see Antonio Salieri (1750-1825), the great Italian opera composer who was then holding the vice-directorship at the opera house. Salieri became Kelly's employer. He informed Kelly that his own opera, "La scuola dei Gelosi", was to be the first production and that in this work Michael would make his debut. He then showed the young tenor the apartment which had been provided for him, an elegant duplex suite. In addition Kelly was to receive a daily ration of fuel and four wax candles as well as the services of a carriage to take him to the theatre whenever he performed.

It was only natural that Kelly should be fascinated most by the gay and colorful society life in the Austrian capital: The "Prater" (which he likens to Hyde Park) with its culinary attraction, the famed "Backhendel" (fried chicken), so highly praised by him, the famous Viennese carnival with all its masquerade balls, where the waltz (at that time yet unknown in England) played such an important part, and last but not least the pleasures of the theatre—all this is mentioned with great enthusiasm in his reminiscences. The artistic-minded and music-loving Austrian nobility of those days, among whom we find the friends and patrons of Haydn, Mozart and Beethoven, and above all the music-loving monarch Joseph II are the persons we meet so often in Kelly's memoirs.

In these writings, bubbling over with wit, music plays the main lead. Kelly paid a visit to Haydn who, at that time, lived at the court of Count Esterhazy in Eisenstadt. He was Haydn's guest for three days and Kelly maintained that it was a pleasure of the highest order to ride with the great composer in the Count's elegant carriage, gazing at the beautiful landscape surrounding Eisenstadt.

One day Kelly attended a concert at which the famous Leopold Anton Kozeluch (1752-1818) soloed on the piano. On that occasion, Kelly met two composers: Johann Bapt. Vanhall (1739-1813) and Karl Dittersdorf (1739-1799). Kelly always refers to him as Baron Diderstoff but "what was to me", he writes, "one of the greatest gratifications of my musical life was that I was there introduced to that prodigy of genius: Mozart. He favored the company by performing fantasies and capriccios on the pianoforte. His feeling, the rapidity of his fingers, the great execution and strength of his left hand particularly, and the apparent inspiration of his modulations, astounded me. After this splendid performance, we sat down to supper, and I had the pleasure to be placed at a table between him and his wife, Madame Constanze Weber, a German lady, of whom he was passionately fond, and by whom he had three children.* He conversed with me a good deal about Thomas Linley, with whom he was intimate at Florence, and spoke of him with great affection. He said that Linley was a true genius, and he felt that, had he lived, he would have been one of the greatest ornaments of the musical world."

The mention of Thomas Linley, that ingenious youth who, at the tender age of 14, stayed in Florence to study violin with Pietro Nardini (1722-1793), leads us to Mozart's sojourn in Italy (1769-1771). Young Wolfgang Amadeus made the acquaintance of the youthful English violinist at the house of the famous female improviser Corilla. The two boys were inseparable, while Mozart stayed in Florence making music together without tiring. "Little Tomaso (Linley)"—so tells Mozart's father, Leopold, in a letter to his wife—"accompanied us to our house and cried bitterly, because we were to depart the following day. He found out that our departure was set at noontide and so came to us at 9 o'clock in the morning. With many embraces he presented a poem to Wolfgang which he had made Signora Corilla

---

*Of the 6 children born to Mozart only two, Karl and Wolfgang Mozart survived.

write for him the previous evening....". Thomas
Linley died in 1778 through an accident on a boat
trip; he drowned.

Let us return to Kelly's memories of Mozart. Kelly
names the great master's passion for dancing as one
of his most outstanding characteristics. Madame Mozart was supposed to have aired her ideas on this point,
according to Kelly, by saying that "his taste lay in
that art rather than in music." A peculiar remark
of the good Constanze, to be sure! "He was," Kelly
continues, "a remarkably small man, very thin and
pale, with a profusion of fine hair, of which he was
rather vain. He gave me a cordial invitation to his
home, of which I availed myself, and passed a great
part of my time there. He always received me with
kindness and hospitality. He was remarkably fond
of punch, of which beverage I have seen him take
copious draughts. He was also fond of billiards, and
had an excellent billiard table in his house. Many
and many a game have I played with him, but always
came off second best. He gave Sunday concerts, at
which I never was missing. He was kind-hearted and
always ready to oblige, but so very particular, when
he played, that if the slightest noise were made, he
instantly left off. He one day made me sit down to
the piano, and gave credit to my first master, who
had taught me to place my hand well on the instrument. He conferred on me what I considered a high
compliment. I had composed a little melody to
Metastasio's 'Grazie agl'inganni tuoi', a canzonetta

which was a great favorite wherever I sang it. It was very simple, but had the good fortune to please Mozart. He took it and composed variations upon it, which were truly beautiful; and had the further kindness and condescension to play them wherever he had an opportunity. Thinking that the air thus rendered remarkable, might be acceptable to some of my musical readers, I have subjoined it."

In fact, we find the little aria, in the style of Paisiello, reproduced in Kelly's book, very charming, even if the solid professional development is lacking. Mozart's variations mentioned by Kelly have never been found. Perhaps Mozart did not write down the variations at all, only played them as he often did from memory. Nevertheless, under No. 532 of the "Koechel Verzeichnis", we find a terzetto upon the same text by Metastasio, and the music Mozart wrote is almost identical to that of Kelly. The Mozart terzetto which is in B flat is in series 7 (No. 35) of Mozart's complete works. Mozart did not hesitate to use the melody which he chanced upon, but it is also possible that Mozart notated Kelly's in order to use it for his variations. Evidence of this fact may be that Mozart's autograph has no text.

It is interesting that Kelly's melody was published in 1790 in a collection of "Six English Airs and Six Italian Duetti for the Harpsichord" (Longman & Broderip, London) and dedicated to "Her Grace, the Duchess of Leeds", as "Duetto III" in form of a terzetto almost identical to that of Mozart and also written in B flat major.

Kelly relates that, flattered by Mozart's recognition, he composed a couple of arias and showed them to the great master. "He kindly approved them so much indeed, that I determined to devote myself to composition." Kelly wished to train himself better in counterpoint and asked Mozart to suggest a teacher. Mozart was of the opinion that he should rather continue as a writer of melodies, for melody was Kelly's real field of talent. Besides, Mozart said, his career as an opera singer would take all his time. A writer of melody, observed Mozart, was to be compared with a race horse, a contrapuntist with a dependable coach horse. It is interesting, however, that Kelly played an important role in the history of Mozart's operas.

At the premiere of "The Marriage of Figaro" (May 1, 1786) in the Viennese Burgtheater, Kelly sang the part of Basilio. Mozart had the highest esteem for this versatile tenor who was always very successful in serious as well as comic roles. To a certain extent Kelly owed his success to his prodigious ability as an actor. He himself wrote that his mimic art evoked such enthusiasm from the famous librettist Casti as well as from Paisiello that they entrusted him with the difficult role of Gafforino in "Re Theodoro". Kelly's interpretation of this part earned him the greatest success.

In the creation of the various parts in "Figaro", Mozart undoubtedly considered the individuality of the performers. Kelly (in Vienna he chose to call himself O'Kelly and that is the way his name appears in Mozart's writings, in libretti, etc.) wrote about Mozart:

"In the sestetto, in the second act, I had a very conspicuous part as the stuttering judge (Basilio). All through the piece I was to stutter; but in the sestetto, Mozart requested I would not, for, if I did, I should spoil his music. I told him that although it might appear very presumptuous of a lad like me to differ with him on this point, I did; and was sure, the way in which I intended to introduce the stuttering would not interfere with the other parts, but produce an effect; besides, it certainly was not in nature, that I should stutter all through the part and when I came to the sestetto speak plain; and after that piece of music was over return to stuttering; and I added (apologizing at the same time for my apparent want of deference and respect in placing my opinion in opposition to that of the great Mozart), that, unless I was allowed to perform the part as I wished, I would not perform it at all. Mozart at last consented that I should have my own way, but doubted the success of the experiment. Crowded houses proved that nothing ever produced on the stage a more powerful effect. The audience were convulsed with laughter, in which Mozart himself joined. The Emperor repeatedly cried out: 'Bravo!' and the piece was loudly applauded and encored. When the opera was over, Mozart came on the stage to me, and shaking both my hands, he said: 'Bravo, young man, I feel obliged to you; and acknowledge you to have been in the right, and myself in the wrong' . . ."

In this connection it should be mentioned that Kelly was not the only Englishman in the cast. The female lead in the opera, the charming Susanna, was sung by Nancy Storace (1766-1817), an English girl. Nancy's father came originally from Italy, but later settled in Ireland; his family became completely anglicized. Kelly tells the amusing story of how he made the acquaintance of Nancy and her brother, Stephen Storace (1763-1796) on a boat trip near Livorno. Michael was a blond and very boyish looking youth who might well have been taken for a girl disguised in men's clothing. On shipboard he overheard one of the passengers, a girl, addressing herself to her escort in English: "Look at that girl dressed in boy's clothes!" To her astonishment, Kelly called out in the same language: "You are mistaken, Miss, I am a very proper he-animal and quite at your service." "All three," Kelly continues, "laughed immoderately, and from that moment was formed a firm friendship which was to have important developments in the musical world of the coming years."

During Kelly's stay in Vienna, Stephen Storace became a well known composer and also Mozart's pupil. He wrote a number of sound chamber music works.

Another member of Mozart's English circle was Thomas Attwood (1765-1838), also a pupil of the great master. In later years, Attwood made quite a reputation for himself in England as a fine church composer.

In February 1787 Kelly bade farewell to Vienna. The Emperor had granted him a year's paid vacation—Kelly never returned, however. His English friends, Attwood and the Storaces were Kelly's travelling companions. On the eve of their departure, at a ball, Stephen Storace had an encounter with an officer who was dancing with Nancy. Because he wore his spurs and carried his sabre while dancing, Stephen —under the influence of too much wine—insulted the officer. Young Storace was put into jail for the night and Kelly had to negotiate with the Emperor for his release so that the travelling party might depart.

Bidding farewell to Mozart must have been a painful task, indeed. On their way through Salzburg, the party stopped at Hannibal Square dropping in on Papa Leopold Mozart to transmit his son's greetings.

Mozart's English friends had left no stone unturned in their attempt to persuade the great master to go to England with them, and Mozart had almost decided to join them, because he thought Vienna ungrateful and unappreciative of his efforts. The somewhat frivolous Madame Mozart went so far as to want to leave the children under the care of her father-in-law in Salzburg, but Leopold wanted no part of this bargain. This refusal, coupled with Mozart's negotiations (which were just then getting under way) with the Prague theatre-entrepreneur Guardasoni, who invited

Mozart to the Bohemian capital, were the reasons which prompted Mozart's final resolution to remain in Vienna.

* * *

What about Kelly? His visit to Vienna marked the climax of his career. His later successes were a mere echo of his former glory. He became first tenor at the Drury-Lane-Theatre in London, sang at the concerts of the "Society of Ancient Music" and took part in the performances of Haendel's works in Westminster Abbey. He never forgot Mozart's praise of his canzonets and wrote songs and incidental music for a number of plays. After he lost his voice he took over the management of a theatre and also opened a music shop which went bankrupt as he did not possess a keen mind for business.

The Kellys had been wine merchants for many generations and, since he had acquired an expert knowledge about wines in Austria as well as in Italy, he opened a business in 1811. This fact, with the then current opinion in London that Kelly leaned heavily on foreign models in his compositions, (on the other hand, also inclined to mixing his wines), was supposed to have inspired Sheridan, the theatre entrepreneur, in voicing his classic statement that the sign hanging over Kelly's wine establishment should in reality read as follows:

"Michael Kelly,
Composer of Wines and Importer of Music."

CHAPTER EIGHT

SCHUBERT'S CZECH PREDECESSORS
JOHANN WENZEL TOMASCHEK
AND HUGO VORISEK

IT was in the summer of 1822 that Goethe met a musician in the German-Bohemian town of Eger. His name was Tomaschek who had come from Prague to meet the 73-year-old German poet whom he greatly admired. At that time Goethe was taking the waters in Franzensbad, a spa about two miles from Eger. He was very much interested in Tomaschek's music which had been set to some of his poems. Having corresponded with Tomaschek for some time, he was anxious to hear these compositions.

At Eger, the composer and the poet went together to the house of the lawyer Franck, who owned a good piano, and there Tomaschek sang about fifteen of his songs for the great poet. When he came to his version of Mignon's song "Knowest thou the land", Goethe is said to have remarked: "I cannot understand how Beethoven and Spohr could have so misunderstood the spirit of the poem when they wrote their musical settings for it. Surely, the punctuation of the steps coming at the same place in each verse should have been sufficient indication for the musician, that all I expected him to do was to write a simple song. It is against Mignon's temperament to intone a formal aria."

Incidentally, Beethoven's version of Mignon's song is not "durchkomponiert" but "strophic" with only very slight modifications.

One year later, Tomaschek met Goethe again, this time in Marienbad, another spa in Northern Bohemia. Here the latter wrote two verses of his poem "Aeolian Harps" into Tomaschek's album and gave it the title, "Lovelorn Duet, sung after parting." This poem is one of those that originated in the sorrowful days after the aged poet had separated from his young beloved, Ulrike von Levetzow. It seems that at this very period Goethe was greatly moved by Tomaschek's songs, because from them emanated that rather mournful, slightly erotic, and musically not over-distinguished spirit of early romanticism which appealed to Goethe at that time.

There was another reason by which Goethe may have felt attracted to Tomaschek. When, in 1819, a translation of the spurious documents of the Königinhofer Manuscript, issued by Hanka, had been published, Goethe greatly admired it, and Tomaschek had composed several of those poems. Their gloomy melodies seem to remind us of the Slavonic type rather than that of the traditional Czech folk song, because Tomaschek—in spite of the fact that he had spent his youth in Bohemia—had no real insight into the spirit of Czech folk music. Where he wished to appear primitive and natural, he conjured up an erotic, melancholy landscape. The songs of the Königinhofer Manuscript by no means contain any of the bright major moods of the Czech people. But we must not forget that the Czech folk song is a product of the late seventeenth or eighteenth century and shows all characteristics of central European homophonic style, the style of that period. Tomaschek's compositions, however, are characteristic products of an early romanticism.

At about the middle of the nineteenth century, a yearbook written in German was published in Prague under the title of "Libussa". Its purpose was to outline the history and the inner meaning of the Bohemian people and their country. The editor of this book was a German who, like so many other Germans of that time, wished to do his share towards the revival of Czech culture. This trend became apparent at about 1800 and persisted well into the middle of the 19th century. At that time no Czech nationalism existed in the sense of an exclusive and aggressive racial consciousness. The two ethnic groups, Germans and Czechs, living together as neighbors, with Germans occupying higher social ranks than the Czechs, found common ground in their mutual love of their beloved native country. They both rejected the Hapsburg idea of a centralistic federalism of a greater Austria. Even as late as 1900, those who considered themselves "Bohemians", who spoke both languages and refused to adhere to a narrow-minded nationalism, were called "Utraquists". Characteristically, the country's literati, its poets and writers felt themselves thoroughly a "part of Bohemia" and wrote and thought in the "Bohemian way". Tomaschek's wife was the sister of the German-Bohemian Karl Egon Ebert, a fervent patriot, who treated of Czech subjects in his works, as for example in his heroic epic of "Vlasta" which describes the war of the Czech amazons. Another representative of this group is the poet Alfred Meissner, who chose a Czech hero for his "Žižka". The same holds good for Tomaschek as well as for a number of other Czech musicians, such as Joh. Aug. Wittasek (1771-1839), Hugo Vořišek (1791-1825), the great musicologist Aug. Wilh.-Ambros (1816-1876) who, though German, wrote a nationalistic opera, "Bretislav and Jitka", besides a great many Czech songs; furthermore, there were Frederic Dionysus Weber (1766-1824), Johann Frederic Kittl (1806), and many others.

The "Libussa" yearbook contains an autobiography of Tomaschek which, in spite of its form, is an excellent source for the musical history of that period. The best known anecdote in this biographical study is the one about Tomaschek's meeting with Beethoven, written in the form of a dialogue.

Tomaschek, born in Skuč, East Bohemia, on April 17, 1774, was the son of a flax-weaver. He went to

Iglau, Moravia, where he became a chorister in the monastery of the "Minorites" and, at the same time, attended High School. In 1790 he moved to Prague to study law at the university of this capital. He was a self-taught person as far as music goes, although he may have had some lessons from a certain Franz Duschek, a rather mediocre Czech composer, whose name became well known because of his wife Josefa, who was Mozart's friend in Prague and a good singer. Mozart dedicated to her one of his concert arias, "Bella mia fiamma" in 1787; and Beethoven, who was also among her famous friends, wrote for her his aria "Ah, perfido" in 1796.

For some time Tomaschek lived on the Duschek estate, in the same villa in which Mozart finished his "Don Giovanni". No wonder then that Tomaschek's youth was dominated by the spirit of Mozart although he had no chance to witness the first performances of "Don Giovanni" (1787), nor that of "La Clemenza di Tito" (1791), because, as he puts it, "he wanted to save his father the expense of a journey to Prague."

He tells of having given lessons in Mr. and Mrs. Duschek's house, the "Bertramka". His admiration for Mozart was so fervent that he failed to do justice to Beethoven whom he visited in Vienna in 1814. He even refused to acknowledge the value of "Fidelio" and did not hesitate to make disparaging remarks about "The Battle of Vittoria". He was sorely grieved to find a Beethoven among "a company of the grossest materialists." Late in his life, though overwhelmed by the great master's titanic stature, he was frightened of him. Mozart remained his ideal and, because of his influence on him, he never departed from a conservative standpoint.

It is quite interesting to listen to a conversation between Tomaschek and Beethoven as Tomaschek tells us in his autobiographical sketch. It was on October 10, 1814, when Tomaschek accompanied by his brother visited the great composer. The conversation did not take place in writing as was usual with the deaf master, but orally. Of course, Tomaschek had to shout:

Tomaschek: Herr von Beethoven, I hope you will forgive us for disturbing you. I am from Prague, composer with Count Buquoy, my name is Tomaschek. I have taken the liberty of calling on you with my brother.

Beethoven: I am very much pleased to make your acquaintance—you aren't disturbing me in the least.

T.: I bring you best regards from Doctor R [eger].

B.: How is he? I haven't heard from him in a long time.

T.: He would like to know how you are getting along with your lawsuit.

B.: One can't make any headway with all these circumstantialities.

T.: Herr von Beethoven, you seem to be very diligent.

B.: Don't I have to be? What would my fame amount to?

T.: Does my pupil Woržischek often come here?'

B.: He has been here several times, but I haven't heard him play. The other day, he brought me some of his compositions. (Beethoven spoke here of the "Twelve Rhapsodies for the Pianoforte" which were dedicated to him and which appeared in print some time later.)

T.: You rarely go out, do you?

B.: I hardly go anywhere.

T.: They are playing an opera by.... today, but I don't feel like listening to music of that kind.*

B.: Good heavens, we must have such composers too, otherwise what would the mob do?

T.: I am also told that a young artist, a newcomer, is staying here (Meyerbeer) and is supposed to be an excellent pianist.

B.: Yes, I too have heard about him, but I haven't heard him play. Good heavens, he is supposed to stay here for three months, after which we'll know what the Viennese think of his way of playing. I know that everything new is very much liked here.

T.: And you have never run into him?

B.: I made his acquaintance at the performance of my "Battle"† on which occasion several of our composers played instruments. That young man took charge of the long drum. Ha! Ha! Ha! I was not satis-

---

*This must have slipped his memory, because no opera performance was scheduled for that day. The only theatrical performance that evening was a drama, "Moses" by Aug. Klingemann with music by Ign. von Seyfried, played in the Theater an der Wien.

†The Battle of Vittoria

fied with him at all, he didn't play it right, he always came in too late so that I had to scold him. Ha! Ha! Ha! That must have annoyed him. He is not good, he hasn't the courage to hit at the right moment.

My brother and I laughed heartily at this story. He invited us to stay for dinner which we refused and took leave of him with the promise to see him once more before we would leave....

* * *

It is understandable that Tomaschek, at a time when Meyerbeer's reputation had reached its climax in 1847, wished to smear the composer, whom—though he was his friend—he very much envied because of his successes and good fortune that followed him. He did the same again when mentioning his farewell visit with Beethoven and was even more malicious about it:

"I was at the opera ('Die beiden Kalifen' by Meyerbeer), it began with a hallelujah and ended with a requiem." And then he has Beethoven rail against the young composer: "He is a miserable fellow..."—and this is the least he has Beethoven say about him!

Well, even great masters have sometimes been jealous of their colleagues' successes. Why should Tomaschek have been an exception? It seems as though his jealousy was the expression of his dissatisfaction and petty envy which somehow was in keeping with his provincial position as a miniature master. And, above all, out of him spoke the traditional opposition of the Bohemian against Vienna, against Austria.

On reading Tomaschek's life story and his letters as well as reports of his contemporaries about him, we learn he aimed to play the part of a Czech arbiter of music and to be its supreme authority. We find that there developed in him a certain opposition to German supremacy and, above all, a rejection of Viennese trends. He admired Vienna, but one cannot help being aware of his resistance to the all-powerful city and capital. This becomes particularly apparent in a letter dated January 12, 1834, in which he writes the following to a German musician:

"Beautiful Prague, the capital of a conquered province, has for the last forty years been lacking the wherewithal, the indispensable state of prosperity which might serve to draw its attention to art and science." This spirit of contradiction, visible in the very expression of his face as we know it from portraits, caused him to be an "outsider" in spite of the fact that he was the most accomplished musical personage in Bohemia at that time. He was not even a professor at the Prague Conservatory, he had no state or other official function, but remained a domestic musician attached to Count Buquoy, though he had become famous as a teacher of musical theory since 1810. His provincialism kept him in Prague, contrary to the habit of former generations of Bohemian musicians, who went to live outside their native country. As a result he was not very much known in musical circles in Europe and has remained obscure to this day.

Berlioz's memoirs illustrate this point. When the French composer was introduced to Czech musicians by Ambros during a visit to Prague, he declared that he had never heard any of Tomaschek's music. Ambros had to tell him that Tomaschek had written a magnificent requiem. Berlioz, on being presented to the musical pope of Prague, at once took the opportunity to compliment him upon his achievements, and Tomaschek was highly gratified. According to Berlioz's memoirs, thirty-one of thirty-two pieces played at a concert he attended were composed by Tomaschek.

It is interesting to discover that the visit to Tomaschek related by Berlioz is also told by Hanslick in his autobiography, "Aus meinem Leben". Here Hanslick substitutes himself for Ambros, and it is an interesting question whether Hanslick was really the one who introduced Berlioz, and whether Berlioz confused the two men in his memory.

Hanslick was a pupil of Tomaschek, and he says "he (Tomaschek) recalled the appearance of Spohr, even down to the badly made wig. He was full of self-confidence, and the proverbial phrase of Dingelstedt (the Viennese theatrical director) 'You can't imagine how much praise I can bear' could easily be applied to Tomaschek."

"This self-confidence," Hanslick continues, "was not without justification. He was an inspired composer, inventive, prolific, and full of character; sensitive without being feminine in his songs, witty and vivacious without coquetry in his piano pieces, and dignified and splendid in his church compositions. But he never reached the audience outside of Prague, and in that respect he shared the fate of so many other Prague artists who hulked in Prague."

It seems to the present writer that Tomaschek belongs more to the so-called 'Biedermaier' group which had that somewhat philistine attitude which became the object of Schumann's expressive criticism, the criticism which found its best expression in the "Davidsbund".

Hanslick goes on to tell about his lessons with Tomaschek: one hour weekly devoted to piano, and two to theory. Tomaschek's bible was Bach's "Well-tempered Clavier", as well as the sonatas of Beethoven, with the exception of the last ones. Otherwise, they studied only the works of Talberg, Chopin, Handel, or some by Liszt. His theory course with Tomaschek was shared by Julius Schulhoff, Wilhelm Kuhe, who later became an Englishman, and Hans Hampel. It is interesting to hear that Tomaschek had little interest in music history or the aesthetics of music.

On the occasion of the Czech master's death an anonymous article appeared in the "Frankfurter Konversationsblatt" in 1850, telling of a visit which a Viennese had paid him. The visitor describes how he found the composer dressed in a ghostly costume playing his Faust composition at midnight. The old musician sang the parts in a hoarse voice, impersonating Gretchen with her lament and Mephistopheles in his scornful moods, and rendering the mighty harmonies of the choral songs. Altogether, it is a tale of magic and mystery, emphasizing the romantic aspect of the Prague quarters across the river; but between the lines it shows clearly how lightly Tomaschek was esteemed outside Prague. "The gentlemen in Vienna," he supposedly said, "behave as though I do not exist at all. Well, never mind, I shall have to be patient now until after my death."

Tomaschek's contemporaries describe him as a stout tall man, who strutted about with a magisterial air, pleased with himself, not very friendly, staring at people arrogantly, shouting at them, tearing them to pieces with his sarcasm; and yet at bottom an upright and honest man.

Clara Schumann, who gave a concert in Prague in November 1837 and on this occasion met the Prague pope of music, gave a somewhat negative picture of his character.[1] "But this Tomaschek is nothing but an awful prattler, who is furious about you," she wrote to Robert on November 19, "because you have rebuked Dreyschock (his pupil). Nothing annoys me more now than that I played some of your compositions for them. Tomaschek does not understand them, or does not want to understand. I quarrelled with him about Bellini, Spohr (you know my weakness), Mozart, etc. When he then told me that Gluck was the foremost composer of the world and that I

---

[1] Berthold Litzmann, "Clara Schumann", I, pg. 146

do not know anything about real music, I said: 'When I am an old woman, then shall I also swoon over Gluck—but now I'll still live for everything that's beautiful in art and feel happy that I am not yet narrow-minded.' He left—and did not come back again."

But Tomaschek was that way, conservative, provincial and a bit jealous of the new and great era of music that was emerging at that time.

Tomaschek's and Voříšek's influence on Schubert has already been pointed out by Willy Kahl in the third volume of the "Archiv fuer Musikwissenschaft". It is true that one cannot regard Tomaschek as the originator of the lyrical pianoforte piece, particularly when one considers the illustrative keyboard compositions of the French clavecinists or Beethoven's Bagatelles as belonging to this category. However, it was Tomaschek who first introduced the exposition of a lyrical concept on the pianoforte, its development by means of keyboard technique and the outlining of a poetical mood which in a way approached the world of the romantic shepherds and shepherdesses as portrayed by Watteau.

As early as 1810 he had published a set of "Six Eclogues" with Kuehnel at Leipzig. They were actually written in 1807, long before Schubert composed his "Impromptus" and "Moments musicaux". It should, however, be mentioned here that another Czech composer antedating Tomaschek by more than a generation, wrote successful lyrical pianoforte music:

Mozart's friend Joseph Myslivecek. In the National Museum of Prague there is a manuscript of six "Divertimenti per cembalo" in which this composer laid down the form of the lyrical pianoforte piece, for the first time. These charming, playful, and light pieces revealing their composer's gay and carefree spirit, are mentioned in a letter written by Leopold Mozart to his son[1] in which he says: "Mr. Misliwetcek (sic) sends me six short clavier pieces for Nannerl." And after Tomaschek and Vořišek, the former's pupil, Johann Frederic Kittl, published his opus 1, "Six Idylls", which, though not as excellent as the works of Tomaschek and Vořišek show a remarkable gift for the evocation of pastoral moods, as Schumann justly pointed out.

Not until 1827 did Schubert begin the composition of his "Impromptus", that is 17 years after Tomaschek's "Eclogues" appeared. During that time Schubert had come to know Bohemian lyrical pianoforte music, not only composed by Tomaschek, but also by his pupil Vořišek. Born at Vamberg in Bohemia, in 1791, Vořišek died in Vienna in 1825. He was a great master of the pianoforte. Although he took Hummel as his model, we do not find among Hummel's pianoforte works any lyrical compositions that might be so designated from the romanticist's point of view. Hummel wrote rondos, dances and bagatelles, using this last name for rondos, variations and scherzos. Thus the only composer who could possibly

[1] October 29, 1777

have served as an example for Vořišek, as far as his pianistic romanticism was concerned, was Tomaschek. Vořišek was on excellent terms with Beethoven. When Tomaschek visited Beethoven, as mentioned before, he spoke of the young composer's "Rhapsodies": "The other day he brought me one of his compositions which I consider nicely worked out for one so young."

Vořišek belonged to that group of Austrian musicians who were forced by financial circumstances to divide their time between work in an office and devotion to their art. Although he had renounced his artistic ambitions in 1822 by becoming a functionary in the State Council for War, he soon exchanged this position for the one of a court organist. He was an invalid all his life. After a cure at Carsbad he returned to Vienna in 1825, an incurable victim of tuberculosis, and died on November 19th of that year, three years to a day before Schubert.

During his stay in Prague, Vořišek had already published a number of pianoforte pieces. His 12 "Rhapsodies" came out in 1818, probably in connection with Tomaschek's compositions bearing the same name; and we find in them the same pastoral moods as in Tomaschek's pieces, the first pianoforte compositions to appear under this new designation. In 1822 Mechetti of Vienna published Vořišek's opus 7, the "Impromptus", in which he somewhat leans on Tomaschek's "Eclogues". The word "impromptu" as a title for music originated with Vořišek, but is closely related to and dependent on Tomaschek's designations, such as "Eclogues" and "Dithyrambs". While Tomaschek patterned his work on that of Mozart, Voříšek took Beethoven as his ideal. Tomaschek was more Czech and more akin to folk music than Voříšek who, though not being so close to the soil, handled the pianoforte better in his compositions.

Schubert's two sets appearing in the years 1827 and 1828 under the title of "Impromptus for Pianoforte", op. 142 and 90, are directly influenced by the keyboard compositions of these Czechs. Schubert did not confine himself to taking over the designations and forms of such music from the Czech musicians, he is also related to them in spirit. Tomaschek's preference for thirds and sixths, a peculiarity which Schubert derived from light popular music, proves the point. Schubert's folk-tone and his delight in Hungarian (Slovakian) treatment is closely akin to that of Tomaschek, whose first composition for the pianoforte was a set of "Hungarian Dances". We find in Schubert all the touches characteristic of the Bohemian masters: a preference for the less usual keys, so often found in Voříšek's music, the frequent appearance of lyrical passages, the interweaving of a sustained melody with the accompaniment, the frequency of episodes in octave unison, the sudden reappearance of a minor theme in the major and the converse —he has all these features in common with them.

Just as we find reminiscences of Czech folk melodies in Tomaschek's pianoforte compositions and songs,

we can easily see how the music of the Viennese suburbs and Austrian peasantry became embodied in
Schubert's work a few years later. So evidently is this
the case that Schubert's music seems to us to give in
crystallized form what has come to be considered the
typically Viennese musical style of the period. As
far as the Czechs are concerned, Tomaschek was not
ready to attain such a typification, nor was it reached
until several generations later in the work of Smetana.

Tomaschek's creation of the "Eclogues" was based
on his objection to the vapid variation compositions
of the time. "The current commonplace taste of the
age forced me," he says in the introduction to the
"Eclogues", "to seek refuge in poetry, to try to find
a way of using its technique in the field of music and
thereby to broaden the already greatly limited poetic-
creative scope of the tonal art."

Particularly in the "Dithyrambs", published in 1823
by Marco Berra at Prague, he showed himself Schubert's predecessor as a keyboard composer. In this
work, especially at the opening of the first of the three
pieces, we find the same rhythm, the same stately
treatment, the same peculiar use of octaves as we
find in Schubert's "Wanderer Fantasy". Here we have
the same long pauses and other Schubertian characteristics, too. Above all, we find the same romantic alter-
nations from a tragic mood into a lyrical one, so conspicuous in the music of the early romanticists, and
this is combined with the portrayal of the Czech landscape, a quality which is pastoral rather than national

in feeling. For Tomaschek's music resembles in its mood that fertile summer landscape watered by the Vltava or Elbe, flanked by hilly vineyards.

Tomaschek's songs no less than his pianoforte pieces express the charm of this Bohemian landscape, which so greatly attracted Goethe. This is particularly true of his settings of Goethe's poems. The song "Nur wer die Sehnsucht kennt" from "Wilhelm Meister" is definitely Czech in tone, with its wavering between 'Sturm und Drang' and sentimentalism, and this is equally true of "Wer kauft Liebesgoetter", sung in Goethe's unfinished sequel to "The Magic Flute" by Papageno. There is a pianoforte prelude which introduces the song with a trumpet-call pointing to the "Cries of Prague", the calls of the Italian street vendors of statuary, who used to entice buyers out of their houses with a trumpet. No less characteristic are "Die Sproede" and "Die Bekehrte", both written in that mellow, almost sentimental, naturally primitive mood which, as in the "Eclogues", shows us Tomaschek's inclination towards the bucolic and rustic. For this true Czech cannot hide the peasant in his make-up, though he sublimates the rustic elements into something pastoral and idyllic.

To a high degree, many of these songs possess the intensity of feeling we find in Schubert. The song "Naehe der Geliebten" ("Ich denke Dein") is composed with a different air to each verse, not strophically as Schubert treated it. It is a masterpiece of romantic lyrical composition, rising from simple but intense emotional melodic expression to dramatic passion, and it is all done quite simply, as Goethe intended when he wrote the poem. All these songs are part of the five volumes of Tomaschek's opus 53—published by Marco Berra in 1815—, which as a whole offers some of the best songs of that time. Those resembling closest Schubert's work are "Mit einem gemalten Band" and "Die Nacht"—published 1822—, the latter in every respect, and almost word for word, the ancestor of the graceful Goethe-Schubert song "Geheimes". Though Tomaschek's style is more primitive than Schubert's, this song shows in every detail how great the Czech musician's influence was on the Viennese master.

CHAPTER NINE

MUSICAL MONARCHS

IN his drama, "Die Jungfrau von Orleans", Schiller, the great German poet, has King Charles VII say:

"Drum soll der Saenger mit dem Koenig gehen.
Sie beide wohnen auf der Menschheit Hoehen."

The days when kings and princes regarded the cultivation of the arts as one of their most essential duties are certainly past, and modern heads of state are so overburdened with urgent affairs of government that they must of necessity subordinate their own personal interest in art; and they have even less time for their own expression of art. But to be up-to-date and correct, we must refer to President Truman, a good pianist and an enthusiastic lover of music. At any rate, he was the first "potentate" of world history to perform on the piano before a forum which represented the world's greatest powers. His playing at Potsdam made such a hit that even Stalin did not find it difficult to play "first violin".

Yet, President Harry Truman was not the first musical president of the United States. Thomas Jefferson, for instance, loved to play the violin. But opinion about his ability to make music varied. Some thought him to be an excellent player, while others disagreed, labelling him "the worst performer of Virginia".

While visiting New York, Béla Bartók, the Hungarian composer, was proclaimed President of Hungary by a patriotic Hungarian party. He never assumed this position, although there was a precedent in the great Polish composer Ignace Jan Paderewski, who was—if not President of Poland—Minister-President of that country in 1919.

Early Musical Kings

One must delve deeply into legend and history to find the early musical kings. The archetype of these royal musicians was King David who, when still a simple shepherd, secured entrance to King Saul's court as a result of his excellent musicianship. But in the final analysis it was probably not his harp-playing which procured for him the throne of Judea. The Roman Emperor Nero, who considered himself the best actor and musician in Rome, often emphasized his artistic abilities much more than his political potentialities. When he felt that his end was near, he called out: "What an artist is going to die with me!"

Speaking of modern history, we may conjecture that Hitler might not have hurled Germany into catastrophe and the world into the bloodiest of all

wars, had he not, as a young man in Vienna, learned
that there was no future for him as a painter. His
ambition to become an artist is said to have transformed itself into an almost pathological will for
power. But even at the height of his power, he did
not stop dreaming of becoming an artist, painter, architect, builder of cities. It is well known how he wooed
for the favor of many a great musician. He pretended
to be the representative of Bayreuth's true tradition
which, after a victorious war, would flourish again in
a new and magnificent way, according to his concepts.
Hitler considered himself a regent somewhat in the
style of Richard Wagner's operatic king-heroes. It
may not be too fantastic to assume that, when the
Reich toppled and Berlin burned, Hitler's thought
was like Nero's: "What an artist is going to die with
me!" These words could also very well fit into Wagner's vision of the downfall of the gods in Valhalla.

Legend and history point to a number of royal
singers and minstrels of olden times. When the Vandal
King Gelimer was besieged by the Byzantines and
hopelessly awaiting the victorious enemy, he requested
bread for his hunger, a sponge for his tears and a
harp to sing of his sadness. Legend has it that an
Anglo-Saxon king, who went to Rome in disguise,
betrayed his royal origin by his harp playing. The
Danish King Holger (or Holther) was able—according to the saga—to arouse great emotion by his artful harp playing. And the legendary King Rother is
said to have "played the harp for the departure of

his bride from his residence at Bari."

The Carolingian kings, Pipin and Charlemagne, play important parts in the history of music. It was Charles who organized Gregorian chanting in the land of the Franks. He was greatly interested in music and maintained at his court an academy for performing plays and music as well as for the reciting of poetry. The participants had academic titles. Charles himself—with reference to his royal position—was called David. His daughters received music lessons three hours each day and sang songs of their teacher Alcuin at meetings of the academy.

Conrad I, attempting to test the students at the cloister, had a basket of red-cheeked apples strewn under their feet during a procession in order to see whether the temptation would interrupt the singing of the young singers. It did not; the marching musicians did not even glance at the luscious fruit. Otto I, during a solemn hymn performed in his honor, had his staff pound the ground, also to see how serious the singers would take their musical duty. He was greatly surprised and satisfied when not one of them lost his composure.

Musical Princes

There were also composers among the medieval royalty. Compositions of the Prince Wizlaw of Ruegen (c. 1280) appear in the famous Jena Manuscript of minnesongs. When he wanted to send a musical greeting to his adored lady, he did not have to ask one of his court composers to write the song for him, as did the Salzburg Archbishop Pilgrim, who employed a ghost writer, the Minnesinger Hermann of Salzburg. In 1392, Pilgrim travelled to Prague planning to enter negotiations with King Wenzel—who does not know his name in connection with the famous English Christmas carol?—and from the city on the Moldau, the Archbishop sent back to his adored lady in Salzburg, Dame Ehrengeil, a tender musical love letter. But he was by no means the author. His ghost writer had done it for him.

A characteristic example of the ardent relations that existed between minnesingers, minstrels and their royal masters is evidenced by the legend about Richard I (Coeur de Lion), this typical representative of knighthood whose life was marked by a succession of feuds, adventures, dazzling festivities and tournaments. On his return from his crusade (1190-92), Richard was taken prisoner by Duke Leopold V of Austria and held captive in Duernstein, a castle near Vienna. The legend tells of Blondel, the king's minstrel, and of his search for his royal master. (There is no connection between this legendary Blondel and the historical Trouvère Blondel de Nesle.) After many months Blondel found his imprisoned master through a song which was known only to him and the king. The source of this legend is the Chronicle of Reims stemming from the latter part of the 13th century. Richard the Lionhearted himself was a talented poet and singer.

We are of course more certain of facts when dealing with the Renaissance. Among the Medici in Florence, among the Estes in Modena and the Sforzas in Milan, there were numerous artistically gifted princes. But love of music was not limited to Italy. Henry VIII of England and the Virgin Queen Elizabeth were passionately fond of music. And Mary Stuart, the unfortunate Scottish queen lost her reputation, throne and life because of her love for the musician David Rizzio.

According to Burney, Henry VIII studied music very seriously. The attention which was paid to choral music during his reign prior to his break with the Roman Pontiff, can be gathered from a set of regulations given to the royal household by Cardinal Wolsey, about 1526. There it says that "when the King was on journeys or progresses, only 6 singing boys and 6 gentlemen of the choir would be part of the royal retinue—". The king was not only able to perform the music of others, but was sufficiently skilled in counterpoint to compose those pieces that go under his name. One of his compositions was found in Royce's collection "Catholic Music", another one "Passetyme with good cumpanye" and "The Kynges balade", a three-part composition, are found in John Stafford Smith's "Musica antiqua".

Queen Elizabeth

"Elizabeth as well as the rest of Henry VIII's children and, indeed, all the princes of Europe of that time," Burney asserts, "had been taught music early in life." Sir James Melvil gives an account of a curious conversation which he once had with the English Queen.

"The same day after dinner, my Lord of Hunsden drew me up to a quiet gallery, that I might hear some Musick (but he said that he must not avow it) where I might hear the Queen play upon the virginals. After I had hearkened a while, I took the tapestry that hung before the door of the chamber, and seeing her back was toward the door, I entered within the chamber and stood a pretty space hearing her play excellently well. But she left off immediately, so soon as she turned about and saw me. She appeared to be surprised to see me, and came forward, seeming to strike me with her hand, alleging she used not to play before men, but when she was solitary, to shun melancholy. She asked how I came there? I answered, as I was walking with my Lord Hunsden, as we passed by the chamber door, I heard such a melody as ravished me, whereby I was drawn in ere I knew how. Excusing my fault of homeliness, as being brought up in the court of France where such freedom was allowed; declaring myself willing to endure what kind of punishment Her Majesty should be pleased to inflict upon me for so great an offense. Then she sate down low upon a cushion . . . ; but with her own hand she gave me a cushion to lay under my knee; which at first I refused, but she compelled me to take it. She inquired how my queen dressed?

What was the color of her hair? Whether that or her own was best? Which one of them was fairest? And which of them was higher in stature? And whether she or my queen played best? Here I felt myself compelled to assert that she played reasonably well for a queen, but that I had to give Her Majesty the praise."

Burney continues: "If Her Majesty was ever able to execute any of the pieces that are preserved in a MS which goes under the name 'Queen Elizabeth's Virginal Book', she must have been a very great player."

We hear that this famous collection of harpsichord compositions, which formerly was named after the Queen, never belonged to her. It was written some time after her death. There is no doubt, however, about her ability to play the difficult pieces composed by Tallis, Byrd, Farnaby and Dr. Bull. She was not only a performer on the lute and virginal but also on the violin and on the poliphant, a wire-strung instrument, invented and evolved from the manifold forms current about the year 1600, by Daniel Farrant, one of the court musicians to James I and Charles I. Playford in his "Introduction to the Skill of Musick" (1654) tells that the "Queen did often recreate herself on an excellent instrument called the poliphant, not much unlike a lute but strung with wire."

The Hapsburgs of the Renaissance

It might prove interesting to trace the musical history of the Hapsburg dynasty. About its first ruler, Rudolf I (1273-1291), who put an end to the fatal interregnum, the "terrible times without an emperor," the legend says that during the coronation banquet a singer appeared and, with the singing of a ballad, brought back to the emperor's memory an incident that had occurred when Rudolf had yet been Count of Hapsburg. This legend was immortalized by Schiller in a beautiful poem (set to music by Karl Loewe). It tells of the incident when the Count had offered his horse to a priest hurrying to the bedside of a dying man and had continued on foot himself.

One of Rudolf's great successors was Maximilian I (1493-1519) at whose court musicians of the highest rank were active. The compositions which were composed and performed at his and at his predecessor's (Charles the Bold of Burgundy) court belong to the so-called "late Burgundy School". "The dissonances of a torn, colorful and dying world are resolved in its solemn gentleness and in the ever-present undercurrents of melancholy..." (Besseler, "Musik des Mittelalters").

The court of Maximilian was the center of activities of Heinrich Isaak and his court chapel. We can see this orchestra depicted in old woodcuts of that age which herald the emperor as the "last of the knights". For instance, in Hans Burgkmair's "Triumphzug" (procession of triumph) we find pictured the emperor's court Kapelle. This picture shows a

trombonist and a trumpeter among the group of singers. In the left background we recognize the head
of the orchestra, Bishop Georg Slatkonia, and right
next to him young Senfl, a friend of Luther.

A Burgundian carpet preserved from the late 15th
century shows a young nobleman engaged in a game
of chess. From all indications the music-loving prince
was not content with concentrating on the game exclusively; he had to have musical accompaniment!
We gather this, because pictured in the left fore-
ground are three female singers and one male singer,
while placed to his right are a harp, a lute, a recorder
as well as one fiddle. In another woodcut included
in Burgkmair's work, musicians playing trombones,
"bomhartes" and cornets are to be found.

About Charles V, Sandoval, his biographer says
"that he was a great friend to the science of music,
and after his abdication, would have the church-
officers only accompanied by the organ, and sing
by fourteen or fifteen Fryers, who were good musicians, and have been selected from the most expert
performers of the order. He was himself so skilful that he knew if any other singer pretended, and if
any one made a mistake, he would cry out, such a one
is wrong, and immediately mark the man... The
Emperor understood music, felt, and tasted its charms;
the Fryers often discovered him behind the door, as
he sat in his own apartment, near the high altar,
beating time, and singing in part with the performers;
and if anyone was out, they could overhear him call

the offender names, as Redheaded, Blockheaded, etc. A composer from Seville whose name was Guerrero[1], presented him with a book of Motets and Masses; and when one of these Compositions had been sung as a specimen, the Emperor called his confessor, and said, see what a thief, what a plagiarist, is this son of a...! Why here, says he, this passage is taken from one Composer, and this from another, naming them as he went on. All this while the Singers stood astonished, as none of them had discovered these thefts, till they were pointed out by the Emperor."

The emperor had of course his own court Kapelle, not only in Vienna, but also in Madrid and Brussels. Ferdinand I (1556-1564), when still King of Hungary and Bohemia had appointed for service at the royal court Arnold von Bruck, one of the most outstanding contrapuntists.

Imperial Court Musicians

Ferdinand I's successor, Maximilian II (1564-1576) adhered to the old Hapsburg tradition. Of his two musicians, Jac. Vaet (d. 1567) and Philippus de Monte (1521-1603), the latter has achieved immortality. It is interesting to read the diplomatic letter of the Bavarian vice-chancellor Dr. Seld addressed to Duke Albrecht V of Brussels[2]: "There lives in England serving at present in the royal Kapelle a certain Phil-

---

[1]Francisco Guerrero (1527-1599), Spanish composer of church music and madrigals

[2]Sandberger, "Beitrage zur Geschichte der Muenchener Hofkapelle", vol. I, 55

ippus De Monte, born in Mecheln. He is a personal acquaintance of mine and I know him to be as quiet, reserved and modest as might befit a virgin. He has lived in Italy for the most part and knows his Italian like a native. Moreover, he is well acquainted with Latin, French and Flemish. He is, beyond any doubt the finest composer in this country, especially as regards the 'New Art' and the 'Musica reservata'."

It was not until the year 1568 that De Monte secured the position of "Chief Kapellmeister" in Prague. In spite of several journeys to Northern Italy, he held the post till the day of his death; he passed away in 1603 in the "golden city of Prague". Ranking among the most prolific composers of his time, De Monte's musical output almost equals that of the great Orlando di Lasso—eight books of motets ranging from 5 to 12 voices, 39 books of religious and secular madrigals, two collections of French chansons, several volumes of masses for 5 to 8 voices and a wealth of other works are authenticated as stemming from his pen. Peter Wagner points out in his "Geschichte der Messe" (History of the Mass) that De Monte's masses bear a closer stylistic resemblance to Palestrina's works rather than to di Lasso's, because De Monte's religious compositions with their genuine religiosity and stylistic uniformity are in accord with the principles of liturgical reform laid down by the Council of Trent. From his native country, De Monte took with him the art of a highly complex and constructivistic polyphony, an offspring of northern Gothic which was termed barbaric by G. B. Doni, who in his writings was so enthusiastic about the Renaissance. De Monte's frequent use of the Venetian double chorus (A. and G. Gabrieli) made an intermarriage between northern art and Italian euphony and sense of form possible. It is well worth while to glance through the documents and papers of the court Kapelle ("Studien zur Musikwissenschaft", VI, published by P. Albert Smijers).

Under the reign of Maximilian II there were two chief Kapellmeisters in the period between 1564 and 1576; the first was the aforementioned Jacob Vaet, and after his death in 1567 De Monte took his place. The position of "Vice-Kapellmeister" was filled by Alardus Gaucquier, a nowadays totally forgotten musician from Lille. He had come to Vienna by way of Belgium and had first held a job as a tenor before he commenced his duties at the court. Four masses ranging from 6 to 8 voices (published in Antwerp 1581), one handwritten mass for 6 voices, one "Magnificat" printed in Venice (1754) and one handwritten manuscript of an "Ave Verum" composed for five voices comprise the list of his works known to us.

No less than four organists were employed by the Imperial Kapelle: Wilhelm Formellis (who died 1582); Wilhelm von der Muehlen; Paul von der Winde (died 1596); and Hans Perger (died 1576).

The Kapelle numbered among its members 25 basses, 20 tenors, 23 altos, 7 treble-singers, 2 "concorderi", 2 music-copyists, 4 preceptors for the choir boys. One of the preceptors, Johann Lotinus, had to instruct the boys "in litteris"; two of them were taught music by Jacob Regnart, an important musical figure of his day. About 20 to 30 choir boys, headed by the prefect, were at all times kept in the service of the Kapelle. Among this group of youngsters, we frequently come across a few names which we encounter later on. Many of them eventually became renowned composers and Kapellmeisters, such as Carl Luython, whose name appears on a list of choir boys dating from the year 1571. Only one year later he became a full-fledged court musician. In 1582 he was promoted to Kapell-Organist and by 1603 he had climbed to the post of court composer. He was pensioned off in 1616 and died four years later in the city of Prague.

Fight about an Organ

Luython was an excellent organist, but he got into quite some trouble about the organ in the royal castle church. The files contain a letter of the musician addressed to the court marshal, in which he complained that the organ builder Albrecht Ruedner "came toward me in premeditated spite, not being incited by me in any way, while I was doing my duty in the castle church. This having taken place some months ago for the first time, when he, as it seemed to please him, fingered the keys, saying: 'This is the way to handle the register!' 'And not so agitated!' etc. Though I had reason enough to let Your

Grace know about it, I spared him because of his drunkenness, hoping he would refrain from such evil behavior and vile words. But when I was on duty again during the Christian festivals and Christmas, he again came to me during the Mass, had smeared my honest and good name, injured and vilified me, saying that it was I who falsely and, to report with reverence, roguishly accused him of not doing his work properly at the organ in the castle church and that it was I who had so told the Bohemian court counselors, whereupon and in front of many people he had called me a knave ten times, had also with his fist hit me in the face while threatening me that he would put his skin upon mine and, though the pharisee had been knifed, the rogue was still alive in me, etc. . . ."[1]

This is the way in which the enraged Luython continued with his accusation. But Ruedner defended himself violently: "I have learned that the organist Carl Luython has again written and filed a complaint against me, which surprises me not little, since he is otherwise a modest fellow who wants to accept good counsel,. . . as he tries in vain only out of a well-known and furtive hatred and envy to drag me into the mire falsely. . ."

"Well," Ruedner continues, "Luython is a young organist who has not yet had many instruments in

---

[1]These quotes, originally written in old German, are, for the reader's benefit, rendered into modern English, though not completely neglecting the rhythm inherent in the 16th century German.

his hand"..."and who else had the right to say it if not I..." "Moreover," explained the organ builder in a long-winded and baroque speech, "all that Luython says against me is not true."

Again Luython was questioned and finally De Monte, the Kapellmeister, was asked to give his opinion in this fight about the organ. Philipp De Monte examined the organ together with Isaac Karltenprunner, "concordero" or "accordier", that important person today called "tuner".

"First of all," was De Monte's categorical report, "the organ is from the normal tone a semitone or half a voice changed, which causes the choir a great many difficulties and to such extent that, secondly, they must shout instead of sing."

"When some time ago," De Monte continues, "Your Majesty celebrated the feast of the Golden Fleece and a Mass was sung by three choirs with the accompaniment of instruments and the organ, we could not play the organ, but had to use Your Majesty's Regal ... In fact, this Ruedner got the organ into such a condition that there is hardly a master alive who could repair this instrument properly. One part of the register cannot be used any more. The pipes are lying around and some of them have been lost. And all this was done by Ruedner, after so much money was spent for the proper restoration of the organ."

We do not know the final result of this altercation about the organ. But we are familiar with the fact that still more musicians complained about Ruedner who, on December 22, 1590, received the order to restore the organ to good condition, in default whereof he would have to face the severest punishment.

Rudolf II

Rudolf II (1552-1612) was a fortunate prince to be able to call his own so fine a Kapelle which could boast of the finest musicians of the time. He had been brought up in Spain, came into the possession of the Hungarian crown in 1572, and three years later ascended the throne of Bohemia and Germania. Although, like Charles V, he became emperor of Germany through the authority of the Bohemian crown, it was not until 1595 that he added Austria to his dominions. No other German emperor was a man of such high intellect and culture in his time as was Rudolf II. The Hradschin in Prague became the royal residence and also the place to which the greatest minds of his day flocked by his invitation. He employed the services of and championed the cause of the historians Johann Pistorius and Franz Guillemann. Numerous scientists and philosophers of many lands worked at the Hradschin: Czechs, Italians, Silesians and Dutchmen. It was in Prague that Tycho de Brahe conducted his meaningful investigations of the planet Mars (1546-1601); it was here too, between 1600 and 1612, that Johannes Kepler lived and created his monumental works both as astronomer and philosopher.

Rudolf II came to Prague at the age of twenty-four after having spent his youth in the musty atmosphere of the Escorial in Madrid. The spiritual pressure of his childhood experiences influenced him for the rest of his life. The fanatic orthodoxy and the extremely austere religious ceremonial of 16th century Spain had left an indelible impression on his mind. When this youth set eyes on the Bohemian capital with its hundreds of spires, churches, crooked lanes and thoroughfares and its peculiar Czech-German and Jewish people, he must have surely felt that here was the ideal place for his spiritual welfare.

The "Rudolfian Epoch" of Prague is considered one of the most brilliant periods in the history of European civilization. Adventurers from the four corners of the earth converged in the city of Prague. Faraway exotic lands sent their ambassadors to the Bohemian capital. Rudolf was the romanticist, the mystic of the Hapsburgs. Like his predecessor Charles V, he felt the discrepancy between his personality and his authority to rule, an authority invested in him by fate and divine providence. Prague's atmosphere of mysticism intensified his pathological tendencies. During the early years of his reign he attempted to suppress this inclination by surrounding himself with dazzling splendor and luxury. He created the greatest art centre in Europe. The most precious paintings of the Christian era were acquired for huge sums. Oskar Schuerer ("Prag, Kultur, Kunst, Geschichte") tells us about these pictures, about all the Duerers, Titians, Coreggios, Breughels, the magnificent antiques and the myriad of coins, the superb leatherbound volumes and the costly wood carvings which accumulated, filling the treasure rooms of the emperor. Shortly after Rudolf's succession to power, he summoned to his court the young Mantuan Jacopo Strada, a great scholar of numismatics (1577). This Strada was put in charge of Rudolf's treasures and art collection and was entrusted to buy up whatever masterpieces could be had for money. "The quainter or more grotesque, the more precious"—that was Rudolf's motto.

The drive for play entrenched in the child often survives the age of puberty and then manifests itself in grotesque outlets. The emperor's infantile neurosis found expression in his obsession for collecting, in his propensity toward the bizarre and the mystic. The thirst for power was diverted into spiritual channels. He yearned to possess the secrets of the world of stars, to conquer the mysteries of nature and penetrate to the core of all existence.

The emperor's mystical nature exerted its influence on the city of Prague which, in turn, with its mysterious atmosphere, produced its effect on him. For centuries the Jews were considered a people imbued with esoteric learning. In the fields of medicine, chemistry, astrology and philosophy, they were believed to possess secret knowledge, jealously guarded from the gentile world, the "goyim". It does not surprise us then to find threads in the Hradschin's alchemistic laboratories and in the emperor's astrological circles which lead directly to the Jewish section of Prague, whose congregation was headed by the "High Rabbi Loew" (Juda ben Bezalel, 1525-1609). In the year 1592, Rabbi Loew had his famous audience with the emperor. Up to this very day, this visit is shrouded in great secrecy. The emperor had undoubtedly tried to penetrate into the secret world of the Cabala and we may assume that it was by way of the Hradschin that the ancient Jewish mysticism has brought to bear its influence on the mysticism of Eastern Germany, on Jakob Boehme and Angelus Silesius.

The emperor also had a predilection for the ludicrous and the fantastic as well as an inclination toward mechanics. Nowadays it is difficult to imagine that so down-to-earth a subject was at that time enveloped in a cloak of secrecy, even mysticism. The emperor loved to do things with his hands and many a time he shut himself in his workroom for days on end to practice wood-carving or stone-cutting. And outside his door, Europe's diplomats waited in vain to be received by him...

Rudolf took a particular pleasure in baroque forms. He liked, for example, to have semi-precious stones laid in on table tops and to watch landscapes, figures and harmonic compositions take shape from the glittering gems. He sent his court painter Savery into the alpine province of the Tyrol to capture on canvas grotesque mountain formations. He asked the Welser and Fugger in Augsburg to send him rare plant animal species from South America and he established a veritable garden of wonders in the

"Hirschgarten". The most abstruse and fantastic was never abstruse and fantastic enough for his tastes.

The ideals of the Baroque had indeed found their truest disciple in Rudolf. This also serves to explain the baroque trends, the extravagant and outlandish traits evident in the music of a number of his court musicians. Regarding Carl Luython, whose quarrels we have followed in the previous section, we know a few of his compositions which were distinguished as chromatic experiments. These pieces were connected with an enharmonic harpsichord which had been constructed by the composer Jacob Buus during the reign of Ferdinand I. For details of this harpsichord we are indebted to a description by Michael Praetorius, who saw the instrument in Prague. It was provided with keys for C# and Db, for D# and Eb, etc. The keyboard octave was subdivided into 19 intervals and there were provisions for mechanical transposition: from C to C#, to D, D# and E. We can imagine the joy of the song accompanists, when, by simple lever action, they were able to transpose the instrumental accompaniment by one step or even a whole third either to a higher or a lower key!

Luython's specialty was the "Missae Quodlibeticae" on Italian song themes which were written despite the exactions set up by the Council of Trent. This type of Luython's compositions, as well as his playing on the super-baroque enharmonic cembalo must very likely have gone a long way in pleasing the emperor.

Hans Leo Hasler

Browsing through the documents accumulated in the Prague National Archives—some papers were kept in Prague, others in Vienna, as the court maintained its residence either in Bohemia or Austria—we often come upon descriptions of musical contraptions such as mechanical organs or musical clocks. Besides Luython the once famous Hans Leo Hasler should not be forgotten.

Hasler was the outstanding representative of a Bohemian-German musical dynasty founded by Isaak Hasler, who had come to Nuremberg from his native Joachimsthal near Carlsbad. In that age of the counter-reformation, Isaak's Protestantism had evidently forced him to make use of the "flebile jus emigrationis" sometime before 1564. In Nuremberg he became a "Stadtpfeifer" (town piper). Of his three sons, Jacob, Kaspar and Hans Leo, the latter achieved the greatest fame. Hans spent some 15 months in Venice (1584-85) studying with Giovanni Gabrieli and afterwards accepted the position of organist at the Augsburg Cathedral as well as that of chamber organist with the magnate Fugger. We know for a fact that his rich masters sent him to Nuremberg to negotiate a loan; it seems that at times even the great Fuggers experienced pecuniary embarrassment. We believe that during his stay in Nuremberg, Hasler collaborated with the linen-weaver Georg Heinlein, an ingenious inventor, on the project of constructing an automatic musical clock. In 1601 he gave it to Emperor Rudolf II as a present and, when he later made a personal visit at the Imperial residence in Prague, Rudolf commissioned him to build an even more perfect instrument. He left Prague with 50 Thalers in his pocket as well as in possession of a diploma making him an "Imperial Servant". Later he received an annual salary of 180 florins and a title of nobility which induced him to call himself "von Roseneck". He exhibited his automatic organ in Nuremberg, charging admission to the public.

Subsequently Hasler became involved in a lengthy law suit with creditors of his partner Heinlein concerning the legal claim to the invention of the automatic organ.

Hasler was looked upon as one of the greatest composers of his day. This statement is borne out by the following passage from the records of the Nuremberg council: "There exists no doubt that not in all of Germany of today or at any other time has ever been found such a composer."

We can imagine that the baroque-romantic Emperor, Rudolph II, showed the greatest interest in such mechanical instruments as Luython and Hasler constructed. Southern Germany—particularly Augsburg and Nuremberg—was the center of mechanical organ and keyboard construction.

Previously, in my article on "Ein spielender Klavier automat aus dem 16. Jahrhundert" (A playing automatic Clavier of the 16th century)[1] I described an

[1]Zeitschrift für Musikwissenschaft, II, p. 523 ff.

automatic clavier built by Samuel Bidermann of Ulm, working in Augsburg possibly one of the first instruments of this type. At any rate, it is one of the first instruments of this type which still plays today; playing six dances which were evidently, at a certain time, favorites of a lady from either the Fugger or Welser families. At least they are designated as Phillipine Welser's favorite melodies.

The Hapsburg Dynasty in the Baroque Era

During the baroque era the music at the Hapsburg court received an unexpected impetus. A few emperors of the period were renowned musicians and composers, able to hold their own in comparison with the great among professional musicians. Their imperial dignity however eclipsed their reputation as musicians.

Rudolf was succeeded by Matthias (1612-1619) who in turn passed on the crown to Ferdinand II (1619-1637). After Ferdinand's succession to power, the art of music constituted a "provenly important and incessantly cultivated part in the education of princes and princesses," as Guido Adler (in his preface to his two monumental volumes on "Musikalische Werke der Kaiser Ferdinand III, Leopold I und Josef I") said: "The art of music was taught systematically. It should constructively enhance religious practices and also beautify and ennoble the courtly diversions."

On the occasion of Ferdinand II's coronation as King of Bohemia in Prague (1627), an opera was performed, the entire cast of which was brought along by Prince Cesare Gonzaga, the emperor's brother-in-law. Cesare himself reputedly composed this opera which was certainly the first work of its kind to be performed outside of Italy. An account of the coronation festivities reports that this pastoral comedy sung in Italian dealt with the four elements offering their services to Jupiter, and that musical instruments also accompanied the parts which were sung by both men and women.

In my essay "Giovanni Battista Buonamente" (Zeitschrift fuer Musikwissenschaft, IX, p. 528) I have included a more detailed report of that performance and I have also endeavored to show that Buonamente, one of the earliest composers of instrumental music, had participated in these performances.

Emperor Ferdinand's wife, the Mantuan princess Eleonora of the House of Gonzaga, was a highly cultured woman. As is well known, the Gonzagas played a great role in the cultural development of 16th century Italy. Besides Rubens, the court of Vincenzo of Gonzaga at Mantua was also the home of the madrigal and ballet composer Giacomo Gastoldi, that of the Jewish musician Salomone Rossi and, above all, also that of the great Monteverdi whose "Orfeo" and "Ariana" were the first really significant operas in the world history of music.

Thus it was the connection between the Houses of Gonzaga and Hapsburg that effectively shaped the subsequent development of Viennese music. And, the greatest significance in the history of opera should be attached to the marriage between Eleonora Gonzaga and Ferdinand II.

Ferdinand was one of the most fanatic music lovers of his time and also tried to instil his son (later Ferdinand III, 1637-1657) with love of music at a tender age.

One of the greatest authorities in the field of 17th century music, Pater Athanasius Kircher pays tribute to Ferdinand III. Kircher emphasizes that this emperor was one of the most outstanding music experts among all the sovereigns. In 1649, Ferdinand III composed a "drama musicum" which he dedicated to the Pater. The dedication, written by the emperor personally, reads as follows: "Drama musicum compositum ab Augustissimo Ferdinando III, Romanorum Imperatore, Justo, Pio, Felici (!) et, ab eodem ad P. Athanasium Soc. Jes. Kircherum, Transmissum, anno 1649". On the title page Kircher had added an inscription in his own handwriting: "Al Padre Athanasio Kircher donum Authoris". Before the outbreak of the last war, this manuscript formed part of the A. Posony collection in Vienna.

This musical drama, one of the oldest preserved works of its kind has as its plot the struggle between human love and the love of God. The latter chosen by "Giovinetto" emerges victorious. The work is a typical example of Venetian opera. The introductory sonata orchestrated for four "viole da brazzio" bears a resemblance to the sonatas of Cavalli. The muffled tone of the viols is in keeping with the allegorical nature of the work. We find ample evidence that the emperor was intimately acquainted with scores of Venetian operas, as exemplified by the frequent barcarole-like rhythmical patterns and above all by the fanfare-like "alla guerra" phrases constructed upon the basic triad. Ferdinand was in all likelihood a pupil of Giovanni Valentini, who had been court organist starting in the year 1621 and who subsequently from 1629 or 1630 until 1649 occupied the position of second Kapellmeister. But it might equally well have been that Antonio Bertali (1605-1669) had been the emperor's teacher, a court musician in Vienna since 1637 and successor to Valentini in 1649. At any rate, it was this composer that exercised the greatest influence on the development of early opera in Vienna. He composed numerous operas, cantatas, madrigals, oratorios and orchestral sonatas in the style of Giovanni Gabrieli.

Ferdinand III has many compositions to his name: a mass for five voices, four motets, ten hymns, one "Popule meus" and one "Stabat Mater" as well as one printed "Miserere" comprise the list of his known compositions. The "Miserere" had been favorably noticed as late as 1826, when a visitor in Vienna wrote the following words in the "Allgemeine Musikalische Ztg." upon hearing the composition: "Although the genuine contrapuntal art is being looked for in vain, the manner of writing is nevertheless so noble, the vocal parts so fluent and appropriate to the text that I could not refrain from copying out one particular choral phrase."

An especially interesting composition of Ferdinand, written in the polychoral Venetian style, is his "Lauretanische Litaneien". The repeated outcries in this piece, "Miserere nobis" and "Ora pro nobis", effected by chromatic shifts in Gesualdo de Venosa's style, convey a strong impression of a genuine Catholic-mystic atmosphere. The madrigal "Chi volgene la mente" is written in the same style. If Tassoni's assertion (told by Burney) is true, namely that James I of Scotland had written chromatic music even before Gesualdo, one might be strongly tempted to label this style "typically royal".

One of the emperor's compositions—if one may so call it—has been handed down to us in the form of variations written by his organist Wolfgang Ebner. Ebner, it is believed, was born in Augsburg in the year 1612. He left his native city to accept Ferdinand's offer as court organist in Vienna where he later also attained the position of organist at the St. Stephen Cathedral. His many compositions include organ and clavier works, religious compositions and ballets. I have done some biographical research on his life and published my findings in the monograph "Die Wiener Tanzkomposition in der Zweiten Haelfte des 17. Jahrhunderts". During the year 1648 the imperial court resided in Prague and it was at that time that Ebner wrote the above mentioned variations under the title:

Aria
Augustissimi ac Invictissimi Imperatoris
Ferdinandi III
XXXVI modis variata, ac pro Cimbalo accomodata
Eidemo
Sacrae Caesareae Majestati
humilissime dedicata
a
Wolffgango Ebner Eiusdem
Sacr. Caes. M. Camerae Organista
Augustano
MDCXLVIII

The title page, a copperplate engraving by the painter Skreta shows the melody being sung by idealized feminine figures who accompany their song on a lyre, a lute, a cembalo and a flute. The melodic theme does indeed lend itself well to variations. Adhering to the form of a variation-suite, the work does not merely consist of formalistic variations, but also includes a courante, a gigue and a saraband. On these dances in turn, variations are composed, a procedure which was later adopted by Joh.Jak.Froberger (also a protégé of the emperor) in his variations "Auff die Meyerin".

Johann Jakob Froberger and Johann Kaspar Kerll, other important organists and harpsichordists at the court, were also good friends of the Emperor.

Both Froberger and Joh. Kaspar Kerll were sent to Italy by the emperor in order to do some additional study with the great organist Girolamo Frescobaldi.

The emperor's action was not prompted by his interest in art alone; he had the ulterior motive of converting the Protestant Froberger and of leading him to the only salvation—to the bosom of the Catholic Church. (I published the document about this historical incident.) On the whole, this emperor contributed a great deal to the development and organization of the Imperial Kapelle. In the regulations regarding court musicians, which he probably wrote himself, we find the following words:

"The Almighty God bestows his divine grace and gifts to us mortals in His own manner, blessing some more than others. Thus it ought not be that one person should despise his fellow men, because he might be gifted with a superior musical skill, nor should he because of it be deserving of undue personal glory."

The emperor took his musicians along on all journeys undertaken by the court. On his journey to the "Reichstag" at Regensburg he was accompanied by sixty musicians and he had his own large theatre built by the great theatre architect Ludovico Burnacini. The expense was immense—but was that to discourage an emperor of the baroque era?

Leopold I, A Great Emperor and Composer

Ferdinand III's successor, (Leopold I, 1658-1705) was the most musical emperor of the Hapsburg dynasty. He was originally slated for a learned and ecclesiastical profession and thus enjoyed an all-embracing humanistic education. But it was music for which he showed the strongest inclination from his earliest youth to late in his life. We are not sure about the identity of his teacher; perhaps it was the court organist Ferdinand Tobias Richter (1649-1711); but it is more likely that he was instructed by several composers, by Antonio Bertali, Ebner and Johann Heinrich Schmelzer (1623-1680). It was Ebner who compiled Leopold's early compositions in a single volume called "Spartitura compositionum" in the years 1655 to 1657. Bertali, on the other hand, has to his credit the viola accompaniment to "Regina coeli", a work composed by Leopold in May 1655. Schmelzer, too, was always in close contact with the emperor; this was—more likely than not—the most intimate relationship of all. In one of Leopold's suites which has been preserved in Kremsier, the following remark is prefixed to a sonata therein: "This done by Schmelzer alone". No doubt, Schmelzer lent a helping hand to his royal master at times.

The historians have found words of praise for Leopold's well-balanced personality. He bore the hard blows dealt by fate with stoicism and resignation to God's will. In the face of such cruel blows as the death of his two beloved wives, Margarita and Claudia Felicitas, the loss of his children, the murderous plague (1680) and the Turks' siege of Vienna (1683), Leopold withdrew into a shell and then wrote numerous compositions, mainly his religious works of which no less than 79 have been handed down to us. Included among these works, are 2 masses, 20 motets,

9 psalms, 12 hymns, 14 chants of the Holy Virgin (Mariengesaenge), 4 litanies, 5 masses for the dead and 13 smaller works for various celebrations. In addition he composed 8 oratorios. The number of his secular compositions is even larger: 155 vocal selections for one or more voices, serving to a large extent as inserts for the operas and oratorios of his Kapellmeisters. Along the same line there are 9 "Feste teatrali", a vast number of dances (Balletti) which have been preserved in Vienna and some of them in Kremsier where I also happened to find four of his songs. Two of them I have published in my book "Das Wiener Barocklied". Guido Adler informs us in his preface to the "Kaiserwerke" that Leopold I composed music for all occasions, but that he especially liked to write music for the birthday and name day celebrations of members of his family. When the court was in mourning, Leopold supplied the accompanying music to the respective church ceremonies. On the occasion of his uncle's death, the Archduke Leopold Wilhelm, it was Leopold who wrote the "Dies Irae" for the exequies. In honor of his bride's arrival, the Princess Margarita of Spain, the world famous equestrian ballet "La Contesa dell' Aria e dell' Aqua" was performed (1666), in which he was seen as horseman and tournament fighter. When his beloved died, he wrote a great requiem in her honor. At the death of his second wife, the Tyrolese Princess Claudia Felicitas, he composed three "Trauerlektionen" (lessons in mourning), works of

great grief and great melancholy. Even the introductory sonata, in which two solo trumpets (Cornetti muti concertanti), two trombones and one bassoon alternate with a sombre viola ensemble, expresses unspeakable grief—a genuine manifestation of the Baroque spirit in despair.

Marshal Grammont, who witnessed Leopold's coronation (1658) in Frankfurt, has this to say about the emperor[1]: "He loves music and has such a deep understanding of this art that he is able to compose pieces of true sadness; his only pleasure consists of composing sad music." It seems as if the "Trauerlektionen" had been close to the emperor's heart. These compositions were also played at his own funeral (May 5, 1705)—presumably at his request—and when Eleonora Magdalena Theresia, his third wife, was buried, again the "Trauerlektionen" resounded above her grave. Annually, they were played at the anniversary of the emperor's death, and this custom continued until, at least, 1740. Emperor Joseph I and Charles VI had Leopold's works performed again and again. On the day of St. Leopold, they staged court performances at which the deceased emperor's works were played exclusively. His "Missa Angeli Custodis" was always presented on his Saint's day and "Oratorio of St. Joseph" was given a performance every year on the day of St. Joseph (March 19).

The emperor, of course, wrote music of a cheer-

---

[1]Memories du Marechal Grammont", Petitot, 2nd series, tome 57, pg. 21

ful note too, whenever the occasion called for it. The arrival of his Spanish bride in 1666, an event to which he had looked forward with eagerness and impatience, prompted the monarch to write (from his place at Laxenburg, May 25, 1666) to his confidant Count Poetting, the Imperial ambassador at Madrid: "As a sign of the joy felt by all of us here, I had the Te Deum sung on Sunday and also ordered a few salvos to be fired." A couple of months previously (March 17, 1666) he sent Poetting the following lines: "Considering the fact that we are in mourning here, I should have spent a quiet carnival season; however, we did enjoy a number of festivities in camera, because after all being sad does not help the dead in any way."

The emperor loved to arrange festivities at which the whole royal family participated. During the performance of the opera "Il Re Gelidoro" (1659) the emperor himself walked on stage in the intrada, leading a procession of courtiers. During the carnival season, the archdukes and princesses danced in the ballets and also participated personally in the "Wirtschaften", "Merenden", and peasant weddings to which Leopold composed the music.

Whenever the emperor left on some journey with the intent of staying away for a while, he took along the court Kapelle, or at least the greater part of it. In 1665 he set out for Innsbruck and took with him the musicians Johann Heinrich Schmelzer, Paul Pichl, Friedrich Holweg and Johann Paul Heinrich. There,

at Innsbruck, he attended one of the opera performances incognito. On October 27, he informed Poetting
about his "adventure" in a letter written from Woergl:
"While the aristocrats were making merry with food
and drink, I too wanted to have a good time, so I
went to the theatre here in Innsbruck. As the musici
were just then ready for a performance (et ut verum
fatear, ita disponente Serenissima Anna), I went to
see it the very evening. I chose to remain quasi incognito, as there were not supposed to be any people attending; however, a goodly number managed
to sneak in somehow. This is to let you know about
it, ne forte aspergatur nos loco funeralium comedias
exhibere."

Leopold's apology for having attended an opera
performance in spite of the fact that the court was
in mourning, refers to the death of Philip IV of
Spain. This was not the first time the emperor deemed
it necessary to offer an apology to his Spanish ambassador for indulging his love of music.

We encounter here a curious connection between
music and politics. A similar apology is on record
(dated the 27th of September 1666) when Leopold
made his excuses to Poetting for having attended a
French ballet at Grenonville's house, Louis XIV's
Viennese ambassador. It should be kept in mind that,
in those days, Spain had an alliance with Austria
against France. Leopold complains in an amusing
mixture of German, Italian, Spanish and Latin about
the presence of a number of stool pigeons and petty

spies at the Spanish Embassy who liked to make a mountain out of every molehill. On the whole we cannot help but wonder whether the emperor might not have thrown the Spanish alliance to the winds rather than curb his passion for music.

We know from available documents that Margarita, his Spanish bride, was also musical, and we may imagine that she had a predilection for Spanish music. In fact, we read in a letter of Leopold to his Spanish ambassador Poetting, dated Jan. 6, 1667, "the Empress always demands to hear 'sonos humanos' of three-part compositions". In another letter he says that "the Empress still only asks for music of Spanish composers".

More interesting is the fact that in a late 17th century manuscript of Austrian origin, I found a suite entitled "Aria Imperatricis Margaretae", referring, undoubtedly, to the Spanish princess. Whether the suite was actually composed by the Empress herself, or just represents some of her favorite tunes, is an interesting question. At any rate, we have here another document of the musical culture at the court of Leopold I.

The first part of the suite is almost identical with Schmeltzer's "Gavotta Tedesca", and the fourth dance is closely related to an aria which I printed on p. 142 of my "Wiener Tanzmusik in der 2. Haelfte des 17. Jahrh." These "Empress dances" show strong evidence of having been influenced by Austrian folk music, and there is a probability, that the Empress, after she made her home in Austria, showed a predilection for Alpine and Austrian folk tunes.

Leopold had been brought up in the Italian tradition. He mastered the language to the point of even writing poetry in Italian. His library contained a collection of music scores which, to this day, are the pride of the Austrian National Library—sumptuous leatherbound, gilt-edged volumes filled with the music of Carissimi, Caprioli del Violino, Francesco Federici, Tenaglia, Ercole Bernabei, Bernardo Pasquini, Alessandro Stradella and many others.

Leopold's own operas are modelled after the style of the Venetian school, after such composers as Cavalli, Cesti, Valentini and Bertali, Vismarri, Pietro Andrea Ziani, etc. Leopold's arias are fraught with noble and inspired melos. These arias are bracketed between instrumental ritornelli and more than often these pre- and postludes are of greater importance than the aria proper. As mentioned before, the musical interludes which Leopold composed for the operas of his Kapellmeisters, comprised a major part of his works. As soon as the Italian maestri Bertali, Ziani, Cesti and Draghi had completed a new opera score, they turned to His Majesty to ask him whether he might not like to grace their new work with one of his own arias. And who can conceive of a composer— even if he were the ruler of the Roman Empire— who would not love to hear his work performed! And thus, nearly always, an "imperial aria" was inserted and we can picture the court audience trying to guess which one of the beautiful arias was the brain child of their Leopold. And almost invariably it was the finest aria in the lot! In this connection, Leopold's biographer, Rink, ventured the statement—possibly a mild exaggeration—that in Vienna "there was never an opera performed which did not in some place contain one of his passages which always seemed to be the finest part of the whole opera."

The ritornello is also used by Leopold in his German songs. This practice is also evidenced in the compositions of Adam Krieger, the great song composer of the Baroque. There is a peculiar incongruence between the gushing instrumental passages and the simple contents of the songs themselves, a remarkable characteristic of baroque taste.

The intermingling of Italian opera tradition with the music of indigenous composers and minstrels was a typically Viennese phenomenon. The emperor did not derive enjoyment and pleasure from Italian opera exclusively; he was also fond of German comedy and did much to contribute to its development. As a matter of fact, he was one of the first writers of German *Singspiele* (musical comedy). Three such works have been authenticated as his own.

During the year 1680, Vienna was caught in the grip of the plague which had raged in a form and magnitude as never before. Thousands upon thousands fell prey to its ravages; some died in their homes, many while practicing their professions, they died in the churches while praying, they died on the streets. The Imperial court fled to Prague, but before long the murderous epidemic reached them there too. All precautionary measures were in vain, all quarantines of no avail. But the Imperial residence in Prague, the Hradschin, was the scene of gaiety and merriment. They sought escape from those sad times in song and play. These were the days that marked the first performance of a comic opera in Prague. The work was Antonio Draghi's "La Pazienza di Socrate con due moglie", a gay affair in which the Greek philosopher married two women, as if his first wife, the notorious Xanthippe, were not enough for him. At that time, the most unlikely "accidenti verissimi" were dreamed up as supplements to the historic facts—in this instance, it happened to be the farcical second marriage of Socrates.

The emperor too made his musical contribution to the "program of festivities" of that pest-ridden time, "Die vermeinte Bruder und Schwesterliebe" (The alleged brother and sister love); the libretto was the work of the German court poet Schlegel—and what a poor text it is! Leopold wrote his musical drama, "Der toerichte Schaefer" (The foolish shepherd) in the year 1683, a year of dire need and emergency, with the Turks at the gates of Vienna. Two years later, a similar work followed: "Die Ergetzung Stund der Sklavinnen auf Samie" (The hour of delight for the slaves on Samos). These "operettas" were comedies with musical numbers.

A comparison of the miserable German texts with Leopold's scores leads to the inevitable conclusion that the music was "regal" in more than one sense of

the word. We often find ritornellos which are scored
for two violins and bass. Leopold did not mind
composing dance music which was principally played
at balls and other court festivities. In one of the
"Nationalbibliothek's" wonderful volumes, entitled
"Di Sua Maesta Cesarea [Leopoldo Primo] Arie",
we find 102 instrumental compositions which can be
unified (according to Adler) into 16 separate suites.
These suites number from four to eleven distinct
movements, in definite tonal relationship to each
other. They are noted down on two staffs, in a kind
of keyboard scoring (Particello) in which the first
violin and bass parts are recorded. This two part
notation was by no means intended to indicate an
upper voice solo part (possibly played by a violin)
and a "Figured Bass". In other words, this mode of
notation was not meant to suggest a violin piece with
cembalo accompaniment as might seem the practical
thing; it should rather be thought of as a short cut
method of notation, employed by the Kapellmeisters
and music scribes for writing down dance tunes which
were in reality composed for and actually performed
by four or five instruments. Many dances of Schmelzer and those of other dance composers have been
handed down to us in this form. The suites are so-
called "Aufzugssuiten" (entries) meant to be performed at the end of a spectacle or at some "Entrée".
The first suite found in this collection begins with
an "Intrada"; to its strains the members of the Imperial party probably made their entrance on stage

or into the audience. The "Intrada" was followed in turn by a "Saraband", a "Trezza", a "Gagliarda", an "Aria", a "Minuetto", a "Gavotte", an "Allemande" and "Bourrée" and finally by a "Retirada" which accompanied the exit of the aristocracy.

The cultivation of music as an art reached an all time high at the Austrian court during the reign of Leopold I. The span of Ferdinand III's reign (1630-1657) saw a mere 16 performances of operas and oratorios compared to the 400 and some presentations which took place during the years of Leopold's Imperial rule (1658-1705). One might almost be inclined to speak of a hypertrophy of music, although one does not have to go quite as far as a contemporary observer[1] who wrote these words during a visit to Vienna: "Even if one were the greatest music lover, a few months' stay in Vienna is enough to kill this love forever. The poor musicians have to be on duty at least 800 times annually for chamber music recitals, banquet music, oratorios and theatrical performances—and this number does not include rehearsals."

The emperor did not tolerate any slackening of zeal or industriousness. He himself drew up those "Punti ch'io voglio che siano delli miei Musici sempre inviolabilmente osservati": Every musician had to be punctual in line of duty. No one was allowed to leave his post before the end of a performance and every musician was obliged to accept and play the part del-

---

1. Magoletti in Giornale storico degli Archivi Toscani, IV, 334

egated to him, whether first or second violin. The musician performing in the church was expected to conduct himself in a manner befitting the sanctity of a place of worship. He was supposed to show the Kapellmeister his due respect and should he have any grievance or argument with his superiors, it was to be taken up officially with the Lord High Steward.

The life of the emperor and that of the entire court was saturated in an atmosphere of music. Therefore, it does not surprise us that, at times, music invaded the sphere of politics as was the case with the French ballet incident mentioned before. Rink, the emperor's biographer, acquaints us with another example of political repercussions in the realm of music: "The emperor's second wife, Claudia Felicitas, occasionally availed herself of the opportunity to use an opera plot as an analogy of court life. A striking example is the opera 'La lanterna di Diogene' of 1674, in which Diogenes points out to the court all its shortcomings and even addressed himself to the emperor personally in the figure of Alexander Magnus, chiding the emperor for too much leniency in punishing vice and thus fostering foul deeds."

The story told by Rink was looked upon as a legend until I was able to authenticate it by a copy of the libretto which I unearthed in the Princely library of Raudnitz in Bohemia. On the last page of this libretto, we find the following key written in by some contemporary:

"Vera clavis Personarum:

Diogene - Il Nicolo Minati, Poeta

Dario - Il Re di Francia

Antigene - (Persian prince in Greek disguise)

Il Grenonville, Inviato di Francia

Statira - L'Imperadrice Eleonora

Siroe - La Contessa Harrach

Efestione - Il Principe de Lobkowitz

Parmenione - Il Principe de Swartzenberg

Chalestre is the apostolic nuncio and pictured as a "functionary of Darius", that is, he is designated as belonging to the French faction. The poet sets before us a number of persons, such as the Kurfuerst of Brandenburg, the Kurfuerst of Bavaria, etc. The soldier who brings water to Alexander is the Saxonian Kurfuerst. Greece is identified with Germany, Persia with France, Hungary with Saba, Egypt with England, etc. One must be very familiar with the finesse of the French-Spanish-Austrian political web, the intrigues of the French Ambassador Grenonville, to understand fully the key to this opera.[1]

We can well imagine how the Viennese court gossip blossomed in the theatre wings of opera and ballet. We are told that Empress Eleonora liked operas and scenes behind which real life events were taking

---

[1]Loewenberg, *Annals of the Opera*, has this comment:

"A copy of the libretto at the Brussels Conservatoir contains a MS note (published by Wotquenne) from which we learn the *La Lanterna di Diogene* was a satirical opera "a clef", each of the 26 characters representing members of the European high society, from Leopold I, Louis XIV, Charles XI of Sweden down to various Dukes, Counts and Ambassadors. The 27th character of the opera *Tirreo Eunuco*, has been politely described by the unknown commentator to be an "incerta persona".

place. The emperor himself probably kept aloof from such gossipy interests. He cherished too highly the absolute value of the musical presentations he heard and saw. Or as Rink put it: "His (the emperor's) compositions are in the hands of most of Germany's artists. When the emperor attended a concert of his Kapelle, unparalleled in excellence to this day, he derived so much pleasure from it and listened so attentively as if he were hearing them for the first time; and it is unlikely that he might have taken his eyes from the score during an opera performance, so closely did he follow the music note for note. When one of his favorite passages was played, he listened with his eyes closed so as to afford the music his closest attention..."

Leopold's musical fanaticism persisted to his last hours. He often expressed the desire to pass into the next world carried on wings of soothing music, should death give ample warning before claiming him. When he felt the end approaching, he ordered his Kapelle to stay in the room adjoining his. The musicians had to play some of his favorite music and during this deathbed serenade, the most music-loving of all emperors passed into the land of eternal sleep.

Joseph I and Charles VI

Leopold's successor, Joseph I, also belonged to the musically creative potentates. According to Guido Adler only a few of the emperor's compositions have been preserved, but "were it not for the fact that

Joseph was an emperor, he would wear the immortal crown of genuine artistry."

Rink, who was also Joseph I's biographer,[1] tells of the emperor's extraordinary gift for music and of his wide knowledge: "Oddly enough, his accomplishments in music were so thorough that very few persons were his equal, even among the non-aristocratic musicians. Just as the great Leopold had composed a host of arias and cantatas which later were acclaimed as unsurpassable by the greatest scholars of music, Joseph, too, enjoyed so thorough a command of music that he was able in his leisure hours, without neglecting his business of state, to compose finished masterpieces which delighted all those who subsequently heard them performed. He was an accomplished performer on the clavecin and flute, and also played a number of other instruments with so much amenity as to make even the professional musicians admit that they themselves could not outdo him in charm and that whatever superior skill they possessed, was due solely to their playing the instrument day in and day out."

Glancing through Joseph's compositions, we are struck by their Italian élan and grace of style, almost resembling that of Handel and certainly that of Caldara. Joseph mastered the aria form prevalent in his days to a high degree. His "Sepolcri" (passions) and his arias, as those for example from "Chylonida", are

---

[1] Josef's des Sieghafften "Roem, Kaysers Leben und Thaten", Coelln, 1712

certainly worthy of being revived. A fetching composition of his for lute (aria), which also sounds lovely on the cembalo, indicates to us that the emperor also mastered the favorite instrument of the lords and ladies of his age.

Of Joseph I's successor, Charles VI (1711-1740), only two compositions have been preserved through the ages, but it is an established fact that also this monarch was a composer whose music was performed. Like his predecessor, he too was a masterful musician. When the operas "Euristeo" of Caldara (1724) and "Elisa" of Fux were performed, the nobility participated in the performance, headed by the emperor himself, who conducted from his place at the cembalo. We read in a contemporary source:

"I cannot begin to describe the enthusiastic reception enjoyed by 'Euristeo' . . . Leading the orchestra from his seat at the cembalo was His exalted Majesty, displaying on that instrument the eminent skill of a professor." It is said that it was during this performance that Johann Josef Fux, the court Kapellmeister, composer and great theorist (whose famous theoretical work "Gradus ad Parnassum" was printed by Charles VI at his own expense) was supposed to have addressed the emperor as follows: "It is a great pity that Your Majesty hasn't chosen to become a virtuoso!" Charles turned to his Kapellmeister and retorted with dry humor in his tone: "Never mind, I get a better break this way!"

PART TWO

FIVE
EIGHTEENTH CENTURY MUSICIANS
AS
THEY SAW THEMSELVES.

The eighteenth century is the age of memoirs, confessions, and autobiographies: a time when men believed in an even somewhat exaggerated individualism, when people who didn't reach the laurel of immortality had the urge to reveal their experiences and their feelings. We may consider ourselves fortunate to have a number of autobiographies of musicians of lesser rank because they show us the typical background and development of those musicians who, although they were not outstanding, were important. Although these composers did not make an epoch, they helped to build up the musical culture of their time!

Karl Ditters von Dittersdorf, born Nov. 2, 1739 in Vienna; died at Castle Rothlhotta, near Neuhaus in Bohemia Oct. 24, 1799, was one of the most popular and prolific composers of his time. He wrote several

oratorios and cantatas, symphonies for orchestra, and
Ovid's Metamorphoses, a remarkable specimen of early
programmatic music. He also wrote a ballet, a concerto grosso, 12 violin concertos, numerous string
quartets, divertimenti, and piano concertos. Among
his dramatic works, the famous "Doktor and Apothe-
ker" was performed in 1786 with great success, and we
are told that Emperor Joseph II, like many other contemporaries, preferred Dittersdorf's music to that of
Mozart.

Dittersdorf's autobiography is among the most colorful of the time. It appeared for the first time in
Leipzig in 1801 in an edition of Spazier; because of
its length we have presented an abbreviation.

Franz Benda, born Nov. 25, 1709 in Staré Benatky,
Bohemia; died March 7, 1786,—was a famous violinist
who may be considered as one of those typical Bohemian musicians trained in the primitive country
schools about which Burney tells us. He became the
leader of the orchestra of the Prussian crown prince,
later Frederick II, whom he accompanied in hundreds of concertos during his forty years of service. A brother of Georg Benda, he was one of the
best performers of his time, and also a composer of
violin concertos, trio sonatas, symphonies, etc. His
autobiography appeared in the Neue Berliner Musikzeitung, vol. 10, p. 32, having been submitted by
C. Freiherr von Ledebur in 1856. Since that time it
has never been republished either in German or another language.

Among the teachers of Beethoven, Christian Gott-lob Neefe and Johann Baptist Schenk are well worth mention. Neefe was born in Chemnitz Feb. 5, 1748, died at Dessau, Jan. 26, 1798. As a law student in Leipzig he had lessons with J. A. Hiller. He was a conductor in Leipzig and Dresden, later of Seyler's itinerant opera troupe, and in 1779 of the Grossmann-Hellmuth Company at Bonn, where he was deputy organist, succeeding van den Eeden as electoral musical director. He was one of Beethoven's most important teachers. He wrote operas and singspiele for Leipzig and Bonn, a double concerto for piano, violin and orchestra, sonatas, variations, songs (among them some for Masonic lodges). Neefe's autobiography, which was originally published in the Allgemeine Musikalische Zeitung, 1798/99, Nr. 16, 17, 18, and 23, was republished by Alfred Einstein.

Johann Schenk was born Nov. 30, 1753, in Wiener-Neustadt, Austria, and died in Vienna Dec. 29, 1836. He was an important musician, operatic composer and theoretician, brought up in the old school of strict counterpoint. At Baden he was a pupil of Stoll (known as a friend of Mozart), and of Schneller and Wagenseil. He became one of the most popular composers. His "Dorfbarbier" ("Village Barber") was presented in 1796 with striking success. It was republished in the Denkmäler der Tonkunst in Oesterreich. He wrote a great number of other "singspiele", and symphonies, harp concertos, trios, quartets, songs and other compositions. It was Schenk who, at Abbé

Gellinek's house, heard the young Beethoven playing, and became highly enthusiastic about his genius. When he visited Beethoven he found on his desk some compositions in counterpoint which proved that the young composer didn't know too much about that art. He advised Beethoven to study the Fux "Gradus ad Parnassum". When Schenk learned that Beethoven studied with Haydn, and when he learned that Haydn hadn't been too eager to correct Beethoven's contrapuntal mistakes, he accepted him as a pupil, under the condition that the whole affair was to be done secretly, and that Haydn shouldn't learn about Schenk's teaching of Beethoven. Beethoven was supposed to recopy all exercises which Schenk corrected in order to avoid Haydn's mistrust; but the secret was betrayed by Gellinek and Beethoven's brothers. Schenk's short autobiography was preserved in his own manuscript.

The author of the present edition recalls a strange event which took place when he was an associate of Guido Adler, the famous musicologist in Vienna. It happened that a certain student at the musicological institute was writing a thesis on Schenk, and was permitted to use the autograph of Schenk's autobiography. Its use, of course, was reserved to the confines of the institute, but, per nefas, the student took the work home with him to study it better. Alas, the manuscript was lost on a suburban train . . . Fortunately a copy was extant, from which the publication was made in the Studien zur Musikwissenschafft, V. 11.

The eighteenth century composer and flute-master of Frederick the Great, Johann Joachim Quantz was a most interesting man. He was born on Jan. 30, 1697 at Oberscheden, Hanover, and died in Potsdam, July 12, 1773. In 1728 he played before Frederick the Great, then Crown-Prince at Berlin, and so pleased him that he engaged Quantz to teach him the flute, and to make two long yearly visits to Berlin for that purpose. When Frederick assumed the throne in 1740, he called Quantz to Berlin and Potsdam as chamber musician and court composer. Quantz left in manuscript about three hundred concertos for one or two flutes, as well as numerous other compositions for flute. His most important contribution was his "Versuch einer Anweisung, die Floete traversiere zu spielen", written in 1752. It is, along with Leopold Mozart's "Violinschule" and C. P. E. Bach's "Versuch ueber die wahre Art das Klavier zu spielen", one of the best sources for the history of musical performance in the 18th century. Quantz' autobiography was first published in Wilhelm Frederick Marpurg's "Historisch-kritische Beyträge zur Aufnahme der Musik", volume I, p. 197-250 in Berlin in 1755. It was recently republished by Willi Kahl in his book "Selbst-Biographien Deutscher Musiker".

1

KARL VON DITTERSDORF'S LIFE

I was born in Vienna on December 2, 1739. My father hailed from Danzig. He was Imperial court and theatre embroiderer under the reign of Charles VI and, since he was also a good designer, he was eventually commissioned as a First Lieutenant in the artillery during the Bavarian war and put in charge of the so-called Loebel-Bastei (bastion) with 20 cannons.

His merit netted the necessary means to afford his five children a somewhat better education than was customary among common people. His three sons—I was the second born—were sent to a Jesuit school and in addition my father engaged a lay priest as a private tutor who received a salary and boarded in our house.

I was hardly seven years of age, when I felt a particular inclination for music. I begged my father to let me take music lessons. He granted my request and within the span of three and a half years I had made such remarkable progress that my teacher—Koenig was the good man's name—admitted that he had taught me everything he knew and that it was necessary to find another teacher so that I could learn to play with concert proficiency. "My conscience doesn't permit me to retard your son's progress any longer," he said to my father, "because he is sufficiently gifted to become a far better instrumentalist than I would ever make."

My second teacher was Joseph Zuegler, a fairly good violinist and also a talented and renowned composer of chamber music. He took great pains with me and my diligence and my liking for the violin made his efforts worth-while. In order to train me in sight reading, he advised me to assist in the performance of the "choir" (Catholic church music) on every Sunday and church holiday. He praised above all the Benedictine choir at the "Freyung", because there, in addition to a large orchestra, I would have the benefit of hearing performed the best in masses, motets, vespers and litanies.

The following Sunday I went there. I reported to the Regens Chori, a certain Mr. Gsur, and asked his permission to play in the orchestra. He looked me up and down and answered in a gruff tone of voice: "The very idea! This is not the sort of choir where any boy can be allowed to scratch and scrape!"

Young as I was, I took great offense at the expression "scratch and scrape" and I wasted no time in talking back: "You don't even know how I play and whether I am able to carry an orchestra part. If I couldn't do it, I am sure that my teacher, Master

Joseph Zuegler, would not have suggested I should ask your permission to play."

"Well, if that's the case," he replied in a friendly manner, "if he really has recommended you, it is all right as far as I am concerned." He told me to pick up a violin and to sit down beside the first violinist, who kept a watchful eye on me to find out whether I could really play. During a fugue he went so far as to stop playing himself to see whether I would make the correct entrances. I did not miss a note. "Bravo, my son," he said after we had finished, "I didn't think you could do it." The Regens, too, had witnessed my performance; he expressed his satisfaction and added that I was welcome to join them as often as I pleased.

Thus I never missed a chance whenever church music was performed. After doing this for about a year, I had gained so much experience that I had become a proficient choir player and a musical "note eater", as they say.

During the course of that year, it often came to pass that Huber, the first violinist, was called upon to play solos in church. His tone, his method, his intonation and his pleasant delivery made an enormous impression on me. I practiced indefatigably in the hope of becoming as good as he. When some time later, we were to perform a mass, unfamiliar to me, in which a violin solo occurred, Huber said to me: "Do you have the courage to play the solo?"

"I guess I'll be able to get through it," I retorted,

"but I won't be able to play it as nicely as you."

"Never mind that. Just go ahead and play. I'm sure that you'll do fine," he encouraged me and even gave me his own violin.

With my heart beating violently, I started to play the solo. I gained a little more confidence after a few minutes, because I felt that I was doing better than I had anticipated and when I had finished playing I received widespread approbation.

On this day, as was usually the case, a great number of music lovers had come to church. After the solo, a few of Huber's admirers came up to him and praised and congratulated him in the belief that it was he who had played. One can hardly imagine their astonishment when Huber introduced me to them with these words: "Gentlemen, it isn't I who deserves your praise, but this young man here." Among Huber's admirers was the famous French Horn virtuoso Hubaczek, who was in the service of the Imperial Field-Marshal and General of the ordnance department, Prince Joseph Friedrich von Hildburghausen. This man came over to me just as I was about to go home. He asked my name and who my father was, then took my address and promised that he would come and see me one of the next days. He kept his word. A few days later he came to our house and told us that his master kept a fine Kapelle which met for rehearsal three times a week at eleven o'clock. He asked my father if he would allow me to come to rehearsal from time to time. My father didn't object and, on the very next day, Hubaczek came to call for me. Of course, I took my violin along.

I was more than surprised when I was offered to take the concertmaster's chair. We had hardly finished tuning and distributing the parts of a Jomelli symphony (which I had played previously) when the court composer Bonno entered the room. He stopped short at seeing an eleven or twelve year old boy as concertmaster. He stood watching me, until the symphony was over and then left, probably to tell the prince about me, as both men came in shortly thereafter. The prince called me over and asked in a kind tone my name and age, who were my father and my teacher, and many other questions. After I had answered him fully and without embarrassment, he wanted to know whether I was able to play everything at sight. "If the piece isn't too difficult," I replied. He had brought a simple flute concerto and a flute sonata and I sight-read the former quite cleanly.

By that time it was well past noon and the prince was so kind as to invite me, with humorous remarks, to have lunch with him at his royal table. He asked me to bring my father to him at five o'clock and the two of them withdrew into the adjacent room. After quite a while, the two reappeared, the prince addressing my father: "Well, you and I see eye to eye. Now the final decision rests in your son's hands. Would you like," he said turning to me, "to leave your father and come and live here? You shall be well taken care of, but in turn you will have to apply yourself diligently to the study of music and languages."

I was so overcome with joy that I fell on my knees, crying: "O yes, kindest Prince, I would very much like to!"

"Get up, my son," he said, "only in church—before God you must kneel, but not in front of me!"

On March 1, 1751, in the morning, my father brought me to the prince's palace where I was to start upon a new life. The prince was not at home and we were referred to the head steward, a distinguished and respectable man by the name of Johann Ebert. He led us to the room of Bremer, a clerk. On the way, he gave me some instructions in a rather paternal tone of voice. Bremer was a handsome young man of about 26. He greeted my father very cordially and showed me to my room which was very close to his. I had to discard every stitch of clothing and I received a brand new outfit from head to toe. The coat and trousers of my everyday suit were ash grey but the vest was red. Every garment was made of the finest Dutch cloth and the button holes were trimmed with silver thread as was the fashion in those days. I also received an abundance of undergarments. Moreover, I was equipped with silken stockings, new shoes, and silver trousers—and shoebuckles styled in the latest fashion. And all this the prince had planned without my knowledge, for the tailor, shoemaker and seamstress had to work on these things in my own house without my noticing it.

"You see," said Mr. Bremer, "that is just like the prince; he is kindhearted and likes to prepare pleasant surprises for everybody. Be sure now to keep everything in good order and to conduct yourself well and you will have a nice life here. There is your key so that you can come and go as you please."

"It is almost eleven o'clock," he then said. "Go to the salon because the rehearsal will start presently." When I came there most of the others had already gathered. They all congratulated me on my having become a page, who was now entitled to join the rest of the musicians.

A few minutes after we had finished the symphony, Madame Tesi came in and wanted to try out two new arias which Bonno had just composed for her. She was a woman in her fifties, but very well preserved and pleasant. Bonno took out the music and sat down at the cembalo; Madame Tesi took her place behind him. She had a round and clear contralto voice and her majestic delivery delighted me no end. I believed that nothing more beautiful could be heard on this earth.

The thrice-sounded chime of the doorbell announced the arrival of the Prince. He immediately went toward my father and most graciously conversed with him for quite a while. He then called me over and said: "Well, I hope you will be satisfied with your room and all that you found in it. You will have to be industrious and well-behaved so that I can also be satisfied with you."

He had a flute and a concerto brought to him, whereupon he sat down and started to play. In all honesty I must admit that he was not a magician on the instrument, but he kept strict time and had an exceedingly nice embouchure. The rehearsal ended with the concerto and the prince went to have his lunch.

The description I have given before is probably enough to give my readers an idea of the noble and philanthropic disposition of the prince. They will, some pages later, become even better acquainted with the incomparable kindness of this great nobleman. Before continuing, I might as well tell the story of Madame Tesi, as I can think of no better place to insert it.

Vittoria Tesi-Tramontini had achieved fame as the foremost singer and actress of her time all over Europe in the prime of her life and she preserved this reputation even into her old age. Completely captivated by her extraordinary acting ability, [Pietro] Metastasio wrote his Zenobia, Didone, and Semiramide especially for her. The most distinguished theatres in all of Italy competed for her and rewarded her so generously as to enable her to make a small fortune. She also appeared in Madrid where she made her debut with Farinelli, the most famous castrato, who was held in such high esteem by the King of Spain that he eventually appointed him minister of state. Farinelli was enchanted by Tesi's talent to such a degree that he frankly told the king he never wished to perform with any other female singer as long as he lived. His request was granted and she was engaged for a number of years, until finally Farinelli gave up singing, since his voice lost power as he grew older. During her career in Spain, Tesi not only earned fabulous sums of money, but received in addition jewelry and gems from the king after every opera performance. In short, she earned the greatest part of her wealth in Spain.

During the reign of Charles VI she left Spain for good to accept a well-paid engagement in Vienna. For many years she sang at the Vienna court theatre for kingly sums. When she approached her fiftieth year, she withdrew from the theatre and decided to spend the rest of her days in peace. Prince Hildburghausen, who had always admired her outstanding talent, offered her a permanent home at his house and suggested a reasonable salary. She accepted his invitation, but would not hear of any salary. Neither did she ever accept any gifts offered her by the prince; and one should not be led to believe that anything but pure friendship and mutual love of art ever existed between them.

I could dwell at length on the many fine aspects of her personality, but I shall limit myself to relating the story of her marriage, a tale which by no means shows a mediocre character. Wherever she performed, Tesi was accustomed to receive a great many visitors, but when it came to suitors she had such a knack of preventing any of them from giving voice to their proposals that only few dared to broach the subject to her. Among her many followers who yearned for her, was a certain Duca di N. One evening when through coincidence he found himself alone with her, he took the opportunity to declare his love formally. Tesi refused him in a very refined and genteel manner. Taking her refusal for a sheer matter of convention, he became all the more obtrusive and made the wildest promises. Tesi answered him with dignity and decency and finally the Duca felt put to shame and withdrew. But this only made his passion grow with each day. He confided in one of his courtiers, who tried to negotiate for his master, but was just as formally rejected. "I must possess her if I have to marry her legitimately!" blurted the Duke. "Tomorrow night I'll surprise her with a formal proposal. But be careful," he said to the courtier, "and don't breathe a word of it!" He promised strictest discretion. But, in order to ingratiate himself with the future Duchess, he went immediately to Tesi and disclosed the great secret under the seal of secrecy.

Well, what did Tesi do? To rid herself of the obnoxious Duke once and for all, she summoned the hairdresser of the theatre to her that very evening and when the handsome man appeared she formally asked him to marry her. "If you want to do it," she said to the pleasantly perturbed Tramontini, "I accept you as my husband on the spot, and we can be married tomorrow morning. I'll put a nice sum at your disposal with which you may do whatever you please. But my main condition is that you forego the idea of living with me as my husband. A physical defect makes me unfit for marriage. If, knowing this, you decide to marry me, we shall be wedded by noon tomorrow."

One can easily imagine that the delighted hairdresser snatched at this offer with both hands. The next day at eleven o'clock the wedding ceremony was over, and after a festive luncheon Tramontini's belongings were brought to her living quarters where she paid her newly wed husband, who was as in heaven, 2,000 sequins in cash.

The Duke's surprise and embarrassment can be easily pictured, when, the next evening, he saw the transformed Tramontini in holiday clothes beside his adored Tesi in an intimate attitude and heard the explanation of this, for him, painful riddle. However composed he acted, he could not hide the feeling of hurt pride and took leave in a cool and formal way. She never saw him again.

By the way, her marriage turned out to be quite happy. When, many years later, the prince decided to settle down in Hildburghausen, she was unable to undertake such a journey because of her age and bad health. That is why she had to separate from her royal friend and to stay in Vienna, where she died a few years later.

* * *

I lived in the house of the prince true to my regulations, which I repeatedly perused. Thus the first three months went by and I must say that I recall this time with great pleasure. The prince introduced me to a certain Mr. Trani who was to become my violin teacher, and I can state in all honesty that this man did his very best for my musical development.

At the beginning of June, the prince and the entire royal retinue left for Schlosshof which was an ideal summer resort. Castle and garden were magnificent, and the village gave the impression of a small town. The national hero Eugene, Prince of Savoy, who lives on in the memory of every patriotic Austrian, had built and furnished Schlosshof.

A few days later, Trani arrived in the company of Signor Pompeati who, in his younger years, was one of the foremost solo dancers; but he left the theatre when he grew older and gave lessons in dancing and Italian. He also became my teacher in both subjects.

Trani brought with him an exceedingly fine violin which the prince had asked him to buy for me. Though many a buyer was interested in it, I have kept this violin all my life and only two years ago gave it to my eldest son.

My instructions, to which horseback riding was added, were properly continued here as well as in Vienna and, despite the many diverting entertainments which made my sojourn in Schlosshof paradisaic, I cannot say that they caused any negligence in my studies.

In the first days of November we returned to Vienna again. I had no longer to take lessons in horseback riding and dancing which gave me more time to practice which is the main thing for anyone who wants to make progress on his instrument. Trani informed me that now I had to be ready with a solo for every *Akademie* (the name for concerts in Vienna at that time) which the prince usually arranged for the high aristocracy on all Fridays throughout the entire winter. "The pieces by Locatelli, Zuccarini and Tartini are good for practice but not for recitals; besides, they are too well known here. Well, you will play something by Ferrari whenever you perform."

Although Trani no longer played solo, he nevertheless had the gift to teach his students what he himself could not do any more. So it happened that I learned to play Ferrari's pieces as their creator visualized them, which made many Viennese jokingly call me Ferrari's little monkey.

Two years before I entered the prince's service, Ferrari, who was a great virtuoso on the violin, had stayed in Vienna about three quarters of a year and had had the greatest success at the royal court, with the theatre managers and the public. I never heard him play.

When I appeared before the high aristocracy for the first time, my recital was generally approved. My teacher was greatly praised by all those present. Some of them even said that he was about to create a new Ferrari.

The same year in December Gluck came to Vienna. The prince was already informed through his correspondent that the success of this worthy man in Italy had been tremendous. The prince was eager to meet Gluck personally and this was arranged by Bonno, who brought about the introduction. Gluck was a jovial man and, since he was not only well versed in music, but was a learned man as well as a man of the world, he soon became a good friend of the prince. When present at *Akademien* Gluck seated himself opposite the violin. The prince's Kapelle was strongly increased by a number of the most selected orchestra players on rehearsal and recital days. Small wonder then, that our *Akademien* were considered the best in all Vienna. As singers, there usually appeared: Madame Tesi, whose acquaintance we had made; Mlle. Heinisch, who was a wonderful soprano and beautiful to boot; Mr. Joseph Fribert, a tenor, one of Bonno's students and in the service of the prince. As instrumentalists usually heard were: Mr. Gentsch, violoncello; Mr. Tuene, fagotto; Mr. Schmit, oboe and English horn; both Hubaczeks, French horn; and finally my little self.

Gluck permitted the prince to copy many of his compositions, such as symphonies and arias, and every piece from the pen of this worthy composer was a new and delicate delight for our ears.

The prince was often a guest at the royal court. Once he came back from there with the news that the emperor had promised him to visit at Schlosshof for a few days the following July and intended to bring the empress and some of the older archdukes

and duchesses with him. The prince therefore decided
to leave for Schlosshof with all his people at the beginning of April instead of in June (as he usually
did) to begin with the necessary preparations early.

When we arrived at Schlosshof, we found the place
crowded with all kinds of craftsmen and artists, with
carpenters, joiners, painters, lacquerers, gilders, etc.,
and wherever one went one ran into people who
busied themselves and labored doggedly for the expected royal party.

At the prince's order, Bonno had to compose two
dramatic pieces by Metastasio, and Gluck also had accepted the commission to compose another Metastasio,
"Il ballo cinese". The singers in our service were
joined by a certain Mlle. Starzer, a sister of the famous ballet composer Starzer, whose works were sur-
prisingly well met and not only successful in Vienna
and Paris, but even in Petersburg. Mlle. Starzer had
a deep contralto and sang excellently. She was one
of Bonno's students, and this says everything. Also
the unique and great singer Therese Teiber, who
was the sensation of Vienna, Dresden, of London and
even Italy, was one of his pupils.

The faster the time of the royal visit approached
us, the busier we became, and the opera rehearsals
were coming along nicely. Then the necessary arrangements had to be made to receive the royal family. To assure and preserve good order the prince
asked the commanding general in Vienna for two
companies of infantry and two squads of cavalry.

This small brigade camped on the Hutweide.

The day of their arrival came in all its glory—it was the most wonderful weather in the world, and at one o'clock noon the august guests with their suite drove in at Schlosshof. Their entrance took place without much ado. On purpose, the prince had avoided all pomp to make the other spectacles appear all the more surprising. He himself and his courtier Beust received them under the main gate. After luncheon they drove to Niederwenden. After the prince had accompanied his royal guests from one party to another, he finally guided them to an open-air theatre with the background view of the blue mountain range of Pressburg. Immediately after their arrival, the overture of the drama began, during which a great many peasants appeared some of whom remained standing at some distance, but some climbed up nearby trees. The emperor was well pleased with it. But how pleasantly surprised was he, when all the peasants, men and women, boys and girls, those who were standing around or sitting in the branches of the trees, joined in singing the last stanza whenever it reappeared in the drama, and this chorus of more than 200 voices sang clearly and correctly as though they had been professional singers. This chorus had an extraordinary effect. It was generally considered sensational and the emperor did not remain untouched by it.

There can be no doubt that the emperor loved nature and simplicity, that he spoke and acted with

gentleness and kindness. It is impossible to describe
in detail the many festivities, fireworks, feasts of Bac-
chus, hunts, etc. which took place here, and, moreover, my readers would hardly appreciate it. However, I would like to say a few words about a water-
carrousel, the memory of which shall never fail me.
I also still recall the exceedingly beautiful performance of the little comic opera, "La Danza", which
Metastasio had fashioned after his play, "Il ballo cinese", and to which Gluck had written the music.
The décor by Quaglio was transparent and done in
Chinese style.Lacquerers, sculptors and gilders added
to it whatever their art permitted. But what gave the
décor its great splendor were prismatic glass bars
ground in the Bohemian glassworks and in exact
arrangement placed into those spots which were im-
pregnated with various oil colors. It is hardly describ-
able—this magnificent and highly surprising sight of
prisms lit up by the innumerable lights and their
total effect on the spectator. Picture to yourself the
mirror reflection of the azure-lacquered fields, the
gleam of the gilded foliage and then the play of the
rainbow colors as created by the many hundred prisms
as if they were the finest diamonds,—and the strongest
imagination will remain far behind this magic. And
in addition the divine music by Gluck! It was not
alone the lovely score of the brilliant symphony accompanied as it was in part by little bells, triangles,
little tympans and cymbals, which enchanted the listeners even before the curtain went up, but the entire

music which throughout was pure magic!

After six days of gaiety and jubilation the highly satisfied royal party returned to Vienna.

The three months thereafter we lived as we had done last summer with the only difference that the prince received several visitors from Vienna and from the vicinity. On such occasions the new operas were repeated several times.

On our return to Vienna the prince stayed at another palace and changes had to be made as to the accommodations of his entire retinue and the Kapelle. I with my brothers (whom the prince had meanwhile also taken into his service) went to live there with him and received a monthly salary of 37 florins and 30 kreutzer. At the same time I was exempted from all previous duties at the table and in the chambers and I stopped wearing a uniform. I had saved so much money as to be able to buy some quite decent clothes.

I no longer took French and Italian lessons, since I spoke both languages well; but my lessons on the violin continued, and Trani who lived pretty far from the palace was called for daily in a royal carriage. One day he remarked to Bonno that he thought I had an inclination to composition, because my cadences betrayed a certain creative power. Bonno, who seemed also interested in the little talent I showed, offered to give me gratis lessons in composition and I received from him permission to come to him three times a week. Delighted about it, I kissed his hand and felt very happy about this prospect.

The first time I came to him, he gave me **Fux'** "Introduction to Composition" as a present. At that time, this work was one of the best of its kind. It was written in Latin and consisted only of dialogues between teacher and student.

After a few weeks' instruction, Bonno asked me to compose a sonata for myself. I did so and brought it to him. He corrected a few notes in the bass and asked me to try to make a concerto of it. I started to work on it and after an interval of 14 days I handed it in. With full-voiced accompaniment, however, I failed badly; I had not only made many a mistake against the rules of the thorough bass, but also against the golden rule: one must not cover nor drown out the vocal part with the accompaniment. It took four lessons, before I had everything corrected. When this was done, he said to me: "Now study thoroughly the Principale under the guidance of **Signor Trani,** write out the voices from the score, and when everything is done correctly, let the prince hear it."

I played my concerto. But how could I describe the delight I felt, when, for the first time, I heard my poor piece of work accompanied by a large and magnificent orchestra! I was enchanted. This attempt which had not quite failed, encouraged me to take all possible pains to learn the rules of counterpoint. The more I worked, the greater were the difficulties which I encountered. But nothing could discourage me.

At that time, Gluck was called to Rome where he

met with much approbation and became "Cavaliere dello Sperone d'oro". One received this distinction in Rome and those who were the bearers of this order had the title: "Comites palatii romani". They were given a diploma written on parchment and certified by a big seal. Moreover, they enjoyed all liberties of the aristocracy in Rome as well as in the papal state and could enter the Pope's palace without restriction. In order to encourage the arts and sciences, the Pope distributed this order to the great and distinguished talents, such as to Metastasio, Bibiena, Guarini, etc. Gluck also received this distinction and thereafter called himself: Cavaliere, Chevalier, or Ritter (knight) Gluck.

The reader should not take amiss that I dwell on the description of this order so intensively. But I myself became a member in 1770. That, however, is not the reason why I call myself "von" Dittersdorf. I was knighted by the royal court in 1773, an incident of which we shall talk in due time.

In the year 1758, [!] the Seven Years' War broke out. The following year the prince took over the command of the *Reichsarmee*. He chose 14 persons of his Kapelle to accompany him in his campaign, and I and my two brothers were among them. In the middle of April of that year the prince's entire outfit began its journey under cover of cavalry, and after 4 weeks we arrived in Fuerth, near Nuremberg, which was the rallying point of the army. We stayed there for about 2 months, before the army which consisted of

90,000 men was assembled. We then marched to Erfurt in Thuringia, where the French General Soubise waited with his 25,000 French soldiers to unite his forces with those of the Reich. A great many incidents could be told, but they do not really belong here.

With the advance of both armies, the suite and baggage of the prince was brought back to Hildburghausen, guarded by 2 squads of cuirassier. We passed the huge forests of Thuringia and went across the depression between two high mountains. Our route of march hit Saalfeld and the famous University of Jena, and on the tenth day we happily arrived in Hildburghausen, the residence of the reigning Duke, where we stayed throughout the winter. Once a week there was a concert at the duke's castle, at which we had to make our appearance.

We stayed there until March, when we began our long and wearisome journey for Vienna. The prince, who preferred life in the country to city life during the summer months, then made the decision to rent a hunting lodge in Austria or Moravia. Thus he travelled a great deal, which made us live in idleness for many months. This was my undoing. I was drawn into loose company, and my salary was no longer sufficient. Notwithstanding that I earned some nice ducats, I could not make both ends meet; billiards, bowling, and the playing of cards were the reason for my being broke by the middle of the month more than once. Of course, sometimes I won pretty sums playing billiards at which I was very good, and then I could pay my debts and received new credit. But such luck only drove me deeper into a loose and careless life. Nevertheless, my musical studies—and this was the best I could make of it—did not suffer from it. I did not fail to play the violin industriously and was seriously occupied with compositions. I wrote 6 symphonies which caused some stir in Vienna as well as in Prague.

The reigning Duke of Sachsen-Hildburghausen, whose granduncle was the prince, my patron, died when the hereditary prince of the dukedom was a child of about 6 or 7 years. Consequently, my prince was offered the guardianship of his ward as well as the regency and administration of the dukedom which he neither could nor wanted to refuse. But this forced him to move to Hildburghausen for good. As there already was a Kapelle at that court and as he was very busy with the education of the prince and the administration of the country, he had to dismiss the greater part of his own Kapelle. To assure those who were dismissed their daily bread, he arranged with the Count Durazzo, who at that time was the chief administrator of the court theatre, for us to continue to work for him. We received a contract for three years and were supposed to work for the orchestra of the theatre as well as for the court Kapelle for the same salary we had received from the prince.

No one was worse off than I. Now I had to be present at the opera—and ballet—rehearsals almost daily from 10 o'clock in the morning until 2 in the afternoon and in the evening at the performances in the theatre from 6:30 until 10; furthermore, I had to accompany the performers at the Friday *Akademien* and play at the concerts every second week. I was also obliged to play solos on holidays and gala days at the Imperial court.

More than a year had passed, when Gluck told me one day that a contract called him to Bologna where he was to compose an opera; and he also asked me whether I would like to travel with him to Italy.

"Oh, with the greatest of pleasure!" I answered enthusiastically. "But—" I added sadly, "I don't have the money necessary for it."

"In that case," Gluck answered in a cold tone and turned away, "we can't do anything about it." A man like Gluck, who knew so well my circumstances and my love for art, ought to have respected my feelings better.

The same evening I had dinner with the former court agent, Herr von Preiss, and told him about Gluck's proposition. "Ah, that's grand!" Herr von Preiss said, "say yes and take Gluck at his word!"

"Yes," I retorted and shrugged my shoulders, "where shall I get the money? True, Gluck wants me to come with him, but I am supposed to share expenses with him."

"Bah," said this honorable man—may he rest in peace!—"I'll find a way. I'll lend you a hundred ducats which you may repay when your circumstances

have improved. Come for dinner tomorrow night.
I'll invite Herr von Allstern and try to convince him
over a glass of Gränzinger [!] that he ought to advance
you the same amount. Besides, for cases of emergency
I'll give you a check amounting to 600 florins, so
that altogether you'll have about 1,500 florins with
you."

With tears of joy in my eyes I thanked the noble
man. Next day I went to Gluck. He was exceedingly
pleased about it.

On the seventh night of our journey we arrived in
Mestre. It was the night between Palm-Sunday and
the Monday of Passion Week.

Gluck decided to stay there for the next eight days.
How we regretted that our sojourn in Venice coincided with Passion Week, during which no theatre
was open and we heard no music except an oratorio
agli incurabili! To make up for the loss of music I
saw two festive spectacles which aroused my full admiration. The one was the celebration on the evening of Maundy Thursday when our Saviour was
carried to the tomb. The other was occasioned by
the burial of the doge, who had died two days prior
to our arrival. Both times the Marcus Square was
illumined, namely two torches as big as an arm and
one fathom long burnt in front of each window of
the palace and created the most magnificent sight.
Both times solemn processions were arranged around
this grand square; it would have been difficult to
determine whether the burial of Christ or that of the

doge was celebrated with greater solemnity and pomp.

At night, on the Saturday before Easter we continued our journey to Bologna. On the next day was the inauguration of the newly built opera house, built superbly with freestones. The director of the opera, Count Bevilaqua, chose for the opening night the opera, "Il trionfo di Clelia", by Metastasio and had engaged Gluck for the adaptation of this piece.

The orchestra consisted of about 70 persons. As they were used to having two harpsichords for such orchestras in Italy, the well-known Kapellmeister Mazzoni was asked to play the second one. He was a resident of Bologna and worked in some of the most esteemed churches, cloisters and prelacies as Kapellmeister. Count Bevilaqua received us with great kindness. Gluck introduced me as his student, for we had agreed that, before we heard the best violinists, I should not mention I was a virtuoso.

The Kapellmeister Mazzoni learned by chance that I was a violin player. After he had heard me, he asked me to play a concerto at the great church festival near San Paolo during the High Mass in the morning. I agreed.

On the day before the great festival I went to the church with Gluck in the afternoon to hear Mazzoni's first vesper. The music was presented by a choir and instrumentalists of more than a hundred persons. The composition was beautiful and of great quality, it only seemed to me to be somewhat profane and too gay for church music; for it resembled—with the exception of perfect fugues—more an opera seria than church music. Spagnoletti played a concerto by Tartini between the psalms which I had studied a few years ago. The whole church was full of connoisseurs and music lovers, and the expression of the listeners showed that the violinist found general approval.

It became known that a German virtuoso would be heard at the High Mass the next day. When we left the church we heard one gentleman say to another, "Tomorrow morning we'll hear a German virtuoso," whereupon the other man replied: "I'm afraid he'll be laughed at after the great Spagnoletti." But when I played one of my concertos next day, I was not laughed at as that gentleman had predicted.

The claustral prior accompanied by two of his brethren approached me and they expressed their gratitude for my troubles. He also asked me to play another concerto during the vesper. In the evening the church was overcrowded, in fact, a great many people could not find room and had to leave. If I played well in the morning, I was certainly twice as good in the evening.

* * *

While I was in Italy, the great violinist Lolli came to Vienna where he stayed for some months and acquired much money. On the first evening after my return, my elder brother was full of praise for him and told me of his sensational success wherever he played. I inquired about the manner in which Lolli played, and he gave me one of his sonatas which he was able to get hold of. My brother assured me that this sonata would give me a good idea of his virtuosity. I looked it over and the quite peculiar passages made his success clear to me.

I locked myself in my room, pretended to be sick and studied from morning until nightfall. Before four weeks had passed, I reported to Count Durazzo and said that I was now ready to appear before the public again. He arranged for it the next *Akademie* in the theatre.

I played my new concerto—and I had the good fortune to outdo Lolli. It was generally said in Vienna: Lolli aroused surprise, Ditters does it too, but at the same time touches our heart.

During the rest of the summer and the following winter I often spent many hours together with the amiable Joseph Haydn. What music lover does not know this name and the beautiful works of this excellent composer? I can only advise any would-be composer to come in close contact with one of his colleagues who harbours neither jealousy nor ill-will, and to do what I and Haydn did; I guarantee that nothing will do more for development than such amicable exchange of ideas without any prejudices. It is certainly not new what I am here saying, for it is well known that criticism—the genuine, impartial criticism of someone who is an expert—has been exceedingly useful to all art and science at all times.

At the time of Archduke Joseph's coronation, the bishop of Grosswardein, a member of the famous family Patachich in Croatia, came to Vienna. He heard me play at the royal court, summoned me to come to him and told me that he was not only a great friend of music, but also had his own Kapelle. Since his musical director Haydn (Michael Haydn, a brother of Joseph Haydn) was about to leave for Salzburg where he was to be concertmaster, he offered me this position with an annual salary of 1200 florins, including board, and also free board and a livery for my servant.

When I happily arrived in Pressburg, the bishop told me during our first conversation: "Now that I have engaged you, I feel strongly inclined to satisfy my pet project as much as I can and I don't see why I shouldn't do it on an income of 80,000 florins. I have decided to spend 16,000 florins for my Kapelle every year. Here is a roster of the members of my Kapelle and here is another one of those musicians I want to engage. Well, I commission you to travel to Vienna and Prague at my expense to act on my behalf. My steward will accompany you so that the contracts can be signed at once."

After my return to Pressburg the bishop had all the musicians gather in the big dining room—those who had been in Grosswardein all the time and the newly engaged ones from Vienna and Prague as well as those who worked in the cathedral—and he formally introduced me to all of them as the director of his Kapelle. I had eight days in which to prepare for the first complete musical performance. Meanwhile, I had long desks and benches made, for I wanted to introduce the Viennese method of sitting while playing; I arranged the orchestra so as to have every musician face the audience. Every Sunday and Tuesday was an *Akademie*. The orchestra consisted of 34 persons.

At the first rehearsal at which the bishop was present we played a new symphony of mine with trumpets and tympani. I got up and said: "Gentlemen! I cannot help making reference to the weaker among us. It seems to me that some of you played incorrectly, and I shall never tolerate that. First, some of you have not tuned your instruments, secondly, some of you did not keep time, were either too fast or dragged behind, and finally others of you have made the unpardonable mistake of not pausing correctly. When we play it again, I hope that everyone will notice his mistake and correct it. However, should my words be without avail, contrary to all expectation, then everyone will have himself to blame for being reprimanded publicly from now on. Now, let's tune up first—and then da capo!" The symphony was repeated and it went off as it ought to. "Bravo!" I said.

The bishop expressed his appreciation "for my firm talk". "I'm more glad each day that I engaged you," he said. "And I'll prove to you my satisfaction immediately." In Vienna I had given him a receipt on the advance of 100 ducats, which he asked to have brought to him and which he tore up in front of me. I seized the bishop's hand, kissed it and said: "Your

Excellency is so gracious today that I dare ask for another favor."

The bishop was taken aback and then asked to hear my request. "My former master, the Prince of Hild-burghausen, who acted like a guardian to me, called me his son," I said, "and addressed me informally. Now that you have acted like a father to me, I dare ask for the same favor."

"Well," the bishop said after a short pause, "granted if you really want it so badly. And if you want me to act like a father, then I must be permitted to consider you my son." At that he dried his tears which were running down his cheeks.

The excellent tenor Renner finally arrived with his family. His wonderful gift for recitation, his good pronunciation of the Italian language, his beautiful and clear voice and perfect technique made him one of the foremost singers. Beside him and Unger-icht, we had engaged a few castrati, and one of them was a good violoncellist, the other was a fair violinist. We had 12 instrumentalists and 4 singers in our orchestra. Besides myself, Fuchs and Pichel for the violin; P. Michael on the harpsichord; Pohl and Stadler for the oboe; Fournier for the clarinet; Satza for the flute; Himmelbauer for the cello; Pichelberger for the contrabass and Oliva and Pauer for the French horn. I made it a rule that everyone had to be prepared and ready to be called up at any time.

It was already September when I started the preparation for the celebration of the bishop's name day which happened to be at the end of December. I discussed it with Pichel, who was not only well versed in Latin, but showed much poetical talent and was able to make nice Latin verses. We decided to get together on a panegyric cantata for 4 voices and chorus. The concert took place on the eve of his name day. The arrangement of the orchestra and particularly the tasteful uniform of the Kapelle (for which I had received the bishop's approval), all this made a very good impression on the audience and was very much liked by the Hungarian aristocrats. Although this was my first great vocal work and the music of this cantata was nothing to boast of, it nevertheless found approval. At least I learned through the mistakes I made, and in the future I would know how to avoid haphazard passages, unconnected with the text, *sans rime et sans raison,* as I interspersed them frequently.

After the first year we found out that we had saved 1400 out of the 16,000 florins which had been allotted for the Kapelle. I conceived the idea of erecting a small theatre in the castle. Design and estimate were submitted by the bishop's architect Neumann, and the bishop himself approved everything with great pleasure.

Since his name day coincided with the last days of Advent, on which it was forbidden by the court to play profane pieces, operas and comedies, I chose the very beautiful oratorio by Metastasio, "Isacco figura del Redentore". As Pichel did not understand enough Italian, the bishop himself made the translation into Latin. While he worked on the translation, I did not want to fritter away the time in idleness. I composed a great concerto for eleven instruments, wherein every instrumentalist was first heard in a solo in the first allegro movement; then gradually 3, 5, 7, and 9 voices were heard, until in the final solo all 11 came together and ended with a cadence which, by degrees, grew in intensity. We rehearsed this great concerto with ardour, often held secret rehearsals, and, since I intended to surprise the bishop with it, I asked the whole Kapelle not to say anything about the matter. We were hardly ready, when the bishop gave me his text. From then on I worked diligently on the oratorio.

On the eve of the bishop's name day my "Isaac" was performed. Proof of its great success was the fact that its performance was repeated every Sunday in the period of fasting through 4 years. The singers—Renner, Mlle. Nicolini, the castrato who played Sara, and Ungericht—were all excellent, even the boy who acted the angel, and their recitation was very good.

The bishop presented me with his favorite *tabatière* with a few dozens Kremnitzer in it.

* * *

In 1769, *the Bishop, at the request of Maria Teresia, dismissed his Kapelle. Dittersdorf went to Vienna, and from there to Venice, where he met the Prince-Bishop of Breslau, Count von Schafgotsch. The latter invited him to live with him in Johannisberg in Silesia. The*

Prince-Bishop loved entertainment and recognized in Dittersdorf a man who was able to relieve the boredom of the court. Dittersdorf was a good hunter, storyteller, and arranger of festivities—in short, a born maître de plaisir.

The composer received the title and salary of Forestmaster at Neïsse. Dittersdorf succeeded in getting Renner and his stepdaughter, Mlle. Nicolini, together with Ungericht, to come to Silesia. We continue with that chapter which deals with Dittersdorf's marriage.

* * *

Actually, I should start a new chapter here, for we shall have to talk about an important step in my life. But since little happens in it that is romantic and full of adventure, on the contrary, since everything reels off in an almost philistine manner, I shall continue without interruption.

It so happened that I gave Mlle. Nicolini daily lessons, I—was in love with her?—Well, if one wants to call it that. But that wasn't quite what I wanted to say. In fact, I had so much opportunity to discover her good qualities and her solid character that I decided one day to propose to her without much ado; but, on the other hand, I wanted to postpone our marriage until I could find out whether I would lead a joyful life with her and she with me. When I finally came to a decision, I proposed to her during one of our lessons, but told her at once to take her time and think it over, even if it were a year. She answered that she did not need any time to reflect on it, only her stepfather, Herr Renner, would have to approve it. The least difficulty was to be expected from him, and on the third of March of the following year we were married in the chapel of the castle.

In the year 1773, the head magistrate of Freiwaldau, Cajetan von Beerenberg, died. Immediately thereafter the prince asked me to see him and, in his graciousness, he offered me the position that was open; "But one thing has to be done," he said, "you must be knighted first, otherwise it won't work." The diocese of Breslau had long since adhered to a fundamental rule from which no bishop could deviate; all the more, since such positions were charitable endowments, and the bishop who is forced to keep up a great retinue and a train of attendants can thus provide decently for the poorer noblemen in his suite and also ensure their children an education according to their station. I therefore filed a petition in Vienna to be made a nobleman and soon received the diploma with the title Carl von Dittersdorf simultaneously with all the taxes to be paid and a flattering note saying that the Empress Maria Theresia graciously conceded to reducing the court taxes to half their usual amount. Thus I was installed as the head magistrate of Freiwaldau, took my oath, was acknowledged by the chapter of the cathedral and started formally on my duties on November 4, 1773. But since the prince desired to have me constantly at his disposal, it was arranged that the *Kammerrat* in Freiwaldau would act as the administrator of my duties, for which he received a handsome part of my income.

Our concerts and spectacles were continued in Johannisberg without interruption and our Kapelle was considered the best in the entire royal and Prussian Silesia, and this rightly so. Subsequently, a great many travelling virtuosi reported partly in writing, partly personally with the request to appear in our performances. Even the great virtuoso Lolli happened to come to Johannisberg once. He was a very handsome man, a perfect man of the world, and, in spite of his great talent, a modest, polite and very jovial man. Small wonder, that the prince soon began to be fond of him. Lolli had intended to stay one day only; but the prince wanted him to stay another day and he accepted this invitation with the noblest of gestures. The symphony was hardly over, when he asked the prince for permission to play a concerto which he then played so beautifully—together with a sonata—that it perfectly explained his great reputation.

The Bavarian war of succession, which at that time broke out between Austria and Prussia, necessitated the dismissal of the prince's private Kapelle. He did not do so, however, without the assurance that he would take us back into his service after the end of hostilities and in the event his income was not curtailed. As I had no longer anything to do with the

Kapelle, I moved with my family to Freiwaldau where I performed my duties as head magistrate and did so with all seriousness.

After the Teschen peace the prince stayed in Bruenn for some time to restore the castle which was greatly devastated by the enemy. After his return to Johannisberg some members of the court Kapelle, who had been dismissed before the war, reported to him, and the prince hired them immediately. For those who did not report for duty, other musicians were engaged, and at the beginning of that winter the Kapelle began to work again. As far as I was concerned, I still lived in Freiwaldau; but every now and then the prince asked for me and I had to go to Johannisberg where I often stayed 8 to 14 days. It seemed I had become indispensable to him. But my duties as head magistrate suffered from such long periods of absence. This was the reason why—as years previously—an administrator had to be installed to act in my stead and I moved back to Johannisberg. There I bought a lot, built a house on it and laid out a beautiful garden.

Some years before I was asked by the musical "Widow-Society" in Vienna to compose an oratorio on their behalf. I finally decided to do it and in the year 1786 the performance of my "Giobbe" or Job took place there at the end of Lent. The papers in Vienna had a great deal to say about it; but it would be unbecoming to mention some of it here.

About three years ago I had the idea of using some

of Ovid's Metamorphoses as subject matter for symphonies and, when I arrived in Vienna I had already finished 12 of those symphonies. In order to cover my travelling expenses to Vienna I embarked on an enterprise which I must relate in great detail because of an attendant incident.

With Emperor Joseph's special permission I advertised the performance of 6 of those symphonies in the great hall of the royal *Augarten* for an admission fee of 2 florins, and even the Baron van Swieten had consented to distribute a hundred tickets. With the approaching day of the performance bad weather set in, and my subscribers asked me to postpone it until the weather cleared up.

I went to the police for permission to cancel the announced performance and fix its date according to convenience. But I was told that a new order of the cabinet was necessary for that; of course, I might get it any time that day if I desired it. "Why don't you go to court," the president said, "to the so-called control-corridor. The door in the middle leads to the emperor's private office. On your right, in a small room, you will find some of the emperor's lackeys, ask them to call Herr von Bourguignon. He will get you the permission and maybe—even the emperor will talk to you!"

"All the better," I said and went immediately to the palace.

I was well informed that one had to be concise, clear and bold when speaking to the emperor, without crouching in fear and humility, so I decided to follow this rule of conduct. The lackey announced me to Herr von B.; but in his stead the emperor himself approached me, and the following dialogue ensued.

Emperor: Aha! Well, what do you want from me?

I: I don't want anything from Your Majesty.

Emperor: How come?

I: Because the affair is too insignificant to bother you with it. I only intended to speak to Herr von B.

Emperor: (good-humouredly) Well, if it's no secret, I'll tell it to Bourguignon.

I: (in the same good mood) Oh, that isn't necessary. Your Majesty could decide yourself. I would prefer it.

Emperor: (as before) Come with me! (He led me into a small room which was next to the private office) Well, what's the matter?

I: The president of the police sent me here.

Emperor: (in an even more humorous tone) Oho! The president of the police? What have you perpetrated? Did you by any chance get into the hands of the chastity commission?

I: (in the same tone) Ah, in that case the police would have found a niche for me and I would not have had the pleasure of—

Emperor: Well! Get the pig out of the poke!

I: My subscribers have asked me to postpone the performance of my music in the *Augarten* because of the uncertain weather. The president of the police can't give me his permission without court approval and that is the reason I am here.

Emperor: (stepping into the private office) Do you hear, Bourguignon? Write a few lines to the president of the police that Dittersdorf has my permission to postpone his performance as long as he thinks it necessary. (Turning to me) Apropos! I liked your oratorio "Job" a great deal and have ordered the score copied. I hope you don't mind.

I: I'm all the more happy that it has found the approval of such a great connoisseur as Your Majesty—

Emperor: (coldly) I can't stand flattery. I love the truth alone.

I: All the better; for I speak the truth.

Emperor: (after short pause) Greybig says: As a violinist you resemble a good preacher who proves himself better-read in the Old than in the New Testament.

I: Satirically enough.

Emperor: On the other hand, he says about your compositions that they appear like a nicely set and well-filled table. The dishes are deliciously prepared, one can enjoy a handsome portion from each dish and risk no indigestion. I agree with Greybig's judgment of your compositions.

I: Your Majesty is too kind.

Emperor: To be just to a man is no kindness. Are you still employed in Silesia?

I: Yes, Your Majesty.

Emperor: In what capacity?

I: As head magistrate and counselor to the government.

Emperor: What are your duties?

I: Publica, Politica et Iudicialia.

Emperor: (seriously) Really? Have you got the necessary capacity for it?

I: I have held this position for the last thirteen years and there have been no complaints.

Emperor: That's nice. But for heaven's sake where did you get the necessary experience?

I: It would be an indelible shame, if I, who was born and educated in Vienna, had learned nothing more than to play the violin and to compose.

Emperor: (still more seriously) Mm, your answers are well put.

I: (in reverential tone) I was told that one must answer Your Majesty in a short, concise and sincere way. If I have failed, I beg your pardon.

Emperor: (milder) You were told the right thing and your answers did not hurt me. (After a short pause in his previous good mood) Have you heard Mozart play?

I: Three times already.

Emperor: How do you like him?

I: As any connoisseur must like him.

Emperor: Have you also heard Clementi?

I: Yes, I have.

Emperor: Some people prefer him to Mozart, among them Greybig à la tête. What is your opinion. Be blunt.

I: Clementi's way of playing is art alone, Mozart's is art and taste.

Emperor: That's just what I said. It is as if we had both studied the same book.

I: We have. The great book of experience.

Emperor: What do you think of Mozart's compositions?

I: He is undoubtedly one of the greatest of all original geniuses, and I have not yet known any composer who has such a surprising wealth of thought. I only wish he were not so wasteful of it.

Emperor: He makes one mistake in his theatrical pieces as the singers so often complain, namely that he drowns them out with his full accompaniment.

I: This surprises me. One can adjust harmony and accompaniment so that the cantilena is in no way hurt.

Emperor: You possess this gift in a masterly way. I noticed it in your two oratorios "Esther" and "Job". What do you say to Haydn's compositions?

I: I haven't heard any of his theatrical plays.

Emperor: You haven't lost anything; for he works the same way as Mozart. But what do you think of his pieces for chamber music?

I: They are the sensation of the whole world, and rightly so.

Emperor: Isn't he a bit too playful from time to time?

I: He has the gift for it without losing the high

standard of art.

Emperor: There you are right. (After a pause) Some time ago I have drawn a parallel between Mozart and Haydn. Won't you do the same so that I can see whether we agree?

I: (after a pause) Will Your Majesty permit me to ask one more question first?

Emperor: Go ahead!

I: What kind of parallel does Your Majesty draw between Klopstock and Gellert?

Emperor: Hm! Both are great poets. Klopstock must be read more than once to get behind the beauty of his work, however, the beauty in Gellert's works lies unveiled before you at first sight.

I: Your Majesty has replied for me.

Emperor: That means that Mozart can be compared with Klopstock and Haydn with Gellert?

I: That is my opinion.

Emperor: Charming! Now you have given me another weapon with which I can hit Greybig's chattering beak.

I: May I be so bold and ask Your Majesty for your parallel?

Emperor: I'll tell you. I compared Mozart's compositions with a golden *tabatière* worked out in Paris and those of Haydn with one done in London. (Stepping toward the door of the office) Are you ready, Bourguignon? (He brought him the slip of paper. Then turning to me again) I am glad that I have made your closer acquaintance. I have found you

202

a different man from what you were pictured to me.

I: How was this, Your Majesty?

Emperor: I was told you were an egotist who begrudged the least honor to any virtuoso or composer. This made me feel you out. I am glad that I learned to the contrary. But now I'll tell off a few persons—although one of them has already gone ad patres. (He gave me the paper) Here you have my permission to perform your music in the *Augarten* whenever you want. Adieu! (He went back into his private office and I left for the police.)

On Jan. 3, 1795, the Prince-Bishop died and Dittersdorf received a pension. He had served his master twenty-six years, but Dittersdorf did not have the ability to save money. However, as always, he found a way out of his financial difficulties when his friend, Baron von Stillfried, took him into his castle, Rothlhotta in Bohemia. Dittersdorf died there on the 24th of Oct., 1799.

II

FRANZ BENDA'S AUTOBIOGRAPHY

Potsdam, in the year 1763

I was born on November 25, 1709, in the kingdom of Bohemia, to be exact: in the village Old-Benatky near the mountain town New-Benatky.

My late father Johann Georg Benda was one of the oldest linen weavers there and played the dulcimer, the oboe and shawm in taverns. My late mother Dorothea Benda, née Brixy, was the daughter of a village schoolmaster. After the death of my eldest sister, I was the eldest of their children.

My grandfather was a steward on an aristocratic estate. His first name slips my mind.

Since the town school was almost half a quarter of a mile from where we lived, I learned the alphabet and spelling from a potter, but finally I went to the town school where I learned how to read, to write and to sing and thus laid the first musical foundation with the help of the skilled schoolmaster, Alexius by name. In the year 1718, when I was 9 years of age, my father took me along to Prague to show me the city. There we visited a church composer whose name was Brixy and who was a distant relative of my mother. He examined my soprano and, as I sang the piece put before me pretty well, he immediately offered me the position of descantist in the St. Nicolai Church of the Benedictine cloister.

After I had passed the examination and was accepted, I remained in Prague. My former schoolmaster Alexius intended to send his own son to Prague to get this position, but my father had not known it. He accused my father of having prevented his son from getting it. The clergyman, however, decided in my favor and against his son.

I also attended the Jesuit school there. I often visited those churches where I could hear the best singers. Within one year I too was considered one of them. At first the cloister gave me only free board, but after one year I was promised to be clothed also. One of the clergymen, a certain Pater Hermann, became very fond of me. It happened that, at that time, he received 200 florins from Count Czernin, one of the students, whom he had helped to write a thesis. He used some of this money to dress me nicely from top to toe.

When my mother visited me and thus saw me trimmed, she insisted on my asking permission for 8 days' vacation to come home with her. Not far from our village—to which we went on foot—she went with me sideways behind bushes. First I did not know what she had in mind, but when she took a paper bag with hair powder out of her pocketbook I realized what she was up to. In short, my hair was powdered and I could hardly refrain from laughing out loud. And who was it who got to see me entering the village? No one but a few peasant people, our neighbors. The coming Sunday I sang in the church, and the schoolmaster was very pleased and satisfied; in the afternoon, over several goblets of good Bohemian beer, my father and Alexius became reconciled, whereupon I left for my cloister again.

A certain student, Roscher by name, was commissioned to engage a descantist whom he considered best as a royal *Saengerknabe* for the Catholic Church in Dresden. I became his choice. As the Prague Jesuits were against it and would have liked to send someone whom they favored, he advised me to run away with him furtively. They went so far as to warn the Pater Regens in whose service I was and asked him to keep an eye on me. They only let me go to school dressed in my vest and topcoat and took away my coat. But I left in the company of this student and in my vest only. I had no money about me, my whole fortune were 5 Kronen from the sale of my schoolbooks to the Jews. I sang in the church at Rakonitz where the student's parents lived. The dean made me a present of 2 florins and treated me to a wonderful meal. I felt as if I were one of the richest people in the world. My laundry and beds had remained in Prague. When my good father came to see me, the Jesuits urged him to get me back. The good man could swear to it that he had no knowledge of my flight. His sadness and tears finally proved his innocence.

When I arrived in Dresden and reported to the Jesuits under whose guidance the *Saengerknaben* stood, I found some of my future colleagues playing ball. As I could not speak German, I addressed them in Czech. They were nicely dressed and, since I wore nothing but an old vest, they looked down on me. But after I was heard singing, I was, three days later, just as well dressed.

Now it was time to write to my father, who, soon afterwards, visited me. He was well satisfied with the change I had made.

After one and a half years had gone by, I was overcome with nostalgia. I wrote my parents about my desire. They sent one of our relatives, on horseback and with one horse for me, so that I could ride home. At that time, however, the late Kapellmeister Heinichen had just finished composing a new Regina Coeli which I was supposed to sing in the presence of the royal party. Also in consideration of the approaching holidays, my relative was sent back and his expenses were paid. But my nostalgic feelings grew more and more. As they did not want to let me go, I secretly left with the help of a Bohemian boatsman and slept during the night on the boat near Pyrna.

When I awoke in the morning, two men sent after me found out my hiding place and took me back with them to Dresden. But the cold of the past night made me lose my voice, and since I did not recover I no longer found any difficulties in obtaining permission to leave. But the kindness shown to me so far had turned into a kind of contempt. I returned to my parents.

In the beginning I was a welcome guest at home. But it did not take long before the question arose what was to be done with me and how I was going to earn my daily bread.

A short while after these considerations, I went with my father to the church where they always made music. My father inquired whether I would like to sing again. He first went with me to a Jew who sold alcoholic drinks. He asked for a glass of a certain drink, emptied half of it, and I had to finish the rest. He said it might be good for my voice. I probably was the first and last one to use such means to improve the voice. Then I had courage standing next to the alto singer and tried to sing with him. In the beginning, the voice was not at its best, but it gradually improved. At the vesper I began to feel more secure—and who was happier than I, when all eyes rested on me. The vicar invited me to his house where also the three young Counts von Kleinau were present, who had heard me sing in the church. They were very polite and asked me to come to see them. Shortly thereafter, one of them finished writing a comedy in which I played the part of a woman. Out of sheer delight and also because of habit, the vicar enjoyed the Melnicker wine so much that his tongue seemed pretty paralyzed. He prided himself on the fact that he had baptized me. But who was happier than I to have regained my voice?

After some time I went to Prague again to continue my studies. I proceeded to the Altstaedter Seminary and inquired whether they would need an alto voice. First I was told that they had too many alto voices, in fact, 9 of them, but when I told them that I had sung in Dresden, they were clever enough to listen to my voice. In short, I was accepted. But I had too much freedom there and neglected my studies. I was 14 years old at that time. In that very year Emperor Charles VI had come to Prague for his coronation. In his honor an open-air performance of the wonderful opera "Costanza e Fortezza" by Johann Josef Fux took place, with a hundred singers and 200 instrumentalists. I was part of the chorus which was often employed.

The Jesuits also performed a kind of Latin comedy for the Bohemian nobility. Arias were interspersed. The music was composed by Zelenka, who was then church composer at the Dresden court.

When I was on the stage the first time, my fright was so great that I was quite unaware of what happened, but when the ritornello had come to an end, I collected myself again and, in fact, as the first aria had come off pretty well, I could hardly await the cue for the next.

Among the excellent singers who had parts in this

opera, the contralto Cajetano Ursini was my favorite. It was of great advantage to me that I observed this singer very attentively and in a certain way it influenced my future musical studies. Since I sang alto, I knew all of Ursini's parts by heart. Later on, Latin texts were written for his arias which I then sang in church and most of them are still in my memory.

When the opera was over I received—as all other musicians—12 florins. Now I was able to buy a sword which I desired for a long time. Soon after, when I reached my 15th year of age, I lost my alto. There was nothing else to be done but return to my parents. Here began a period of my life which I did not like at all. I do not recall any more when I began to play the violin, but so much I know that I played dances in taverns at the age of eight. In Dresden where the *Saengerknaben* had their own concerts for themselves, I played the viola. At the same time I practiced playing the violin and knew the concertos by Vivaldi by heart. My father did not permit me to be idle. I had to become a *Bierfiedler* and had to try myself as linen weaver at home. I liked neither one nor the other and must honestly admit that I was ashamed of it. I still dressed very neatly and associated with the best families in town. The daughter of the first burgomaster (or primator) was very fond of me and I must say that by and by I really fell in love with her.

Because of my circumstances her parents had never accepted me, although she would have been willing to say yes. One thought of a strange thing. The town had no gingerbread baker, and therefore I ought to have learned this craft for three years and then settled down and married my beloved. I might have even become alderman in a town which had almost as many aldermen as citizens, for, at least in those days, there were 12 aldermen for 60 citizens. Love made me do everything. But first it was necessary to request the permission of Count von Kleinau whose subject I was. A petition was drafted, I submitted it, but the reply foiled this beautiful arrangement completely. It said that it would be very regrettable if I neglected the music. I had much better go to Prague again to look for a violin teacher and then the Count would take care of everything else. To reduce my expenses, he immediately presented me with 12 florins. My love for music at once lessened the affection I had for my beloved. At that time, the boy in me was still struggling with the would-be man.

Thus I went to Prague again. My cousin recommended me to the then best violinist, Konyczek by name, who was in the service of the house of Lobkowitz; some time later I was favored by His Highness to become his teacher on the violin.

I stayed with an old widow on the fourth floor. Though I had a hard time in getting all the necessary food, I was nevertheless very industrious as far as playing and writing of music was concerned and even worked until late at night. After ten weeks had passed, my master told me that from now on I was on my own. He could no longer keep me from advancing, he said, and take money for his instructions with clear conscience (though he did not get more than a ducat a month). I went back to my parents again with whom I stayed for a few weeks. My father who did not tolerate any idleness forced me again to play in taverns which I utterly disliked.

In those days, an old Jew, whose name was Lebel and who was born blind, used to play for dancing in another tavern. He was a man with quite excellent gifts for music. He himself composed the pieces he played and played exactly and very clearly, even the high notes, and he was able to make his instrument sound exceedingly sweet, although his violin was not particularly good. I often followed him to have the opportunity to think about the way he played and I must honestly admit that I received more stimulation from him than from my master to make my instrument sound as well as I could. Moreover, I am convinced that playing for the dance had done no harm to my artistry, particularly in regard to keeping time.

My Count, who seemed to have been satisfied with me, was just then host to a certain Count von Ostein, royal *Geheim—und Reichshofrat.* He recommended me to him with the intention of taking me into his service as his valet after I had made myself useful in somebody else's service. Count von Ostein took me with him to Vienna at once. I took leave of all my relatives and also of my beloved who now hoped to be called "Frau Valet" in some time.

In Vienna I was recommended to Count von Uhlefeld, who later was ambassador to Constantinople. He learned the violoncello with the famous royal violoncellist Francischello. Thus several times I had the opportunity to hear this particularly skilful man, whose ability surprised me.[1] I gradually made the acquaintance of several musicians. At that time in Vienna it was the usual procedure to have a stranger who wanted to be heard, play an unknown piece. On a certain occasion my fate was no different, but everyone seemed to have been satisfied with my test.

A close relative of mine, a bugler, was in the service of Field Marshal Montecuccoli and was so insistent that I should give up my post with Count Uhlefeld and join him with the Field Marshal, that I agreed. But it did not take long before I was offered a far better position with a higher salary with the Baron (and afterwards Count) Andler which I accepted and moved with this nobleman to Hermannstadt, the capital of Siebenbuergen. Count Kleinau, however, disapproved of my journey which was undertaken without his knowledge. It so happened that a cousin of his served as an officer in the regiment of the Marquis Lugneville[2] which was stationed in Hermannstadt. It was he who went out of his way to make me serve as soldier for some time.

---

[1]Al. Scarlatti is said to have been so enthusiastic about Francischello's artistry that he maintained an angel must have played in F.'s body.

[2]This name is also spelled Luneville.

213

My patrons, however, took sincere interest in me. The Baroness gave word to the Marquis that, should he use force to make me serve, he would be unwelcome at her house and a charged pistol would be at his disposal. This courageous and determined attitude of hers induced the Marquis to pay his respects without asking for me. Notwithstanding this fact, he desired to have me join his regiment and now I was lured with kindness and presents and finally I let myself be duped into giving in, quitting my position, a deed which I soon regretted.

Luckily, the Marquis was called to Vienna. The last evening he decided to take me along. During our journey I sat in his carriage, but in Vienna I was asked to do the work of a lackey which grieved me very much. I had to leave most of my belongings in Siebenbuergen, because it was said that we would return soon. Now I began to think of means to run away secretly. Soon the occasion came.

The Marquis left hastily for his regiment and, since he was to be back again very soon, he only took one valet and one servant along. Meanwhile I remained here and was often asked to play, most often in the suburbs where I occasionally stayed overnight. Subsequently, this served a good purpose. A musician, a certain Herr Czarth, who was in Count Pachta's service, became an intimate friend of mine. As he was just as dissatisfied with his service as I was with mine, we both decided to run away together to Poland. Two other men with whom I had become friendly in Hermannstadt were determined to follow us, and we arranged to meet in Breslau.

Herr Czarth and I had taken some music and a few shirts in a knapsack, 2 violins, and a flauto traverso on which he played. All this we carried alternately on our backs. I had exchanged my suit so that I would not easily be discovered, and we started on our way in the evening at seven o'clock. We avoided as much as possible the main routes and arrived safely in Breslau after a few days.

There we pretended we were a couple of students from Prague and wanted to try our luck in Poland. We made a few acquaintances and each of us played a concerto in the Church *Am Sande* on a Sunday where we were nicely treated. A few days later our two other friends arrived on the stagecoach. These two were richer than we were, richer in money as well as having a clearer conscience.

After a stay of eleven days, Count von Proskau let us know through one of his buglers that a warrant was taken out against two musicians from Vienna and, if we should be these two, he would advise us to take to our heels as fast as we could. We did not wait for a second warning and immediately left our living quarters in the suburbs of Ohlau. We slept beyond the town wall that night. It so happened that a goods van was just leaving for Warsaw. Our two friends put their belongings on the car and walked with us to Warsaw.

In Wartenberg we had to wait for the carters. We

played in the church and on the marketplace there and the noblest among the inhabitants desired to engage us. But our goal was Warsaw. At the frontier we rejoiced that the danger of the warrant was over. We had received word from a friend of ours from Vienna that the Marquis, who was very rich and ambitious, offered a thousand ducats for our arrest.

Our journey went on well in company of the carters. But one day I got very tired from walking, the heat was unbearable. I asked one of the carters for permission to sit on the car for half an hour. After I had repeated my request, he agreed under the condition that I blow the bugle (which I carried but which belonged to one of my colleagues) and that I could only sit as long as I would blow on it. I made an attempt, but as soon as I stopped the fellow, who was one of those callous brothers, said: "Down with you from the car!" Finally it seemed harder to me to play than to walk. So I left my seat which was bad enough anyway and stepped down from the car.

A few miles before Warsaw something happened to us which was so strange that I shall never forget as long as I live. We came through a pretty large forest and, because of the heat, we took a side path. Suddenly a rather large knapsack came falling down on us. We looked at it, stood before it for some time and then called out in the hope that the owner would come for it. Thus we called and waited quite a while. But since no one showed up, we picked it up, put it on the car and asked in the neighboring villages and thus inquired along our way, even in the taverns in Warsaw. As we did not find its owner, we finally opened the treasure and shared what we found in it. Everyone of us got the thing he needed most. I received a suit which fitted me as if a tailor had cut it for me. How happy I was about it! For the jacket I exchanged in Vienna rather looked like a topcoat, because it was very long.

Now we were in Warsaw. Since we had little money (to admit the truth I had almost nothing), we accepted the advice of a friend whom we had met at our arrival to stay at the so-called Casimir palace in the suburb. Nobody had lived there for the last fifty years. Only one small room had a window and a door which, however, could not be closed properly. Not far from here a German painter had his living quarters. His son studied music, and these people were very kind to us. When we practiced in our enchanted castle, the passing Poles thought that something was wrong up there and that we were ghosts. On festive days we used to play in the cloisters where the clergymen gave us raw slices of meat which we then cooked and roasted in the painter's house.

After some weeks had elapsed, we were finally called to a certain Starost Suchaquewsky[1] from the house of Schaniawsky for an audition. This gentleman engaged all four of us and, since it was the custom in Poland that one of the musicians had to be

---

[1]Starost is a Polish governor.

Kapellmeister, I received this title. Our so-called Kapelle consisted of about 9 persons and really was one of the best in the country. Most of the time we stayed on the Starost's estate, but sometimes we also visited other estates and had to travel pretty far. Two and a half years we lived in this service and, in general, had a very good time, for our master was a kind man.

I played first violin, next to me was Herr Czarth, who also played the flauto traverso well. Herr Carl Hoecks, too, played the violin and was excellent as a second bugler. Herr Weidner blew the first French horn and played the viola. Weidner and Hoecks were the two men who had accompanied us on our journey. Meanwhile a violinist of the royal Polish Kapelle died. His name was Willicns. The director addressed a letter to me in which he suggested that, if this position would be of interest to me, I should come to Warsaw for an audition. I took leave, but had to promise to be back in three days, for on the fourth day the Starost gave a party for many of his friends. I had a good horse and a friend of mine let me have his servant for the trip. We rode 12 good miles to Warsaw in one day. I borrowed a violin from a friend and had a few concertos with me in my pocket. I had to play for Count Bruehl, then Minister of King August, who had not felt well enough to hear me play. I left my fate to the musical director who seemed to be perfectly satisfied with me. In fact, when he told me that I was accepted and should begin my work as soon as possible, I did not inquire about my salary, since it was sufficient for me to be accepted. On the third day I proudly rode home. My master let me come to him at once and smilingly asked about my affair. I replied that I was already engaged and, at the same time, begged to be relieved from my duty. He gave me to understand that nothing would come of it, that means could be found to prevent this. At that the guests arrived and I played in good mood. The Starost flattered me more than ever. He offered me a higher salary through a third person. One evening he was ready to give me 30 ducats should I agree to stay, and he was also willing to give me a new contract.

But nothing could persuade me. I esteemed higher than anything else to be called a royal musician. In short, when the next three months came to an end, the Starost's wife asked me to see her and tried her best to convince me that I should stay; she assured me that, should I ever be in trouble, this would be my punishment for having wronged the Starost who loved me like his own child. This conversation really caused quite some struggle, but 'the royal musician' overcame everything. I shall touch upon another very important reason for my action toward the end of this biography. When I intended to take leave of the Starost, he gave me word that he wished me much luck but did not want to see me if I did not change my mind and did not stay on in his service. Thus I was in low spirits when I left, all the more since so many of my good friends remained. Herr Czarth, who was considered my brother—this was part of the plan we agreed upon before we left Vienna—, received my position as first violinist, but it did not take long and he too was engaged by the Polish Kapelle.

When I entered my new service and received my salary for the first quarter, I found out that, in comparison with what I had received from my kind Starost, my income had become a good deal smaller. I longed to get to Dresden if possible and soon an occasion arose. King August died. Count Bruehl sent much of his baggage to Dresden and charged the musical director, Herr Schultze, with its supervision. Among those who accompanied him were Herr Czarth and myself.

After my arrival in Dresden I wrote my parents, who had had no news from me for the last 6 years. I could not have written to them, because Count von Kleinau would have pressed my father to get me back and my parents would have had to bear a great many troubles, but this way he could swear to it with clear conscience that he knew nothing about my whereabouts. My honest parents suffered much grief because of me, for they received much unpleasant news. For instance, they were told that I was hanged, because I had run away from Vienna and more of such comforting things.

One day, my father seemed to be very gay, he confided in my mother that he had a dream the past night and it had given him the hope that he would soon have news from me. The same afternoon, the mailman came, knocked on his window and gave him my letter. My father opened it, with his hands trembling, began to read, but, since he could not keep back his tears, hastily went into the adjoining room. My mother, who saw it, became frightened and followed him. But soon the sadness turned into rejoicing.

Because the snow was high that winter, they took a sleigh, namely my father, mother and one of my brothers, and visited me in Dresden. My intentions were to get entirely rid of my Count. When my parents left me again, I gave them a silver box as a present, together with a letter, for the Count's steward, who had great influence with the Count and was a friend of our house. The steward's reply indicated that the Count was a great lover of wonderful horses and with one such horse I could buy myself out. I arranged for one from Count Bruehl's stables for 100 thaler and, to visit my relatives at the same time, I myself traveled to Prague and my servant, whom I had brought with me from Poland, rode the horse. My cousin Brixy, who was mentioned in the beginning, was very glad to have me with him again and to see me in such improved circumstances. His son— now musical director at the Metropolitan Church in Prague—was, at that time, still in his cradle. In the course of those days, the horse was trotted out in front of the Count, but he was not pleased with it.

My friend, the steward, found a way out and, speaking on my behalf, arranged my release for 200 florins. My mother had to borrow the money from her own brother, who was a materialist [!]; but soon afterwards I paid back the full amount which, by the way, the Count had lost the next day playing cards.

I visited most of my relatives, as I could well imagine that I would hardly come back to Bohemia again. My former beloved had meanwhile married.

I returned to Dresden where they were kind enough to take back the horse (with which I had no luck) into the Bruehl stables without any recompense. Soon thereafter I received the appointment for the position I am now holding. His Majesty the King, at that time still crown prince, happened to stay in Ruppin, when Herr Quantz, one of my best friends now, who had the honor of instructing His Majesty on the flute, sent me a letter. Certain religious reasons which I shall describe at the end made this appointment very tempting and pleasant. I thus handed in my resignation. Minister Count Bruehl tried to persuade me to stay in his service, but all my reasons weighed more heavily.

One of my intimate friends, the late concertmaster Pisendel advised me to travel via Zerbst and gave me a letter for the late Kapellmeister Fasch. He received me with great kindness and gave me the opportunity to be heard at the court. There I was offered the post of the concertmaster, an honor which I could not accept. However, I recommended Herr

Hoecks (now concertmaster), who at that time was still in Poland, a man whom I held in high esteem for his musical gifts, but also for his virtuous and God-fearing character.

When I arrived in Ruppin on April 17, 1733, I stayed at an inn and immediately began to practice. It so happened that just at that time His Royal Highness, the crown prince, was walking by. He and his party stopped and listened under my window for a while. Then they inquired who I was and sent for me. I went down to present myself at once. His Highness ordered me to come to him in the evening and was kind enough to accompany me on the clavier. And this was how I entered the service I am still holding. Here I met the concertmaster Herr Graun, a man of great merits, whom, to this very day, I consider one of my best friends.

Up to then I hadn't heard any violinist whose adagio would have convinced and pleased me as much as his. I sought his friendship of which he found me worthy. He was kind enough to study a few adagios with me which turned out to be of great advantage later on. He was also very helpful in making me handle the bass, since I had started to compose violin solos. His instructions in my study of composition really helped me to a certain perfection, and I profited a great deal from his corrections. I must add that, at that time, I was still a tenor and had to sing a few arias almost every evening. A year later the famous Kapellmeister Graun was transferred.

We had lived together for some time, and he had shown to me much love and friendship.

At the request of the late margravine I was sent to Bayreuth in 1734, where I stayed for several weeks and to which I returned four times thereafter. When I was there for the first time, I took the way back via Dresden to visit my old friends. Against all expectations I met my second brother there, who also tried his luck far from home. At once I took him with me. In the beginning he played the viola, but later received the position of a violinist with the royal Kapelle.

In Bayreuth I made the acquaintance of Mademoiselle Eleonora Stephein. She was engaged as a lady's maid at the court. I married her in 1739. She was born in Colberg, where her late father had been postmaster and duty inspector, but he was no longer alive at the time of our marriage. We settled down in Reinsberg and were hardly married for six months, when a tremendous fire broke out that could not be stopped and destroyed all but 15 houses in the little town. I almost lost all my belongings so that I was forced to take a loan in order to be able to buy the most necessary things by and by.

Some time later His Majesty came to the throne and we moved to Berlin. Herr Quantz was appointed to his duty. This honest man has proven his great love for me in so many instances and, in addition, has given me some instruction in composition.

Because of its consequences I cannot leave one incident unmentioned. My father visited me in Ruppin in 1734. The evening I played in the crown prince's house, he furtively managed to get in to hear me play. His Highness recognized him and asked me afterwards whether I had any brothers who practiced music, which question I answered in the affirmative. He also inquired where my father lived.When, after the death of Charles VI, war broke out and His Majesty found himself in the neighborhood of my native town, he sent to my parents and asked to see my brothers. My youngest brother, Joseph, was still at home, but the elder one, now Kapellmeister in Gotha, studied in Gitschin at that time.

My youngest brother presented himself to His Majesty, who immediately decided to engage him, even without having heard him play. I was informed about it by letter and also that he would be sent to me and I was supposed to give him violin instructions. In my answer I pointed out that this was such a good occasion to have my parents sent too, who always expressed great longing to be near me; thus I begged His Majesty for my whole family. The decision was immediately made. His Highness Prince Leopold von Anhalt-Dessau had his headquarters in the town Jung-Buntzlau, not more than two miles away from Benatky; he received an order from His Majesty, who was still in Moravia then, that my family was to receive all the necessary help for their trip. My parents went via Gitschin and persuaded my brother Georg to come with them, so that I had the pleasure of seeing with me my parents as well as my 3 brothers and my sister.

I had my two brothers Georg and Joseph, live with me and helped them in their musical studies. They are both so well known now that I deem it superfluous to mention much more about their musical achievements. My sister married a skilful violinist, a certain Herr Hattasch and lived at the court in Gotha. She had a nice soprano voice and, without false pretence, belonged to the best singers of her time. My late parents had lived the last years of their lives in Nowawes near Potsdam among the Bohemian colonists. It was a quiet and pleasant life they had, and I had the particular pleasure of celebrating with them their 50th wedding anniversary in 1756. On that day not less than 9 carriages had brought relatives and good friends to the church. Some of my friends managed to erect a theater. A performance was given after the entire party had eaten. They played three pieces. The first of the pieces was enacted by grownups, the second by children of 14 or 15 years of age, the third by the smallest of our family. It was one of the most joyful days I ever had. A few months later the war began and with it a great many sad events. The next year my beloved father died; in the year 1758 my wife, with whom I had lived in great harmony and love for 19 years. We had 8 children, of whom 6 were twins; 4 daughters and 2 of my sons are still alive.[1]

---

[1]His two sons are: (a) Friedr.Wilh.Heinrich, born in Potsdam on July 15, 1745; he studied the violin with his father, composition with

In 1762 my mother died and shortly after her my brother Victor. But the loss of Kapellmeister Graun was the most painful blow to me. We had been the best of friends for 27 years, and for three days I was quite desolate and spent them constantly sighing and crying. He was not only a great artist, but also a great personality whose character needed no improvement. It must have been a great consolation to his family that our Frederick the Great expressed his great affection for him in Leipzig more than a year ago and that His Majesty honored him in a great many ways because of his excellent qualities.

The miseries we had to endure during this long war are only too well known. The year 1761 was a very strange phase in my life. To visit some of my relatives I traveled to Weimar and Gotha. My brother in Gotha had asked me to bring my second daughter Maria Caroline[1] with me, who had taken singing and piano lessons. We were received very kindly at both courts. We also received an invitation from His

---

[1]This daughter of his later married the Kapellmeister Ernst Wilhelm Wolf in Weimar; one of his other daughters, Juliane, born in Berlin in 1752, married the Kapellmeister Joh.Friedr.Reichardt in the year 1799. Juliane not only had a pleasant voice, but was also a very distinguished pianist, moreover, composed odes, Lieder, and sonatas; she died in Berlin on May 9, 1783.

Kirnberger, joined the royal Kapelle in 1765, composed oratorios and operas; died in Potsdam on June 19, 1814; (b) Carl Hermann Heinrich, born May 2, 1748; played as violinist in the royal Kapelle in 1766 and was said to have come closest to his father's artistry in playing the adagio. He also was an excellent piano teacher. King Friedrich Wilhelm III and C. F. Rungenhagen were his pupils. He almost reached an age of 88 (died on March 15, 1836), but he already retired with the title of a concertmaster in 1802.

Highness Prince Schwartzburg to come to Rudolstadt.
At all three places we received so many gifts whose
value we estimated at more than 2,000 Reichsthaler.
My late wife's sister, Caroline Stephein, was first
lady's maid with the duchess in Weimar. I married
her there and my two eldest daughters were taken
in her stead to serve the duchess. This was a particularly happy turn in my fate and it all came about
quite unexpectedly. I can hardly thank God enough
for it, because the circumstances in which I had been
were greatly improved through all this.

I have been the happiest of all men in my first
as well as second marriage and I could well provide
for my daughters, in fact, I could never have wished
for more. May God find me more and more grateful
for it!

During the First War I was forced to go to Wiesbaden because of the gout in my arm. On my way
back I stayed a few days in Frankfort, since I felt
much better. My fellow traveler was a relative of
mine, a businessman from Berlin. As I did not like
the idea of playing in public, I pretended to be a
businessman too. A Prussian officer, who stayed there
at the recruiting station, introduced me to a very
good violoncellist, a certain Monsieur Berdo. I was
of course introduced as a businessman. We were told
that he was on his way to Berlin and asked him to
play for us. He excused himself, since there was no
one to accompany him. There was no other way out
for me than to say that I was a lover of music and if

he would not mind playing with me I would try to play the bass on the violin. My violin case was brought. In the beginning, I purposely made some mistakes so that we had to stop a few times and begin again. His way of playing as well as the sonatas which he had composed pleased me very much and I justly lauded them.

After a while Berdo finally asked me whether I had no music with me, it would be a pleasure for him to accompany me. In my role as a businessman I deemed it necessary to be asked several times. After all, said the officer, what can happen to you? Since it isn't your profession it is of no consequence whether you are good or not. However much you may fail, you are always covered as a music lover.

Thus I took a solo out of my briefcase. Monsieur Berdo saw the name Benda on it and asked me whether I knew him, which question I affirmed. I mentioned that he was my daily companion in Berlin. The next question was: Is he your teacher by any chance? which I could again answer in the affirmative. He replied: I am about to go there and hope I'll be able to meet him.

I began to play my solo, again made mistakes, even struck false notes, and then stopped playing altogether. But he urged me to begin again. After a while I played more seriously. Now he said: It's much better—bravo—very good—bravissimo! But finally he got up and said: Sir, you are no businessman, you must be Benda! The officer burst out with laughter. And when urged to go on, I played another solo without playing the businessman. Thus I unmasked myself completely, and we spent a very pleasant evening together. He hardly let me out of his sight the next few days. Two days later I was visited by musicians who were in the service of Prince Taxis and who wanted to hear me, but I did not play any more.

A few years later I fell very sick and was tortured by the *Malum Hypocondriacum*. But in spite of it I had a strong desire to compose and to read books. I also did my daily duties though often with great difficulties. I used to take a great many medicines which, however, did more harm than good. Finally I was in such a bad condition that I was forced to go to Carlsbad. I was strongly advised to take up horseback riding there, but was forbidden to do any brainwork. If I had not made use of this Queen of all Spas, they would have buried me long ago.

On this occasion I visited Bayreuth the fourth time. His Highness the margrave was kind enough to drive me back to Carlsbad with his horses. He also presented me with a golden snuffbox.

After a fortnight I felt much better. On my way back I was asked to visit the Rudolstadt court. From there I left for Gotha and Dresden where I was favored with the permission to play before His Royal Highness and also to hear Her Royal Highness sing. His Excellency the Russian Ambassador, Count Kayserling, gave me a saddle horse as a present with all the necessary accessories. For three years I have been on this horse almost daily. I have received many more presents at these courts.

The second year I went to Aachen and Spaa with the Chamberlain of His Majesty, Herr Fredersdorff[1]. but I found the Carlsbad waters preferable to both of them. When I had finished my cure in Spaa I was asked to play for His Eminence the Cardinal who gave me a golden repeater as a gift. The Cardinal urged me to take my way back via Cologne and gave me a letter for his brother. His Highness the *Kurfuerst* also received me with great kindness and presented me with a beautiful golden *tabatière* and a medallion with the *Kurfuerst's* likeness.

Meanwhile the Duchess von Braunschweig had asked me in a letter written by my wife not to fail to come to Braunschweig. I followed this kind order and when I arrived in Preussisch Muenden I found a written invitation from His Highness Count von der Lippe to come to Bueckeburg, where I spent two wonderful days. Moreover, they sent me a silver coffee set. In Braunschweig kindness and favors were heaped upon me; the Duke gave me a golden *tabatière,* the Duchess a cane with a golden handle so that, in both years, my travel expenses were covered more than threefold. Besides, I went to Pyrmont with His Majesty twice, but its waters did not help me at all.

---

[1]Michael Gabriel Fredersdorff, Chamberlain to His Majesty Frederick the Great, was an excellent flutist. The King made his acquaintance on a trip to Frankfort at a time when he was still crown prince; on this occasion the students serenaded him and Fredersdorff played the flute. He died in 1758.

Also with His Majesty I travelled to Silesia in 1754 and during the continuation of hostilities I went to Breslau with my colleagues of the Chamber Music in Potsdam in 1757 and three years later we were called into winter headquarters at Leipzig.

I overlooked mentioning the following incident. In Spaa I made the acquaintance of a well-esteemed art patron, who honored me with a great many invitations for dinners and other entertainments. I soon noticed that they desired to hear me play, but abstained from asking me for it, since I stayed there quasi incognito so as not to be disturbed during my cure. The wife of this great patron was a Countess by birth. The last day before their departure they told me: Herr Benda, you must have lunch and dinner with us today, the last time! They also gave me a few nice little things which had been made in Spaa and which I was to take with me to my children.

After lunch I asked the lady of the house whether she would kindly permit me to bring my mistress with me in the evening. She started and seemed embarrassed. Apparently she could not answer. My patron, however, immediately understood and said, Yes, yes, Herr Benda, bring your mistress along, she must be probably very well-behaved, because you have good taste.

I took leave and went out of the room. But I was hardly gone, when the lady said: My dear, how is it possible that Benda has a mistress? From his tales one would think that he loves his wife and children. And yet he keeps a mistress. I thought him a virtuous and Christian person, but now I have lost a great deal of my confidence in him. And I know you won't take it amiss if I am not present tonight. No, it's quite impossible for me to be in the society of such a person. Whereupon my patron replied: You don't have to be ashamed so far from home. All's well that ends well. Take it as it is, tomorrow we are leaving anyway and the whole game will come to an end.

In the evening when I entered their room, the lady expected my mistress to follow me. She seemed very embarrassed. My patron said, How come, Herr Benda, you promised to bring someone with you. I replied that my mistress would have the honor to present herself soon. The door was opened and my violin case was brought into the room. The lady looked at her husband, then at me and again at him, and, since one could not abstain from laughing out loud, she said, O you naughty man, how you had frightened me this afternoon, I no longer liked you half as much as I did! This joke brought about a happy ending.

The publisher and editor of the *Musikalische Lebensläuffe* asked me to enumerate the musical pieces I composed, but I don't think I'm able to do it. The number of my compositions is not so great, because I only began very late to work seriously on them; moreover, the last 12 years I was unable to work on anything new—with the exception of a few violin sonatas which I was willing to have printed on demand of more than one music lover—, since my daily duties as well as my (for many years) weak constitution did not permit much work. In regard to my intention of having those sonatas published, one of my dearest and best friends prevented this; under the condition that I would teach his son, he paid for them very generously to keep them from becoming generally known through print. I could say a great deal that would add to the praise of this noble philanthropist. But I deem it sufficient to mention his name, for everyone who knows the incomparable Johann Ernst Gotzkowsky will give him equal praise.

Altogether I wrote 80 violin solos, 15 concertos, a few symphonies and a great many capriccios. Only time will show whether I shall be able to write anything in the future. This very day I have completed my 53rd year. It is no little gratification for me that I had the great fortune of being in the service of the really great Frederick whom I have accompanied at more than 10,000 flute concerts in all these years. His Majesty's skill on this instrument is world-known.

Now at the end I deem it necessary to touch on the question of religion. I was a devout Catholic until I was twenty. I still remember how I delighted in the fact that, at the time I was in Siebenbuergen, seven churches were taken away from the Protestants on one Sunday and the Catholic service held there. I could witness the tears and laments of the Protestants quite placidly. I was invited to play on the oc-

casion of the inauguration of a church which the
Catholics had taken away from the Protestants in
Hermannstadt.

I played a concerto, but did not quite know what
happened to me when, while I played, my hands
began to tremble and I thought I would have to stop
playing. I have probably never played as badly as
that. I was frightened and thought that I would not
lose this tremble in my hands. But still the same day
at noon—at a great party which my master had given
out of his great devotion to Catholicism—I played
and felt no tremble in my hands. I did not think of
this incident until I came to be converted to Protestantism.

In Poland I had the opportunity to read the Bible
for the first time in my life. The aforementioned
musician Weidner, our first French hornist, a born
Saxonian and devout Protestant, was an honest man
in every respect and God-fearing at the bottom of
his heart. His library consisted of one Bible, Johann
Arndt's Real Christianity, and a hymnbook.

I read his Bible a great deal. In the beginning,
however, I remained true to my principles. On many
an occasion we discussed the issues. He always remained calm, whereas I could easily get into a fit of
anger. Since he proved to be cleverer than I was,
he asked me in all friendship to abstain from such
quarrels and to stick to the faith in which each of
us believed. When, later, I began to talk of it again,
he remained silent. By and by, I became calmer too.

I first read the Old Testament. I then read the Epistles of Paulus and when I read about the Apostle condemning the interdiction of marriage and food as a satanic doctrine, the first scruples of my conscience were aroused, also because of the Last Supper.

I discussed it with several Catholic clergymen, but their replies and interpretations did not dispel my doubts, in fact, they themselves would have liked to condemn Paulus and consider him a heretic. The tables turned. My previous fervor weakened and I began to discuss these things with Weidner very placidly. His excellent way of life convinced me that God was pleased about it. Carl Hoecks, who was far more serious about it than I and who often made me feel annoyed, at least in the beginning, left with Weidner for Saxony where he became a Protestant.

As I could no longer find my peace of mind I went immediately after my arrival in Dresden to the General-Superintendent Doctor Loescher who, however, was too fearful to convert me publicly. Therefore, it had to be done secretly in the Kreutz Church. The Jesuits must have heard of it, moreover, I had already made myself suspicious in Warsaw.

For a short time in Warsaw I ate in a house, the lady of which was a Protestant, but the man a Catholic. She had much confidence in me, complained about how her spouse and the Catholic clergy were all behind her to make her change her religion. I cautioned her against it, tried to strengthen her in her faith through the Holy Scriptures, and finally divulged that I contemplated accepting the Protestant faith. But she was not sincere, and I finally noticed that she would have liked to have illicit intercourse with me. When she noticed that I tried to keep away from her as much as I could, she was annoyed that she went so far.

Shortly thereafter her husband told me that she had become a Catholic. From then on I noticed that his entire attitude toward me had changed. Luckily my trip to Dresden was about to take place. They intended to hurt me and perhaps to frighten me away from my intentions when, the next year, my name was not listed among the violinists in the address calendar of 1733, but at the very end of it next to the instrument caretaker. Count Bruehl as well as the musical director Schultze were very much annoyed about it, but they did not dare examine the affair closer. A copy of this calendar is in my possession; I had it sent to me when I was in Dresden to preserve it as a souvenir. Moreover, the Jesuits sent one of their men to me to let me know that I should not nourish any hope of keeping my position in case I really considered to leave my Catholic religion. I gave him a very short answer saying that what happened was in no way connected with worldly issues and solely with the real convictions of my conscience and that I was sure God would provide for me in the future.

At about that time I received my appointment from Ruppin and went to His Excellency Count Bruehl to take my leave. He tried to persuade me to stay and assured me that the steps I had undertaken or were about to undertake would in no way prejudice him against me, but I stuck to my intentions and went off.

I saw Dresden 12 years ago for the last time. I was then given to understand that I could enter service there and improve my salary a great deal. One of the noblest Catholic priests acted very friendly and offered me his living quarters. But I was not tempted and assured them that I was highly satisfied with my present position, for I realized what was in their mind. They were mainly out to save a so-called misguided sheep and wanted to tempt me with worldly goods. But I have a clear conscience, free from all reproaches. Gradually, my whole family had left Bohemia and was converted to Protestantism. It seems that it was God's will that my parents should have died as Protestants. His holy name be praised forever.

I cannot help mentioning certain incidents which had happened to the late Weidner. These things may not be everybody's dish, but there may be some readers who will not dislike this report. When this honest man intended to leave Warsaw, he was seized by a few priests and dragged into a cloister. There he was accused of having misguided Hoecks and myself and using blasphemous words about the Holy Virgin; he should either renounce his heretic faith and profess his belief in the only true church, or forfeit his life. At that moment, the cloister was thrown into a stage of uproar, the rumor had spread that King Stanislaus had arrived to visit the cloister. Excitement and curiosity made the priests run off to greet the King. At that our honest man thought he should not wilfully wait for his enemies here, and he sneaked out quite slowly.

He ran to the place where he lived and where a sleigh with horses stood ready to take him to Saxony. He did not linger for a moment to get away. But he was hardly a few miles from Warsaw when a pack of Poles stopped him with the intention of robbing him. He prayed for help to God and, at the same time, tried to divert them by persuasion. When the evildoers were about to attack him, they saw a group of German soldiers on horseback approaching them. They lost their lust for booty and took to their heels. The riders spoke to him in a friendly way and gave him good advice as to a safe route to Saxony.

His last few years he spent very quietly in Berlin. He was shabbily dressed and eked out a meagre living for himself and his aged mother by copying music. Finally he became so sick that he was confined to bed. When his mother who had sat up with him for several nights began to complain that she could not stand it any longer, he had spoken these strange words: Dearest mother, only one more night. Tomorrow morning at seven my Saviour will come to take me with him.

She was frightened and said: Ah, my dear son, so you will die and what shall I do then, oh, I poor woman, shall I go begging at my age?

Whereupon he replied with a solemn expression in his face: If you trust God of whose kindness we were so often convinced and which you have just witnessed, then He won't forsake you, He will arouse good heart to take care of you. But if you do not trust Him and begin to doubt in your faith, then I am not sure but that what you fear will really happen.

The next day at the very hour he had mentioned this honest man passed away. Immediately some of his friends took care that he was buried with all honors. One of our mutual friends wrote me about his death. At once I asked my wife whether she would mind taking the mother of this friend, who had been so dear and helpful to us, into our house. Since she did not object at all I immediately wrote to my friend about my plans and since we went to Berlin at about that time, we took the woman with us. I consider it one of my greatest pleasures that I was able to help this wonderful woman to the last day of her life.

When speaking of her son she often had tears in her eyes. She said that God had taken care of her, although she had doubted. She told us how often it had happened that she didn't know in the morning whether they would have anything to eat at noon, because there was neither money nor any food in the house. But he, her late son, was always in good spirits and satisfied. And when she sometimes said, now, my son, it is ten o'clock and we have nothing to eat, then he would reply: Well, what does it matter if we skip one meal. God will help that it will taste all the better in the evening! And he had hardly spoken thus, someone would knock on the door and bring either money or some work to be copied and paid in advance.

He would never let anyone notice that he was in want. He wrote very slowly but correctly and very beautiful notes. Then when the visitor had left he would say, now, dear mother, we were again put to shame unbelieving as we were. Several years before his death he visited the Concertmaster Hoecks in Zerbst, for the two men were intimate friends. He went on foot and when he intended to return, Herr Hoecks decided to accompany him to Berlin, and both walked back. On their way they had spiritual discussions as they used to.

They were closely followed by a young man, who was, if I remember correctly, a wig-maker. He listened to their conversation, and they did not notice it. When they stepped into a tavern to have a rest, he followed them there too. He asked them whether they were on their way to Berlin which they affirmed, whereupon he expressed his desire to accompany them. Gentlemen, he said, your conversation has given me more pleasure and I was edified by it more than by any sermon from the pulpit. Therefore permit me to accompany you, this day will be a blessing to me and I'll recall it as long as I shall live.

I was present at their arrival in Berlin, where this young man said good-bye to them with words which were touching. The sarcastic reader may think or say whatever he wants about the last few stories I have told, they are certainly not fairy tales but the naked truth, which I had never put down on paper if I had ever had the least doubt about their veracity. And thus I shall conclude and recommend myself to my patrons and friends. I shall strive to serve God the few remaining days of my life, praise and devotion be His from eternity to eternity. Amen.

Franz Benda

Potsdam, April 18, 1763

P. S. This is to request Herr Secretary Marpurg[1] to inform the reader in a short note that I was never willing to publish my biography and that I only intended to leave a written souvenir for my family and their children and children's children who, as I hope, will not be ashamed of the humble stock I come from. But, I must admit that I could not resist your friendly request and that I also told of incidents, not in immediate connection with my person because I was asked to (according to your kind letter). But in writing this biography I have certainly thought of no other readers but my family.

This makes me hope that all other readers will interpret those things mentioned which might cause ill will with kindness and overlook those which may

---

[1]This is probably the famous theorist Friedrich Wilhelm Marpurg, who later became Royal *Kriegsrath und Lotterie-Director* in Berlin. He was born in Marpurgshoff near Seehausen in the Altmark on Oct. 1, 1718, and died in Berlin on May 22, 1795.

be a credit to my family, since, on the other hand, I
so frankly revealed what might be humiliating to
me. Moreover, I leave it to you, dear sir, to shorten
or to prolong certain parts of this biography and I
am sure you will find better and more pleasant words
for the humorous paragraphs. But everything that
deals with religion I beg you to leave unchanged.

Dear friend, I regret that my hodgepodge report
will cause you much trouble, because I have put
down the incidents as they occurred to me without
any sequence. In case you would like to have my
whole story told in the third person, I would not
object to it. In short, do whatever you deem the best.
I know that you won't be unpleasantly touched by
my reports on the Concertmaster Hoecks, as I was
told that the biography he had sent you was much
too sketchy.

Now the following things occur to me which you
may insert wherever you see fit. Twice I was invited
to Mecklenburg Strelitz where the late Duke Carl,
the father of the reigning Queen of England, arranged
with me that I was to come there for 2 or 3 weeks
each year and advise him in his music. I would have
to bring with me everything I had composed and
would receive 100 ducats quarterly.

When the money for the first quarter was paid,
His Highness passed away. On the occasion of his
death I had the honor of eating at the princely table.
At that time of course I did not know yet that a
linen weaver's son should have the special honor of

dining with the future and now present Queen of England at the same table. On that day I was presented with a wonderful golden watch and received 40 Luisd'or in Strelitz. Also this incident is told for the benefit of my children and children's children and not with the intention of bragging about it.

The following could still be inserted. In my younger years I would have loved to learn how to play the clavier, but hadn't opportunity to do so, and you can't teach an old dog new tricks. This instrument would have been of great service in my compositions; the fact that I did not master it made me shy away from composing "strong" things and fugues. Knowing my limited possibilities I endeavored all the more to write violin sonatas in a skilful and singable manner. Whether I succeeded in it may be left to the judgment of those violinists who tried to play my compositions for almost 30 years.

The late Kapellmeister Graun used to keep me from brooding to which I was strongly inclined and always told me that I should follow the tracks of my innate singing voice whereby I would earn the gratitude of all music lovers. In short, I am not ashamed to confess publicly that I cannot be placed among the great contrapuntists. Everyone has his own gift and should try to do his best with it. I have admiration and due respect for those contrapuntists who also can express beautiful thoughts, for they are rare and therefore all the more to be admired. But those compositions which show an only apparent and inflated mastership remain rare too, for nobody asks for them and their composers are angry with the whole world. To make their creations rewarding, they increase their own enthusiasm and acclamation tenfold; and they never listen to the compositions of their colleagues to enjoy them, only to find something in them they can criticize.

* * *

Berlin
July 26, 1856

Dear editor:

Professor Dr. Rudolph Koepke was kind enough to let me have the enclosed manuscript, the autobiography of the famous violinist Franz Benda. This, for the musicologist important piece of writing, probably was in the property left by Kapellmeister Joh. Friedrich Reichardt and has not yet appeared in print, although Joh.Adam Hiller seemed to have used it in his work, "Lebensbeschreibungen beruehmter Musikgelehrten und Tonkuenstler neuerer Zeit".

Should you, dear sir, be inclined to publish it as a whole and in its original form in your musical paper, I would take the liberty of adding a few historical annotations.

Yours sincerely,
C. Freiherr von Ledebur

III

THE LIFE OF CHRISTIAN GOTTLIEB NEEFE

I was born on the fifth of February 1748 in the town of Chemnitz in the Saxonian Erzgebirge. Although my parents were poor, they nevertheless sent me to public school at an early age. I was blessed with an unusually fine soprano voice and thus I soon gained admission to the great choir. There I was taught the fundamentals of the art of singing and was able, at the same time, to help my dear and righteous, but poor parents in defraying my school expenses. I am bound in gratitude to my teachers for their faithful instruction and their infinite patience; foremost among them were the late honorable schoolmaster Hoffman, the late head master Hagen and Herr Juenger, now head master in Freiberg, but then senior assistant of the Chemnitz grammar school. I have mentioned "patience", and rightly so. My youthful sprightliness which often resulted in mischief demanded the utmost of forbearance and I have felt due regret in my later years for my juvenile roguishness. I assimilated the subject matter of my studies fairly rapidly and learned with great facility. I was by no means the most diligent pupil. I was satisfied as long as I finished my work in time as I was praised no less than my most industrious fellow students. Frequently a mood of clowning and joking took possession of me and my frankness and lack of inhibitions in doing and saying as I pleased often got me into trouble. Once I almost followed the misguided course of a scoffer at religion. That I nearly went astray, may be ascribed to the many bodily hardships which were connected with the divine service in my youth, to the miserable sermons of a number of priests, their pride and intolerance and generally to their hypocrisy in preaching water and drinking wine; above all, I fell under the influence of a notorious and course mocker of religion. This thoughtless man, a lawyer by calling, provided me, an inexperienced and confused youngster with a wealth of blasphemous writings which I absorbed avidly and, in turn, quoted occasionally.

The task of instructing me in the elements of clavier playing was put in the hands of the town organist, Wilhelmi by name. My lessons were later continued by some Prussian enlisted man who was quartered in our home during one of the winters of the Seven Years' War with Saxony. These were the best teachers I could hope for and which I could afford. It is true that a mere three hours from Chemnitz, in the little "Schoenburgischen" town of Hohenstein, there lived a fiery and skilful musician, the cantor Tag, who is now one of my dearest friends; but even this short distance was more than my modest circumstances would permit when it came to taking music lessons from him. I paid him a visit from time to time only, never leaving his home without having received an encouraging word. I learned a great deal about pianistic skill from Marpurg's "Anleitungen" and also from C. P. E. Bach's "Versuch".

At the age of twelve I felt a strong urge to try my hand at composing. I wrote a number of short pieces under borrowed and fictitious names and listened eagerly to the opinions of the audience. My compositions, rather my musical scribble, were acclaimed by persons who knew as little as I did, or even less about art. For some time, I was intoxicated by these successes; I kept on groping about in the darkness, dulling many a pen point and besmearing many a sheet of paper, until a more mature point of view prompted me—still a student in Chemnitz—to turn to Hiller in Leipzig, who subsequently became my highly venerable friend, and to approach him with written inquiries about the art of composition.

Through some unfathomable causes, I lost my sound health in my 14th year. From that time on, I remained sickly and delicate. Unquestionably, however, I had inherited from my father the tendency to hypochondria. During many periods of his life, he suffered from this sickness. In my early childhood days, I suffered from rachitis and, according to my parents, nothing but the Halle gold tincture cured me.

When I reached the age of fifteen, my father wanted me to follow in his footsteps and take up tailoring as a profession, on the one hand because of my frail condition, on the other because we were in precarious financial circumstances. I voiced my reluctance and told him frankly that it was within no one's power to divert me from my course of study. I called his attention to the Divine Providence which had permitted many poor boys in a similar position to pursue their aims. I quoted actual examples and called to his mind the financial subsidy of patrons which I had enjoyed thus far. I managed to appease him and was able to continue on my path with confidence and good cheer.

In 1767 I went to Leipzig and joined the student body of the "Akademie" under the rectorship of the famous Doctor Crusius. After my return, I taught music and other subjects as I had done before, mainly to increase my own learning, but also to avail myself of the necessary means to acquire useful and pleasant books, such as the excellent writings of Gellert, Rabner and Gessner (among which I found the greatest pleasure in those of Gessner).

At Easter time in 1769 I took leave from my family with a heavy heart. With tears in his eyes, my father asserted that he could never suffer to see me in dire circumstances, even if he might have to sell his small house which he had acquired through unflagging toil and labor. Deeply touched, I left my home to enter the university of Leipzig. My health was in a poor state, but not nearly as pitiful as was my financial well-being. My total wealth consisted of a mere 20 Thaler savings and an annual scholarship of 30 Gulden, granted by the town council of Chemnitz. These comprised my sole source of income from which I would have to pay for my tuition as well as my room and board. The most cutting curtailment on my part, the financial help of a few generous persons and the unselfishness of some of the professors saw me through. My teachers were chiefly Gellert, Seydlitz, Sammet, Breuning, Tobias Richter and Kleemann. Among them, Gellert above all shall always occupy a special place in my heart.

The study of logic, of philosophy of morals, the natural and international law provided food for my mind thirsting for knowledge. In the beginning, I also felt a strong propensity toward civil jurisprudence, at least until I delved into forensic procedure. I soon came to realize, from the countless exceptions to the rules provoked by the unfathomable malice of human nature, how much truth there was indeed in the old proverb: Justice has a waxen nose. At this point, I lost all my desires to become a jurist. This disillusionment, my weak memory rendering me unfit for the legal profession, coupled with my strong tendency toward music and the belief of showing prodigious musical talent prompted me to abandon my initial course of study.

Moreover, the encouragement of my musically inclined and aesthetically feeling friends, such as Hiller and Engel, as well as my hypochondria which had all along presented a great obstacle to my academic studies and which I hoped to dispel partially through the stimulating study of music, influenced my final decision to abandon Themis and to dedicate myself to Euterpe. However, I do wish to state as proof for certain parties, in whose eyes I seem to have idled away my university days and who might accuse me of having put to ill use the scholarship granted by my native town, that before dedicating myself to music, I did complete my legal studies and discussed publicly the question whether it was within the right of a father to disinherit his son because the latter had chosen acting as his profession. I must confess though that I did maintain the negative.

My hypochondria caused me a great deal of suffering. Between 1770 and 1771 my body was weakened to such an extent that I could hardly go from one house to another. My mind too was affected. I was in low spirits and gravely afflicted with imaginary illness; so much so, that I could only rarely bring myself to work. I often forgot what year it was, I saw rain even when the sky was blue and lived in constant fear of the various deaths that might befall me. Very often I was plagued with thoughts of suicide. I was gripped by constant terror and every little sand hill seemed to me an unsurpassable mountain range. A number of sensible physicians, a strict diet and a moderate amount of diversion finally conquered this monster. On the other hand, I owe much to my sickness:

(1) I was again brought closer to religion. Every hypochondriac always imagines imminent death, so I strived for better and more substantial views on religion. I attempted to develop such feelings for it as would permit me to terminate my life with joy and hope in my heart. I succeeded in coming closer to God, mainly through the writings of Bonnet, Moses Mendelssohn, Spalding, Jerusalem and Noesselt. Religion became for me a concept worthy of veneration and I perceived its glorious fruits in my heart and in my life.

(2) My state of health discouraged me from indulging in debauchery, so common with university students. Once I was talked into going along to a village near Leipzig where a brothel was allowed to thrive in those days. The vulgar atmosphere and clothing I saw there, were in themselves enough to drive me away quickly and to stamp in my mind an indelible disgust for such places, their animal-like inmates, for lewdness and corruption in general. In spite of this incident, I always managed to harbor the purest feelings for the fairer sex in my heart.

(3) My own situation put me into the position to comfort and give counsel to my father, who suffered himself such a severe attack of hypochondria as to cause him to fall into a state of melancholic despair. He did not understand the nature of his affliction and therefore attributed his suffering to an improper source. My past experience enabled me to point out

to him the true nature of his affliction. I showed him
that the causes should be traced to the body, not to the
soul, and that the devil certainly had no part in it. I
advised him to discontinue the services of a mental
healer and to adopt a regular physician. I further suggested remedies which had helped me. He showed a
great deal of confidence in me and followed my counsel
by putting himself under the care of a skilled physician. The use of prescribed medicines improved his
physical condition and consequently improved his
mental state.

(4) A closer friendship between Hiller and myself
developed as a consequence of my condition. He too
suffered from the same affliction and similar fates usually bring people closer together.

Now that I have mentioned Hiller again I feel duty-
bound to write about him in more detail. Where can
one find a music lover who does not know and adore
this intelligent, tasteful and sensitive composer, this
musical Gellert! and where can one meet an ingenious
performing artist who does not value him! I have never
seen such all-out patronage of his art as practiced by
him. He used his financial means and exhibited the
most glowing fervor in subsidizing young talent, helping it develop and promoting it.

It is this man then, more than any other, to whom
I am indebted in gratitude. He is the well of my better
musical knowledge, though I have never been subjected
to his teaching in an organized manner. But his conver-
sations about musical matters, the suggestions regarding

my work, his readiness to supply me with the finest examples and to point out their most exquisite beauties as well as the stimulation of further interest by such books as for instance Home's "Grundsaetze der Kritik" and Sulzer's "Theorie", wherein art was dealt with along psychological lines of thought, all this did me more good than any formal instruction might have done. Whenever I came to visit him, he received me most cordially. His friendly manner dispelled my fears of making a nuisance of myself with my frequent visits and questions. Over a considerable period of time I boarded at his house for a negligible sum of money. At that time, Reichardt, now the Imperial Prussian Kapellmeister, was a frequent visitor at the home of Hiller, and the two men discussed and consulted each other about musical matters. Thus I was afforded the opportunity to meet many other worthy musicians from many lands. Hiller also introduced me to other artists, scholars, and great minds. The association with such men of renown as Weisse, Garve, Engel, Oeser, Bause, etc., their artistic output, their impartial recommendations of other works as well as their discussions and evaluations did much to enrich my spiritual learning and to impart to my maturing mind keen discernment and artistic sensitivity. I seriously strove to become worthy of associating with such outstanding people. I believed that they were able to read my ignoble thoughts or base feelings from my face and thus I strove harder toward the good and noble, guided by their fine example and also by my own strong endeavor.

Hiller also used his influence to improve my economic status. He recommended me as music teacher to many distinguished families, asked me to collaborate with him on his operetta, "Der Dorfbarbier" (The village barber), and mentioned me favorably in his weekly musical notes and comments which served as an official introduction into musical circles. He further promoted the publication of some of my later compositions which considerably eased my pecuniary troubles. Among these pieces were songs from the "Dorfbarbier", various short pieces printed in Hiller's "Woechentliche Nachrichten und Anmerkungen"; the three operettas, "Die Apotheke", "Amor's Guckkasten" and "Die Einsprueche", and the piano sonatas dedicated to C. P. E. Bach (1773) all of which I composed and had published under Hiller's surveillance. Here are my other published works:

(a) Six piano sonatas, dedicated to the late Koenigl. Preuss. Kammer-composer, Mr. Agrikola;

(b) Freemason songs, published under the name of Fenee;

(c) Songs with piano melodies (1776);

(d) Heinrich und Lyda, an operetta (1777);

(e) Twelve Odes by Klopstock (1776);

(f) Six Serenades for voice and piano (1777);

(g) Six piano sonatas with optional accompaniment of a violin;

(h) Vademecum for those who love singing and piano playing (1780);

(i) Sophonisbe, a monodrama by Meissner, dedicated to Her Grace Princess von Hassen-Darmstadt;

(j) A piano concerto with complete orchestral accompaniment, dedicated to the Kurfuerst von Sachsen. This work was etched at Goetz in Mannheim; all other works mentioned were published at Breitkopf in Leipzig.

(k) Contributions to various journals.

The manuscripts are:

(a) A score for the opera "Zemire and Azor", text by Herr von Thuemmel;

(b) A score for the opera "Adelheid von Veltheim";

(c) A score for the Latin version of the Lord's Prayer;

(d) Six piano sonatas with violin obligato;

(e) Several parts for a complete orchestral piece;

(f) A score for several pieces of incidental music;

(g) Various songs;

(h) Short theatrical pieces and some unfinished works.

I was very intent on showing my gratitude to this man who had been so kind to me, not with mere words but with deeds. The fact that I dedicated to him my first operetta, "Die Apotheke", hardly deserves to be mentioned. I searched vainly for some opportunity to show my appreciation, but none came to my great chagrin. Finally I was afforded the chance. Hiller had been persuaded to accept the position of musical director for the theatrical producer Seiler. Since many other engagements and duties prevented Hiller from devoting himself fully to his new task which made him lose more than gain, he asked me, a person without any professional obligations, whether I would be willing to step into his place. He supplemented his request by pointing out that my frame of mind was more suited for the job than his own. Although it meant giving up a rather easy and pleasant life, I was nevertheless overjoyed to accept, thus enabling me to do my friend a favor and to help him extricate himself from a potentially embarrassing situation.

I soon came to terms with Seiler and around midsummer 1776 I departed for the Linkische Bad near Dresden where, at that time, Seiler's stock company was temporarily stationed. I took over my dear friend Hiller's position who, in turn, went back to Leipzig. My contract with Seiler was a verbal one and valid for one year. Before the year was over, Seiler's contract with the electoral court of Saxony came to an end and as difficulties arose about various clauses in the new contract, Seiler found himself compelled to forget about Saxony and turn to the Rhineland instead. I felt little inclination to accompany him there, because I was very much attached to my native land, my friends and relatives and also because a fine upstanding young woman kept me tied to my native town. For these reasons I begged Seiler to release me from the six remaining weeks of the contract. He, however, painted the Rhine landscape in the most glowing colors and pointed out that my health would greatly benefit by the new locale (which incidentally proved to be so). He continued telling me about salutary mineral baths and waters and about the strong and pure Rhine wine, both of which might prove so highly beneficial for my hypochondria that I might very well never be plagued by it again. He finally persuaded me and I left with the troupe for Frankfurt on the Main in 1777.

The separation from my home town and from my loved ones weighed heavily on my heart. I was gradually more and more attracted by the magic beauty of the Rhine and Main provinces, and the scenic splendor coupled with the many new experiences and impressions abated my nostalgic grief. I continued to conduct the Seiler opera for another two and a half years, making appearances in Frankfurt, Mainz, Cologne, Hanau, Mannheim, and Heidelberg, until finally, after the Frankfurt fair in the fall of 1779, this once so outstanding troupe disbanded.

For a number of years, I had strongly been attracted to a dear young girl, more so than was good for my peace of mind. She was Demoiselle Zink, born in Warza (in the Dukedom of Gotha) and had at one time been in the service of the Duke of Gotha as a court singer. When I met her she was a member of the Seiler company—Kapellmeister Georg Benda, in whose house she had been brought up, had recommended her. I loved and wooed her secretly and succeeded in winning her affection and respect. For my part, I had long regarded her highly for her gentle heart, her good character and her genteel manners.

I saw no future chance ever to be united with her in Saxony. The sorrow of this unhappy love affected me deeply. I began to neglect my official duties; even my talents suffered. The desire to share my life with this virtuous woman grew stronger and stronger in my heart—I married her in Frankfurt in the year 1778 and she has made me a good and affectionate wife. Our union was blessed with three children, two daughters and one son, who unfortunately passed away.

I have made many pleasant and important acquaintances in the Rhine and Main provinces and have found a few dear friends to whom I have become strongly attached. Among the theatrical people I came across many scoundrels; few to be sure who were a credit to their profession.

In October 1779, after the Seiler troupe had been dissolved, I took my family to Bonn where I joined the Grossmann-Hellmut company. As a matter of fact, I was at that time negotiating with Bondini, the impresario of the "kursaechsischen" theatre. He hesitated when it came to reaching a final agreement, so I accepted the position as musical director with the Bonn company where my wife also joined me in the capacity of an actress. The post was a temporary one without a formal contract, but the conditions were favorable. Some time later I received a letter from Bondini informing me that he was willing to accept my terms. I acquainted the administration of the Bonn group with the contents of this letter and the fact that I had been negotiating with Bondini over the past six months. As I was not bound by any contract and as I knew myself to be among friends who were well aware of my love for my native district, I felt confident about receiving permission to leave my temporary position. I did not suggest to them to simply let go without doing something for them in turn. I therefore suggested that I would ask Bondini to put off my contract until Easter which would give me ample time to put the Bonn opera on a more solid footing and afford them the chance to find someone to replace me. They accepted my proposal and I wrote to Bondini about my plan. He answered immediately that he would not hear of any postponement. His letter was followed up by a contract-like statement and a check for my travelling expenses. He insisted that my wife and I were to come to Leipzig at the latest in the middle of January. I went to the theatre administration right away, reported the change of plans and begged them to let me depart without further delay. They resorted to various means in the attempt to dissuade me from doing business with Bondini. No words of praise, promise of future gains, personal appeals and admonitions were left untried.

Notwithstanding their attempts to hold me, I felt that it was within my moral right to leave, not having made any binding written agreements for any definite period, as is evident from original documents in my possession (which I have sent to Dresden for my exculpation). My honesty did not permit me to disregard my lawful obligation to Bondini even if I had been able to conquer the longing for my native district and no matter how much indemnity the Bonn people might have offered me—which was not the case anyway. When the administration realized that all efforts to detain me had failed they had my personal belongings seized. I sued them, but the final decision was procrastinated from week to week. This was undoubtedly their purpose to begin with. In other words, it was impossible for me to be in Leipzig at the appointed date, and Bondini was forced to engage other persons to fill our positions. I had to annul the contract and stay in Bonn. I cannot voice any complaints about the judges in charge of the case. The light in which the facts were presented to them and certain other circumstances involved—which I would rather not divulge for reasons of modesty—made it virtually impossible for them to take any other course. However, I deplore the abuse of friendship which can produce the most shocking effects upon a sincere person, not prepared for such eventualities.

I hope that this incident will not have to be mentioned or remembered ever again. The whole affair left a deep wound in my heart and has depressed my spirits as well as weakened my health. Moreover, it aroused in me certain sentiments and attitudes which I had never thought myself capable of. A considerable time had elapsed and a goodly amount of effort had been invested before I regained my equanimity and my aroused sentiments died down. Still, I was never again able to develop a friendly attitude toward and show confidence in certain persons. This incident made me view all their other actions from an entirely different perspective. I have, however, always attended to professional duties with my usual zeal and ambition and I still continue to do so.

On the 15th of February 1781 I started a new position as court organist in Bonn. His Excellency, Kurfuerst Max Friedrich of Cologne had appointed me—without regard to my being a Protestant—on the recommendations of the head minister Count von Belderbusch and those of the Countess von Hatzfeld.

In June of the same year I accompanied the court to Pyrmont where Grossmann took over the direction all by himself during our two months stay. From Pyrmont we proceeded to Kassel where we also stayed about two months. There I had the honor and the good fortune of being admitted into a circle of the finest and wisest of men who were all united on a great plan for the happiness of mankind and worked toward that goal. After Kassel, we returned to Bonn and stayed until the 20th of June 1782. On this day we started on our journey to Muenster; the Kurfuerst came along. Only a day before our departure, my predecessor, the court organist Van den Eeden, had been buried. I was granted permission to go along to Westfalen and from there to Frankfurt for the Michael Mass where we inaugurated the "Komoedienhaus," recently built by the town council. During my absence, my post was filled by some vicar (deputy).

This is as far as I can go with the tale of my rather insignificant and simple life. May God grant me to spend the few more years remaining for my ailing body in tranquility. May He grant that I might lead a life of usefulness not only for myself, but for my family and my fellow men as well and that I might then face my Maker with joy in my heart.

Frankfurt, September 30, 1782

* * *

Neefe's widow continued the autobiography of her husband in the Leipziger Allgemeine Musikalische Zeitung, 1798/9. She states that in 1784 he received a position as Director of all the church music in Bonn after the Electoral kapellmeister, Andreas Luchesi, had left that city. However, Neefe lost a good deal of his income at that time, just after Max Franz (the youngest son of Maria Teresia) succeeded Max Friedrich as Elector on Aug. 15, 1784, and he was forced to give private lessons. It is typical of Neefe that at the time he settled in Bonn, he bought a house and planted a garden with trees and flowers. Shortly thereafter he assumed his old position, which he held until the war with France broke out, and the theater was dissolved.

Frau Neefe gives a very sad picture of the life they led for the next two years. Neefe assumed, in 1794, a position in the troupe of the impressario Hunnius, who played at that time in Holland. There he performed with his daughter (she playing the role of Constanza) in Mozart's "Entführung aus dem Serail."

Hunnius and his troupe went to Düsseldorf, and after the French invaded Bonn and forced the Elector to flee, Neefe was compelled by the invaders to do non-musical administrative work as a registrar. Shortly thereafter, Neefe and his family left for Leipzig, where, on his arrival, he found his dismissal from Bonn.

On December 1, 1796, the Neefe family went to Dessau, where Neefe died on January 26, 1798, from a heart ailment which had lasted two years. Two daughters and a son survived him.

IV

JOHANN BAPTIST SCHENK'S
AUTOBIOGRAPHY

Dear Sir: [Aloys Fuchs]

It is not easy to comply with your so often uttered request for my complete autobiography. However, since I expect to remain in the country for the whole summer, I shall use the opportunity to recall my long past childhood and the years that followed and I shall write it all down with a light conscience and in unadulterated truth.

I, Johann Schenk, a native of Wiener-Neustadt, was born on November 30, 1761. The Italian Anton Tomaselli, who was employed as a singer at the cathedral in Neustadt, happened to hear me sing and liked my voice. This noble man went to the trouble of giving me singing lessons. The easy progress I made encouraged him to instruct me in clavier (he himself was a good cembalist). At that time it was my fervent desire to be accepted as *Saengerknabe* in the cathedral; however, there was no vacancy. I was grieved that I should have to go on being a burden to my dear ones, when it so happened that I was accepted as *Saengerknabe* by the school and choir director Anton Stoll in Baaden in 1771. This good man gave me the fundamental knowledge of thorough bass. Besides, I was very anxious to learn more about wind instruments. I had started to play the violin when I was still in Neustadt. My purely intoning voice aroused the interest of Father Ignatz von Froehlich. He often expressed his satisfaction with my possibilities in a kind way, he also gave me some moral books which contained Gellert's ecclesiastic Lieder and odes. I composed some of these Lieder with accompaniments. This was my first attempt at composition. My second opus consisted of 12 dance minuets with full orchestra. Now I took a daring step—I began to compose symphonies. In this respect my paragons were Karl von Dittersdorf and Josef Haydn; these compositions were done by ear. The little I had learned of figured bass was not sufficient background.

In 1773, His Eminence Cardinal Count Migazzi happened to be in Baaden. My benefactor, the priest, who stood in especial esteem with His Eminence, did not fail to warmly recommend my musical talent. That very same year His Eminence was gracious enough to let me come to the archiepiscopal palace and appointed the canon Josef Schneller as my guardian. This honorable priest, who was generally considered a great preacher, furthered my education. While studying I composed some string quartets which Pater Schneller (who was an excellent violinist and also a great con-

noisseur of music) immediately played. One of them
he liked a great deal. Here I must say that canon
Schneller was father confessor to the court Kapellmeister Christof Wagenseil. Thus it was easy for him
to submit my aforementioned score for examination of
my abilities to Wagenseil. Subsequently, the court
Kapellmeister accepted me as his student thanks to the
kind recommendation of my good Pater Schneller, and
I was very glad about it.

I began to study with him in January 1774. Wagenseil's method of teaching composition was based on the
theories of Johann Fux, who had been his teacher.
Because of my easy perception I fully acquired the
rules of counterpoint within one year—from the nota
contra notam to the double counterpoint in the
duodecim. But Wagenseil was not satisfied with my
theoretical knowledge of the rules and my ability to
use them; he wanted me to feel sure about these rigid
theories and made me try the *stilo alla capella* in the
composition of masses and several graduals and offer-
torios. In this respect I chose as my models Giovanni
Palestrina and the compositions of my teacher. In the
course of my studies I devoted some of my time to practicing the clavier. Sebastian Bach's preludes and
fugues as well as the clavier suites by Handel served
for my practice material.

When I had finished these church compositions, my
wise teacher guided me to the art of composing in a
freer style. His intentions seemed to have been to
wean me from the dry movement and to direct me

toward a beautifully blossoming melody. Here my paragon was Adolf Hasse for the serious compositions and Baldassare Galuppi for the comic ones. But the sublime Handel was my highest ideal as far as I was concerned. Alexander's Feast was the first work my teacher called to my attention and followed it with the oratorios Athalia and Judas Maccabaeus. Wagenseil also acquainted me with the beautiful passages which could so frequently be found in Handel's works, and in particular with his choruses, and he used these examples for his instruction. The oratorio Messiah was the last work which I studied under his guidance. Several years later, I also included the great dramatist of the tragic opera, Ritter Christof Gluck, in my studies.

Christof Wagenseil was a very famous composer in his days and even before the advent of Emanuel Bach he was also a well-known cembalist. The pianoforte was still unknown. This noble old man did not cease to teach me with love and patience until his death which took him away on the 1st of March 1777. For more than a decade was this poor man tortured by gout which chained him to his house. His name remains indelibly engraved on my heart.

After the death of my unforgettable teacher I was overcome by grief and pain. Two months later, H. Gallus, a pupil of Wagenseil, performed one of his compositions, a mass, in the Salesian convent for women on the occasion of a great church feast. This truly beautiful composition which was received with much praise by the musical connoisseurs revived my spirits and stimulated me to compete with him. In this mood I first decided to compose a solemn mass. I finished this composition when I had just completed my 16th year. While I was still working on this mass, Pater Schneller received the benefice of the St. Magdalene Church. Therefore, the performance of my mass was prepared for his inauguration, which took place on January 8, 1778. Because of his love for his father confessor, the Vice-President of Appeal, Herr Edler von Kees, engaged the foremost musicians in Vienna to guarantee a magnificent performance. The Kapellmeister of St. Stephen, Herr Leopold Hofmann, accepted the offer to conduct it. This was the first work of mine of which the musicians took notice. Subsequently, I had the honor of showing this mass to His Excellency Baron von Swieten and also to Josef Haydn. Still in the same year, Herr von Kees asked me to compose a lauretanian litany which he needed for Mariazell. Herr Karl Friedrich, director of the choir at the church *Am Hof* made me write a Stabat Mater which, for the first time, was performed in the Italian church on Good Friday 1779. The following Sunday it was played in the church *Am Hof* and on the same evening once more at the house of Herr Regierungsrath von Hering and was, for the fourth time, repeated in the Seminary on Maundy Thursday.

In the same year I wrote two cantatas, one of which was played in the country. In 1780 I composed another mass and at the end of that year I worked on the entr'acte music for Blumauer's tragedy, "Erwin von Steinheim". At that time I began to visit the opera house. The pleasant artistic singing and the graceful impressive melodies awoke in me the hidden desire to devote myself solely to the theatre. In the period between 1781 and 1785 I wrote five operas for which I used well-known *Singspiele* by Goethe, Michaelis, etc. These compositions served, so to speak, as an exercise or preparation for my theatrical career. In 1783, after Easter, the Italian opera company began to give performances in the court theatre. I transcribed the music of the favorite operas for string quartets and for piano score. Now I composed an important harp concerto for Madame Muellner (who later became a lute virtuoso); this concert was performed in the court theatre in 1784. Because she handled the instrument so delicately and produced sweet sounds on it, His Majesty, the Emperor Joseph, presented her with a new pedal harp. I wrote two more concertos for this new instrument.

On the 8th of October 1785, my first opera entitled "Die Weinlese" (The vintage) was staged in the Leopoldstaedter Theatre. I accepted the composition on condition that the author of the text would not make known my name before I myself agreed to it. He was discreet and kept his mouth shut. But my music was received with great acclaim and subsequently aroused general interest. His Majesty, the Emperor Joseph, accompanied by His Highness, the Archduke Franz and Princess Elizabeth, honored the eleventh performance of this *Singspiel* with their presence. In the same year he even came a second time accompanied by His Highness Archduke Leopold of Florence, and the third time he had with him His Highness Archduke Maximilian of Cologne. Of all the contemporaries, who witnessed these events, only a very few are still alive. Later on, I wrote for the same theatre "Die Weihnacht auf dem Lande" (Christmas in the Country), a *Singspiel* in three acts, which was staged for the first time on the 18th of December 1786. These two operettas remained in the repertory of this theatre for more than 18 years.

In 1787 I composed the *Singspiel,* "Im Finstern ist nicht gut tappen" (It's hard to grope in the dark), and opening night was on the 17th of October at the court theatre next to the Kaerntnerthor. Before the première took place I came out with the disclosure that I was the composer of the two aforementioned operettas (kept secret for two years). The Kaerntnerthor Theatre was closed in 1788. Now I diligently composed symphonies which were played on the occasion of Herr von Kees' musical *Akademien.* At every performance His Excellency Baron van Svieten was present and a few times also Josef Haydn, who uttered words of satisfaction and encouraged me in a kind way to go on working.

I composed three operas for the *Theater auf der Wieden* which was situated in Prince Starhemberg's *Freyhaus.* The first was: "Das (unterbrochene) unvermuthete Seefest" (The unexpected feast on high sea), 1789. The second: "Das Singspiel ohne Tittel" (Singspiel without a title), 1790, and the third: "Der Aerndtekranz" (Harvest wreath), 1791. Two of these operas were played to undivided acclaim; the "Singspiel without a title" had not more than 6 performances. In the same year and on the same stage Mozart's eternally young "Magic Flute" was performed for the first time. Pleasant memories are connected with this wonderful period, when Salieri, Haydn and Mozart worked together, and the gay Mozart opened his house to me. I often enjoyed his great artistry. However inventive and brilliant his fantasies sounded, they never lacked the highest clarity and the most perfect contrapuntal purity.

This extraordinary man had hardly reached his 35th year of age, when death overtook him. Had Mozart lived longer, he undoubtedly would have achieved the highest goal in his art. As in a silent summer night when the silent stars twinkle and suddenly, visible to everyone, the moon spreads its full, clear light, so Mozart would have stood out, more radiant than any other genius, alone and unique in greatest glory. So profound, so clear, so all-embracing, so rich and tender was his mind!

In 1792, His Highness Archduke Maximilian, *Kurfuerst* of Cologne, graciously sent his protégé Louis van Beethoven to Vienna to study musical composition with Josef Haydn. Toward the end of July of the same year Abbé Gellinek told me of his acquaintance with a young man, who showed such great virtuosity on the piano as he had not heard since Mozart. In the course of our conversation he also mentioned that Beethoven had begun to study counterpoint with Haydn more than 6 months previously and was still working on the first exercise; also His Excellency Baron von Swieten seriously recommended to him the study of counterpoint and often inquired how far he had advanced in his studies. The fact that he had to hear these frequent inquiries and that he was still in the early stages of his studies aroused displeasure in this anxious student of which he often spoke to his friend. Gellinek, who took Beethoven's suffering and bad moods to heart, asked me whether I would be inclined to help his friend in the study of counterpoint. After all I had heard about him, I desired to make his acquaintance soon. A day was fixed on which I was supposed to meet Beethoven in Gellinek's living quarters and to hear him play the piano.

On that day I saw and heard for the first time that now so famous composer. After the usual polite phrases were exchanged, he expressed a desire to play a fantasy on the piano and asked me to listen to it. After a few chords and somewhat casual figures which he produced nonchalantly, this creative genius gradually unveiled the profound and sensitive image of his soul. The beauty of the manifold motifs, interwoven so clearly with utter loveliness, compelled my attention and I let myself be carried away by this delightful impression. Surrendering himself completely to his imagination, he gradually departed from the magic of his sounds and, to express violent passion, he threw himself into discordant scales with the glowing fire of youth. I was entirely overcome by this agitation and excitement. Now he began to grope his way to heavenly melodies with many a turn and with pleasant modulations, to those great ideas so often found in his works. After the artist had thus masterfully proven his virtuosity, he changed the sweet sounds into sad and woeful ones, then he went from tender and touching effects to gaiety and merry playfulness. Each of these figures were characteristic of their kind and had all the earmarks of the expression of his own passionate feelings. There were nowhere any feeble repetitions, nor any empty condensations of many incoherent thoughts; on the other hand there were no impotent decompositions through constantly interspersed arpeggios which usually give the listeners the feeling of encroaching sleep. This fantasy was throughout correct in its execution.

It was a clear day, full of light. More than half an hour had elapsed, when the master of sound left the piano. This unforgettable fantasy with which he enchained ear and heart and tickled the musical palate is still fully alive in my soul.

The first thing I did next day was to pay a visit to this still unknown artist who had proved his mastership so well. I found a few phrases of his first contrapuntal exercises lying around on his desk. After a short examination I realized that there were some mistakes in every key (however short the exercise may have been). This proved Gellinek's contention. As I was now certain that my student was not familiar with the rules of counterpoint, I gave him the well-known text-book by Josef Fux, Gradus ad Parnassum, for his further exercises.

Josef Haydn, who had returned from the country to Vienna at the end of that year, was anxious to use all his time for the composition of new masterworks. In consideration of this laudable endeavor of his it was understandable that Haydn had little time left to teach the musical alphabet. This made me decide to help Beethoven who was so eager to learn. But before I began to help him I made him understand that our combined efforts must always be kept secret. I therefore recommended that he copy each phrase which I had corrected so that Haydn should never be able to recognize another person's handwriting. After a year's time Beethoven and Gellinek had some kind of quarrel, the cause of which I no longer remember, but it seems to me that both were to blame. Because of this strife, Gellinek was furious and divulged our secret. From then on Beethoven and his brother made no secret of it any longer.

I began to teach my dear Louis in the first days of August 1792 and, without interruption, continued to hold this honorable post until the end of May 1793, when he finished learning the double counterpoint and prepared to go to Eisenstadt. Had His Royal Highness placed his protégé under Albrechtsberger's guidance, his studies would have never been interrupted and been entirely completed.

Several years ago someone stated publicly that Beethoven had completed his studies with Albrechtsberger. This would have been very useful to Beethoven, had he really done so. This assertion, however, misleading as it is, was the first I ever heard after so many years. If there had been any truth in this rumor, Abbé Gellinek would certainly have been the first to tell me about it. Also Beethoven, who always was sincere in his feelings for me, would have never kept secret such a laudable change, on the contrary, he confided to me that he had gone to the court Kapellmeister Salieri to be taught composition in a free style.

In the middle of May he informed me that he was about to leave for Eisenstadt with Haydn and that he would stay there until the following winter. The day of departure was not yet set. One day in the beginning of June I came to give him his lesson as usual—but my good Louis was no longer there. He had left me the following note which I copy word for word:

"Dear Schenk,

I wish I had not been compelled to leave for Eisenstadt today. I would have liked to talk to you before I left. But meanwhile be assured of my gratitude for all the kindness you have shown to me. I shall try to make good for it as best as I can. I hope I'll see you soon again and have the pleasure of your company. Farewell and do not entirely forget your

Beethoven."

It was my intention to touch upon my relationship

with Beethoven only briefly; but the circumstances which brought me together with him and made me become his guide in musical composition, demanded a more detailed explanation.

For my endeavor (if endeavor is the right word for it) I received the costliest gift from my good Louis, namely the strong tie of friendship which remained intact to the day of his death.

Well, here follows the continuation of my biography. Between 1792 and 1793 I composed two more symphonies and also a few concertos for wind instruments. While staying on the estate of His Highness Karl von Auersperg from May 1794 to the end of November of the same year, I wrote two short *Singspiele* which were performed there. In that year Baron von Braun took over the administration and direction of the two court theatres. I composed for him the opera: "Achmed und Almanzine" which was performed in the Kaerntnerthor Theatre on August 14, 1795, and the operetta "Der Dorfbarbier" (The village barber) whose opening night was November 6, 1798. During the same year I was honored by His Majesty with the assignment to compose a short *Singspiel* with pantomime which was performed in honor of Her Majesty, the Empress Maria Theresia, in celebration of her name day, in the castle of Laxenburg on October 15. Next year I again wrote an opera in two acts, "Die Jagd" (The hunt), which was performed on May 7 in the Kaerntnerthor Theatre.

Herr Josef Weidmann, a royal actor, had, many years previously, enacted the part of Zep, an old drunkard, in the *Singspiel* "Der Fassbinder" (The cooper). The audience enjoyed his delightful characterization at every performance, but the old, so often heard French music no longer had any appeal. Since this was the reason that the *Singspiel* was not in the repertory of the theatre any more, my friend Weidmann, who would have liked to play his favorite part again, asked me to compose new music for this operetta. Thus, "Der Fassbinder" was performed again with the new music I had written for it on November 17, 1802, and was kept in the repertory until Weidmann died. This *Singspiel* was my last theatrical work.

Besides my compositions, I have spent a great deal of my life teaching the piano. I was never very anxious to get employment. A sequestered life suited my character better than any post as Kapellmeister.

For a long time I was fascinated by an idea which was incessantly in my mind. It was a dramatic poem which only Ritter Gluck would have been able to compose gloriously. And yet—without closer examination of my abilities—I began to work on this composition. I thought about it, I brooded over it, I probed its depths and possibilities so intensely that I was overcome by sadness and melancholy. This condition grew gradually worse, until a nervous fever kept me in bed. My disease was very dangerous. Much time passed, before I recovered somewhat. After this incident I had lost confidence in my capacities. From then on I was undecided, fearful and not to be persuaded to attempt another performance. In addition, there was no good text available and in consideration of the many unpleasant events connected with theatrical work—which no poet or composer can avoid—I could not be induced to continue my work as a composer. It was reason enough not to jeopardize the small recognition I had gained in the musical world. The only exceptions were two cantatas which I wrote for a friend of the great *Musikverein,* who had done so much to encourage me. The first was: "Die Huldigung" (Homage), performed in the large *Redoutensaal* on February 28, 1819, and the second: "Der Mai" (May), played on the 7th of May.

This describes the entire activity of my life. Only my present sojourn in the country impelled me to write down the so long promised biography. I dare send it to you, dear sir, and remain with expressions of my respect,

Sincerely yours,
Johann Schenk

Baumgarten, next to Krems,
July 28, 1830

V

THE LIFE OF HERR JOHANN JOACHIM QUANTZ, AS SKETCHED BY HIMSELF

I was born in the province of Hannover, in the village of Oberscheden, located between Göttingen and Münden, on the 30th of January in the year 1697, between 6 and 7 o'clock in the evening. I was baptized and reared in the Evangelical-Lutheran faith.

My father, a blacksmith in the same village, was Andreas Quantz. My mother's name was Anna Ilse Bürmannin. She died in the year 1702, and my father remarried. However, in the year 1707, on the day before Easter he also died, in his 48th year.

From the time when I was nine years old he had trained me in the trade of the blacksmith, and on his deathbed he declared that I should continue with this mode of life. But Divine Providence, which always knows better than mortals who believe they have discerned the right way, soon showed me another way toward future happiness.

As soon as my father had died, two of his brothers, of whom one was a tailor, the other a court and town-musician in Merseburg, offered to take me in and teach me their professions, leaving to me the choice of which one I should follow. My father's sister was married to a clergyman in Lautereck in the Palatinate, and this man also wanted to provide for my education and send me to the university. However, since my 8th year I had to accompany my oldest brother—who sometimes, during the country festivals, assumed the place of a village musician—and play on these occasions the German bass violin without being able to read a note. This music, inferior as it was, nevertheless dominated my interests in such a way that I wanted to be nothing but a musician.

Thus, in August of the year 1708, I went to Merseburg to begin my apprenticeship with the former town-musician, Justus Quantz. But after three months he too died, and his future son-in-law, Johann Adolf Fleischhack, received his post. I served with this man as an apprentice for five and a fourth years, and as a journeyman for two and a fourth years. He was, by the standards of those times, not a bad musician, particularly on the violin. He preferred tending to his comfort, however, to giving his apprentices the proper musical instruction. The journeymen, for the most part, were of the same mind. Consequently, there was no instruction available other than that which one apprentice gave, as well as he could, to the other. Under these circumstances I should have undoubtedly lagged as far behind as my comrades, if my burning love for this science, placed within me by the Creator together with a good native ability, had not driven me to independent application and made even the most difficult attempts toward achievement in music a pleasure for me.

The first instrument which I had to learn was the violin, for which I also seemed to have the greatest liking and ability. Thereon followed the oboe and the trumpet. During my years as an apprentice I worked hardest on these three instruments. I was not spared other intruments, such as the *zink,*trombone, *waldhorn, flute a bec,* bassoon, German bass violin, violoncello, viola da gamba, and who knows how many more, all of which the real *Kunstpfeifer* must be able to play. It is true that because of the great variety of instruments which come into one's hands, one remains a bungler on each one in particular. At the same time, one acquires, in this way, a knowledge of their characteristics which is necessary, in fact almost indispensable for composers—especially those who write church music.

Due to my own choosing, I took some lessons at this time on the clavier, which I was not required to learn, from a relative of mine, the organist Kiesewetter. Through his instruction I laid the first groundwork for understanding harmony, and probably first received the desire to learn composition.

My master did not make the mistake that most of his colleagues make, that of falling in love with the rigidity and bad taste of the past, and scorning and condemning everything which is new and good, if they themselves are not able to execute it. He knew how to choose examples, and tried to obtain the best of that which was brought to light. He received much from Leipzig, especially from the famous men: Telemann, Melchior Hofmann, Heinchen, and others. This gave me an advantage which even in later years has been useful.

The Ducal Kappelle in Merseburg was not especially large at that time. We had to fill in at the court, as well as in the church, and also perform table music. This served as no little incentive for me, particularly since musicians from other courts often performed there.

The greatest desire to compose now began to stir within me. I often attempted small things, such as settings of *bicinia* for trumpets, marches, minuets, and other dances. However, I did not dare attempt anything larger without instruction, which I could not have at that time.

At this time my main instrument was the violin. What I lacked in instruction I had to supply by my own industry. I studied diligently the solos of Biber, Walter, and Albicastro until I received those of Corelli and Telemann—the latter spurring me on toward even greater industry. I finally reached a point which enabled me to play some of them for my examination, when I was released in December, 1713. My master absolved me from three-fourths of a year of study, but under the condition that I should serve him another year for half a journeyman's wages.

Dresden or Berlin were the places where, in the end, I wished to take up residence. I believed I could hear much more beautiful music there, and learn much more, than I could in Merseburg.

The death of Prince Friedrich, brother of the reigning Duke, in June, 1714, and the three month mourning period which followed, soon gave me the opportunity to take in hand the execution of my intentions. I travelled from one city to another, and finally to Dresden, in the hope of making myself known. I did not reach my final goal as yet, but had to travel further. By the way of Bischofswerde I came to Radeberg, where a journeyman was needed. Partly because I did not want to travel in the hot weather, and partly because I had not given up my desire to become known in Dresden, (which was only 2 miles from this place) I took a position with the town musician, Knoll, agreeing to serve with him until the end of the mourning period in Merseburg. However, an incident most deplorable for both my master and the whole town, soon parted us again. One of the most terrible thunderstorms that I have ever heard began around 8 o'clock in the evening on the great day of penance which falls after the feast of St. John. With two terrible thunderclaps it struck in three places, and in a few minutes the whole town was afire. The whole town was transformed, within the space of four hours—including the church, town hall, school, parsonage, and twenty houses in the suburb—into a heap of ashes. The fire raged so violently that those who did not get out of town in time were not able to pass the city gates because of the flames which raged around them. They had to seek refuge in the flaming market place, myself among them. The church was set on fire by a burning side of bacon which struck in flight the point of the spire. On the following day one could not get any food or drink, not even water. Twenty some loaves of bread and two barrels of beer, which a sympathetic forester had sent from the country, had to feed (wretchedly enough) all the inhabitants on this day. The town's rector, D. Richter, had on the morning of the disaster concluded his severe sermon in which he had likened the town to Sodom and Gomorrah, with these words:

"Ye shall know it. God will strike with thunder! Amen!"

By this, as well as the fervor with which he pounded his fist on the pulpit, he filled his listeners, among them myself, even then with horror. It seemed even stranger that the house of just this rector remained standing unharmed in the fire, even though it was exposed to the danger of the flames just as the other parsonage and school, both of which burned down. The simplest among the burghers were therefore inclined to place the blame for this on him, and almost declared the honest old man a weathermaker and sorcerer.

Under these circumstances it seemed wisest for me to travel on. I went, urged by the poor town-musician Knoll—who lost everything in the fire—to Pirna, to the town-musician Schalle, one of whose journeymen had become ill. For the time which I had left I entered his service. This was really, I have subsequently realized, the way in which Providence chose not only to fulfill my wish to become known in Dresden, but also further my future happiness. For when the town-musician Heine had to supply music for more weddings than he could manage with his small band of players, as often happened, he used to engage the necessary journeymen from the neighboring towns. On these occasions it was sometimes my turn, and I thus came to know him. He was my first acquaintance in Dresden.

During this period in Pirna I saw Vivaldi's violin concertos for the first time. As they represented a completely new way of composing music they impressed me not a little. I did not fail to supply myself with quite a number of them. The splendid ritornellos of Vivaldi served as excellent examples in the future.

With the end of the mourning period in September of this year, my former master in Merseburg called me back. I went there in order to serve the remaining year and a half which I owed him.

In 1715 I was appointed first violinist in Berenburg, and had to perform at the Lustschloss Friedeburg before a princely gathering. The conditions offered me in regard to my future salary were more advantageous than I could have expected at this time. Since I did not see how I could further my intention of learning more about music in a place where I would be the best among inferior musicians, I declined the offer in order to wait for a more suitable position. Shortly thereafter I was supposed to go to another court to serve as oboist, and finally, Duke Moriz of Merseburg, the great patron of the *Kunstpfeifer,* out of special kindness wanted to allow me to learn the trumpet. The former position I declined, and the latter I did not wait for as just at this time Heine called me into his service in Dresden. This I preferred over the others, and with great joy, in the hope of coming closer to my final goal (which is what actually happened), I accepted.

In March of the year 1716 I went to Dresden. Here I soon became aware that the mere playing of the notes as set down by the composer was far from being the greatest merit of a musician.

The Royal Orchestra was in full bloom already at this time. It distinguished itself from many other orchestras by its French smoothness of performance, as introduced by the concertmaster at that time, Volumier; just as it later, under the direction of its concertmaster, Herr Pisendel, who introduced a mixed style, achieved a finesse of performance which I have never heard bettered in all my travels. At that time it boasted of various famous instrumentalists such as: Pisendel and Veracini on the violin, Pantaleon Hebenstreit on the Pantalon, Sylvius Leopold Weiss, on the lute and *theorbe,* Richter on the oboe, Buffardi on the transverse flute, not to speak of the good violoncellists, bassoonists, horn players, and bass violinists. When listening to these famous people I was greatly amazed, and my zeal for continuing musical studies was doubled. I wanted to prepare myself so that in time I too could become a fair member of this excellent company. For although I was otherwise quite taken with the life of the *Kunstpfeifer*, I found the playing of dance music stood in the way of attaining greater finesse, and I wanted to give up the life of a *Kunstpfeifer*. However, I remained one for two more years.

In the year 1717 the mother of King Augustus II died. The subsequent mourning brought on a three month silencing of music. During this time I took a journey through lower and upper Silesia, Moravia, and Austria, to Vienna, and returned in October of this year by way of Prague to Dresden.

During the jubilee then in progress which celebrated the Reformation, it also happened that I had to concertize on the trumpet in a church. Kapellmeister Schmidt heard me there and proposed that, if I were interested, he would get the King (as was the custom among trumpeters) to let me finish my studies on this instrument, after which I would be taken into the Royal Service as court trumpeter. As in many other places there was at this time a shortage of musically competent trumpeters. However, I declined this kind offer because as I well knew, I could not acquire the good taste I then primarily lacked by playing this instrument.

In March of year 1718 the so-called Polish Kapelle, which was to consist of 12 members, was established. Since 11 members had already been hired and an oboist was still lacking I was proposed for the job, and after a successful test before the director of the Kapelle, Baron von Seyfertiz, I was accepted. The yearly salary was 150 thalers and free lodging in Poland. The others received no more than this. In the summer of 1718 I traveled to Poland with this Kapelle and returned to Dresden the following Spring.

Here I reached a turning point, affecting both my previous way of life and my main lifework. The violin, which until now had been my principal in-strument, I now exchanged for the oboe. However, I was prevented by my colleagues, who had had longer experience, from excelling on either instrument, which I wanted very much to do. My chagrin over this caused me to take up seriously the transverse flute, which un-til then I had practiced only for my own pleasure. On this instrument I did not have to fear any special re-sistance from my colleagues, particularly since the pre-vious flautist, Friese, who had no great inclination toward music, willingly allowed me to take the chair of the first flautist. For about 4 months I took instruction from the famous flautist Buffardi in order to learn the peculiarities of this instrument. We played nothing but fast pieces, for this was the "forte" of my master.

This new occupation brought with it an increased in-terest in composition on my part. At that time there were few compositions written especially for the flute. One had to manage, for the most part, with com-positions for the oboe and violin, which one had to ar-range as well as possible for one's purpose. I composed different compositions for the flute and let one or another correct them. However, at that time I did not enjoy a formal education in the principles of composition. Although the Kapellmeister, Schmidt, promised to teach me counterpoint, he put it off from time to time, until in the end nothing came of it. I didn't dare approach Heinchen for lessons as I did not want to offend Schmidt, particularly since they were not exactly the best of friends. In the meantime, while anticipating a more suitable situation, I studied industriously the scores of acknowledged masters, attempting to imitate in trios and concertos their method of composition without actually writing them down. I also attempted to write fugues, as I always found a great deal of pleasure in this type of music, particularly since in Vienna I had acquired from the artful church composer Zelenka (then a student of Fux) a fair understanding of counterpoint in the octave.

I was fortunate enough to make the acquaintance of Herr Pisendel, the great, skillful violin virtuoso and Royal Concertmaster after Volumier's death. This acquaintance, by and by, grew into an intimate friendship on both sides which to my great pleasure is still continuing until this day. From him—who is as great a violinist as he is dignified a concertmaster, as good a musician as he is righteous a man—I have learned to perform not only an adagio, which he played in an extremely touching way, but also, insofar as the interpretation of movements and the performance of music in general is concerned, I have learned the most from him. He encouraged me to make further attempts in the field of composition. His style at that time was a mixture of the Italian and French schools, as he had traveled in both countries when already a man of mature judgment. In the tenderness of his youth he had sung as a choir boy in Anspach under the excellent singer and voice teacher Franc. Antonio Pistocchi, and thus had had the opportunity to lay the groundwork toward developing good style. From Torelli he had learned to play the violin. His example took root within me so deeply that I later always preferred the mixed style to the national style. I can also thank the attention which I have always paid to good singers, particularly in matters of style.

In the year 1719, during the nuptials of the Electoral Prince, several Italian operas, a pastoral play, two serenades, and a French divertissement were performed. The singers and dancers in the latter consisted entirely of ladies and gentlemen of the court. Herr Schmidt, the Kapellmeister, declared himself the author of the music. For the Italian operas the most famous singers available had been hired from Italy. The music of the two operas *Gli odi delusi dal Sangue* and *Teofane,* and the pastoral was by Kapellmeister Lotti who had been especially commissioned for this. The rest of the music was by Heinchen.

These were the first operas I heard in my life. Not only did they amaze me, but they also gave me some idea of the then pure, but sensible, Italian style, from which the Italians have since strayed too far, in my opinion. The most notable singers which I heard in these operas were: Francesco Bernardi, called Senesino, Matteo Berselli, Santa Stella Lotti, wife of Kapellmeister Lotti, Vittoria Tesi, Durestanti, and Frau Hesse, a German, and wife of the famous viola da gambist of the same name, now minister of war to the Landgrave of Darmstadt.

Senesino had a well-carrying, clear, even, and pleasantly low soprano voice (mezzo soprano), a pure intonation and a beautiful *trillo*. He rarely sang above the fifth line "f." His way of singing was masterful, and his execution perfect. He did not overload the slow movements with arbitrary ornamentation, but brought out the essential ornaments with the greatest finesse. He sang an allegro with fire, and he knew how to thrust out the running passages with his chest with some speed. His figure was quite favorable for the theatre, and his acting was quite natural. The role of a hero suited him better than that of a lover.

Berselli had an agreeable but slightly thin, high soprano, which ranged from middle "c" to high "f" with great ease. He amazed his listeners more through this than through artful singing. In slow movements he showed little emotion, and in allegro movements he did not use many *passagien*. His figure was not bad, but his acting was not very fiery.

Lotti had a very strong soprano voice, good intonation, and a good *trillo*. The high notes were somewhat difficult for her. Her "forte" was the adagio, and I heard the so-called tempo rubato for the first time from her. She made a good figure on the stage and her acting, particularly when playing lofty characters, was unexcelled. Tesi will be discussed later.

After the nuptials Heinchen composed still another opera which was to be performed after the King's return from Poland. At the rehearsal, however, which took place at the Royal Palace in the presence of the music director, Baron von Mortax, the two singers, Senesino and Berselli, behaved like rude virtuosos. They quarrelled with Heinchen over an aria and charged this scholarly man who had spent 7 years in Italy with making an error in the libretto. Senesino, who may have already had intentions of going to England, tore up Berselli's score and threw it at Heinchen's feet. This was reported to the King in Poland. In the meantime, Count von Wackerbart, who usually was a great patron of the Italians, had reconciled the Kapellmeister and the castrati to Heinchen's complete satisfaction in the presence of some of the most important members of the Royal orchestra, such as Lotti, Schmidt, Pisendel, Weiss, etc. However, a Royal order came back demanding the dismissal of all the Italian singers. With this, opera was at an end for the present.

Almost every year I went to Poland and back with the Kapelle of which I was a member. In 1722 our salary was raised to 216 thalers. This time we had to remain in Poland. Meanwhile, several great patrons of mine, especially the Keeper of the Royal Sword (*Cron-Schwerdträger*) Count Lubomirsky, and the Royal Assessor, (*Cron-Referendarius*) Abbot Roseroschewsky, had asked the King, without my knowledge, to send me to Italy. The King had consented and I did not hesitate to return to Saxony as soon as I received the first news of this. But on my arrival in Dresden I heard that the Chief Steward (*Oberküchenmeister*) and Director of the Polish Kapelle, Baron von Seyfertiz—who had been my greatest patron since he took me into the Royal Service and remained so until his death—had pointed out that because of my youth it was too early to send me to Italy, and upon hearing this the King canceled his earlier decision. This action made me feel badly, as I believed he had forestalled my temporary happiness. He assured me, however, that when the time became ripe he would bend all his efforts toward having me sent to Italy. In time I have come to realize that he was completely right.

In the meantime, in July 1723, I traveled in the company of the famous lutenist Weiss, and Herr Graun, who is now the Royal Prussian Kapellmeister, to Prague, to hear the great and splendid opera which was being performed at the coronation of Emperor Charles VI. It was performed outdoors and included 100 singers and 200 instrumentalists. This opera was *Costanza e Fortezza*. The composer was the Imperial Oberkapellmeister, famous old Fux. It was composed more in a sacred than a theatrical style, but was quite magnificent. The contrasting and the binding of the violins against each other which occurred in ritornellos —though to a great extent it consisted of writing which often may have looked rigid and dry enough on paper —had on the whole a good effect. In fact, the effect was better than a *galant* melodic style, ornamented with many small figures and fast passages would have been.

Not considering that a more *galant* instrumental line —
which is better in a small room and with fewer instruments—cannot possibly be performed with the
proper ensemble by so many persons, especially when
they are not used to playing together. The spacious-
ness of the place would have prevented the desirable
clarity of passages consisting of many fast notes. I have
been convinced of this fact on many occasions, including Dresden, where the otherwise somewhat dry overtures of Lully always have a better effect when performed by the whole orchestra than the more pleasing
and *galant* overtures of some other famous composers,
who, on the contrary, were greatly preferred when performed in the chamber.

The many choirs of the Prague Opera also performed ballets in the French manner.

Because of the many performers, the Imperial Kapellmeister, Caldara, had to conduct. Old Fux, who
was stricken with gout and had to be carried, by order
of the Emperor, from Vienna to Prague in a sedan-
chair, had the pleasure of listening to this unusually splendid performance of his work, sitting near
the emperor.

Not a single principal or concertizing singer was
mediocre, all were good. The female singers were the
two Ambreville sisters, Italians, one of whom later
married the violoncellist Peroni, and the other the
singer Borosini. The male singers were the famous
Gaetano Orsini, Domenico, Giovanni Carestini, Pietro
Gassati, a great actor, and Braun, a German and a

pleasant baritone who sang an adagio as movingly as could have been expected only from a good contralto.

Gaetano Orsini, one of the greatest singers who ever lived, had a beautiful, even, and moving contralto voice of considerable range, a pure intonation, a beautiful *trillo,* and an extremely charming manner of execution. In an allegro he articulated,especially the triplets, very well with his chest, and in an adagio he made use of a caressing and touching quality in such a masterful way that he captured the hearts of his listeners. His acting was fair, and his figure not disagreeable. He remained in the Imperial Service for a long time and died only a few years ago at an advanced age, retaining his beautiful voice as much as possible until his death.

Domenico had one of the most beautiful soprano voices that I have ever heard. It was full, carried well, and was pure in tone. But otherwise his singing and acting were not very lively.

Carestini will be mentioned later. All of these singers were actually employed by the Emperor. Only some twenty persons had been brought along from the Viennese Orchestra. The other instrumentalists were gathered in Prague and were composed of students, of members of several kapelles, and of foreign musicians. The leader of the orchestra was the Imperial Concertmaster, Piani. The famous Francesco Conti*, an in-

---

*I take this opportunity to defend this good man against the so-called believable report from Regensburg of Oct. 10, 1730, with which Herr Matheson, member of the embassy staff (*Legationsrat*), had been deceived, and which is included on p. 40 of his *Der Vollkommene Kapell-*

ventive and fiery, though sometimes bizarre composer for the church as well as the serious and comic theatre, and one of the greatest *theorbists* who ever lived, played the first *theorbe*.

The chorus consisted of students and of members of church choirs from the city. Because of the multitude of people present, admittance to the opera was denied to many people, even those of rank, and thus my two comrades and I applied for a place in the orchestra. Weiss played the *theorbe*, Graun the violoncello, and I the oboe, as ripienists. In this way we had the opportunity of hearing the opera often, because of the many rehearsals that were necessary.

During my stay in Prague I also heard Count von Hartig, a great master of the clavier; Frau von Mestel, one of the most skillful lutenists; and the famous Italian violinist, Tartini, then employed by Count von Kinsky. Tartini was indeed one of the greatest violinists. He created a beautiful tone on his instrument, and had equal control of both hands and the bow. He mastered the greatest difficulties without great effort, play-

---

meister. It was not this Conti but his son who struck the clergyman and had to do the prescribed penance. The other circumstances are true. Since his son was then among the so-called Imperial Court scholars and studied composition, it is easy to see that he might have been confused with his father. Besides believable witnesses who were in Vienna at the time and knew both men, there is another piece of evidence proving it could not have been the father, because during the carnival of the year 1732 he composed the opera *Issipile*, performed in the Imperial Theatre, which was published in Vienna. The son was absolved from exile. After his imprisonment he returned to Vienna but could never approach the musical merit of his father. He is always referred to as Contini. I hope that Herr Matheson will not be opposed to this defense of a man for whom he otherwise has the greatest respect.

ing with pure tone. Trills, even double trills, he could execute with all fingers equally well. He mixed double stops in fast as well as slow movements, and he liked to play in the first position. Yet his performance was not moving, nor his style lofty, in fact, quite contrary to good singing style. Locatelli and Piantanita resembled in many ways this famous violinist.

After the closing of the opera, we traveled back to Dresden. At this time the Bishop of Würtzburg, Count von Schönborn, asked, through the intercession of one of my friends, to hear me. I traveled in October of this year to Würtzburg and had the honor of allowing myself to be heard on the flute by the Bishop, in the presence of his father's brother, the Elector of Mainz. I could have joined the service of this gracious Prince under advantageous circumstances, but I found it wise to decline. The Bishop's kapelle at that time consisted of some twenty persons, among them skilled musicians, and various singers. The Kapellmeister was Chelleri, and the Concertmaster Vogler, a not unknown violinist.

At the end of this year I had to travel back to Poland.

In 1724 General Count von Lagnasco, by birth a Piedmontese—whose wife is Countess von Waldstein, a connoisseur of music and a patron of mine—was sent to the Roman court as minister from Poland. This opportunity seemed to me, finally, the right one to take in order to reach my goal of seeing Italy. Prince Lubomirsky not only arranged for Count von Lagnasco to take me along, but also managed to obtain permission from the King through his father-in-law, the

Chief Chamberlain (*Oberkammerherr*) Count von Vitzthum. How great was my pleasure! I immediately made ready for the journey and went to Dresden to await there Count von Lagnasco. On May 23 of this year we left Dresden and arrived via Augsburg, Insbruck, Mantua, Modena, Bologna, Loreto, Ancona, etc. in Rome, on the eleventh day of July. This journey not only cost me nothing but in addition I was given free meals and lodging while I stayed with the Count in Rome.

I was immediately desirous of hearing music, which I could easily arrange because of the multitude of churches and monasteries which I visited as much as I could. The newest reaching my ears was the so-called Lombardic style, heretofore unknown to me, which had previously been introduced in Rome by Vivaldi through one of his operas, and which made such an impression on the inhabitants that they wanted to hear almost nothing that did not resemble this style. Yet in the beginning it was somewhat difficult for me to take a liking to it and to become accustomed to it, until at last I too considered it advisable to join the fashion. In addition to the Lombardic style, the current taste seemed to me still the same which I had noted in the year 1719 in Dresden and in 1723 in Prague, where I heard good Italian opera performed by good Italian singers.

Shortly after my arrival in Rome the extremely hot weather and my frequent running around from one church to the next caused my blood to rise. A careless cold which I contracted, and which I thought would be an antidote to the aforementioned condition, resulted only in a violent fever.

After I had recovered from this, I began to take instruction from the famous Francesco Gasparini, a 72 year-old kind and honest man, who was not only a learned contrapuntist but also an agreeable and lucid opera composer of his time. He taught me the principles of counterpoint. Since I already had some knowledge of composition and did not lack in industry, I reached, within the space of six months, the point where my master did not consider it necessary to give me further lessons unless I wanted to study vocal composition, which I did not care to do for various reasons. Furthermore, he offered to correct anything that I might compose during my stay in Rome without a fee. A rare example among the Italians!

At the same time I had the pleasure of hearing a new work by my master performed. It was the Serenata which Cardinal Polignac had performed in his palace on the occasion of the wedding of the present King of France. This music was so lively and pleasant that the advanced age of its author was not noticeable. At that time he also set certain madrigals which were not only artfully constructed, but were also quite easy to listen to. He is the author of a book called *Musico practico al Cembalo* and among other things, a mass for four voices consisting entirely of canons and judged very highly by the contrapuntists. He is further said to be the inventor of the instrumentally accompanied recitative. Twenty-five operas by him have been performed on the Venetian stage alone.

After I had become rather tired of the contrived "eye music" I turned again to "ear music", and again composed solos, trios, and a concerto. Not considering that through instruction I had advanced in composition as such—which served me well when composing a trio and quartet—I nevertheless had to discard some of my learning when composing solos and concertos, so as not to fall into the stiffness and dryness which attaches to more artificial contrapuntal works. I resolved to keep in view the aim of always combining art with nature, to keep a steady balance between melody and harmony, and to look upon good invention and well-chosen ideas as the most essential thing in music.

Besides Gasparini, there were two other good church composers in Rome, namely: Pittoni, Papal Kapell-meister, and Bencini. The compositions of the former were somewhat artificial, but bizarre and even bold. Those of the latter were not so artificial, but natural and pleasant.

Two papal church singers seemed to me worthy of mention above others, namely: Pasqualino, a contralto with a beautiful voice, and Chechino, a soprano. I did not hear any particularly good female singers except the so-called La Cieca, a daughter of a midwife and born blind, who not only had a beautiful contralto voice but also sang in such good style that she surpassed many virtuosos of her sex. Among the instru-mentalists there were only two who were good and who were particularly conspicuous, Montanari, a skillful violinist and leader of musicians, and Giovannini, a strong violoncellist. Both composed, but this was not their greatest "forte." Mimo Scarlatti, a *galant* clavier player in the manner of the time, also was in Rome. He was in the Portuguese service, but later went into the Spanish service, where he is still employed.

In the year 1725 no operas were performed in Rome as it was a year of Jubilee. On January 13 I therefore traveled from Rome to Naples, where I immediately heard an opera composed by Sarri, almost in the style of Vinci. Farinelli, who was then approaching his famous perfection, Strada, who later became more famous in England, and Tesi, were brilliant in this opera. The others were only fair. Tesi was gifted by nature with a masculinely strong contralto voice. In the year 1719 at Dresden she sang on several occasions the kind of arias which are usually composed for bassos. By now she had acquired, in addition to the magnificent serious tone in her singing, a pleasant softness. The range of her voice was extremely wide, neither high nor low notes being difficult for her. A display of virtuosity was not her strong point. She seemed to be born to impress the audience with her acting, especially in male roles which she performed almost naturally.

The first church composer in Naples was the Oberkapellmeister and Knight, Alessandro Scarlatti, under whom the present Oberkapellmeister of Saxon music, Herr Hasse, was studying couterpoint. The others were

Mancini, Leo, and Feo. The orchestra was fairly good. There were no outstanding instrumentalists except for the incomparable violoncellist Franchischello, who later joined the Imperial service.

Herr Hasse asked me to live with him, and we became good friends. At that time he had not performed any music publicly in Italy. However, a well-to-do Neapolitan banker asked him to compose a Serenata for two persons, which he accomplished during my stay with him, and Farinelli and Tesi sang in it. Through this Serenata Herr Hasse received so much acclaim that he was immediately entrusted with composing an opera, which was to be performed in the Royal Theatre in May of that year. This opera led the way to his future success.

I asked Hasse to acquaint me with his master, old Scarlatti, to which he gave his immediate consent. However, he received the following answer: "My son, (this is what Scarlatti used to call him) you know I cannot stand 'blowing' instrumentalists, they all 'blow' falsely." Nevertheless, Herr Hasse continued to request that the old man see me, until he finally received permission to bring me to him. I heard Scarlatti play on the clavicembalo, which he knew how to play in a learned way although he did not possess as much finesse as his son. After this he accompanied me in a solo. I had the good fortune to win his favour, in fact so much so that he composed a few flute solos for me. He introduced me at various distinguished houses and even wanted to obtain for me a position in the Portuguese service with a substantial salary, but I considered it wise to decline. This man is the Scarlatti whom Heinchen mentioned in various places in his *Der Gereralbass in der Composition*. He was not only one of the greatest contrapuntists of his time, but also one of the most fertile composers that have ever lived. He is not only the author of a great number of operas, but it is said of him that he, not considering Psalms for Vespers and other compositions, has composed 200 masses. In fact, a certain Neapolitan courtier boasted of possessing 4000 samples of Scarlatti's work, mostly solo cantatas, and in many instances the texts were also written by Scarlatti. While I cannot vouch for the exact truth of this number, I do know definitely that the number of his compositions is very large. In Germany, however, Telemann might be considered a strong rival in this respect as the latter has undoubtedly composed even more when all of his work is taken into consideration.

In honor of Count von Lichtenstein, who was in Naples at this time with his wife, several concertos were performed by the greatest musicians of the country. Besides Hasse, Farinelli, Tesi, and Francischello, I too had the honor of being invited to play, and on this occasion gained the personal acquaintance and friendship of Farinelli.

On March 23 of this year I left Naples and returned to Rome to hear the famous *Miserere* by Allegri in the Papal Chapel on Good Friday. Here I was offered a position with the present Bishop of Dornick, who was then Count von Salm, to whom I gave lessons on the flute, and in whose company I climbed Mt. Vesuvius. But again I declined the offer. I remained in Rome until October 21. At this time I was given leave by Count von Lagnasco and now began to travel at my own expense, going to Florence. Here I heard several operas, all of which were patched together with arias of various masters, which is called "pastry" by the Italians, "un pasticcio". The best among the singers were the two tenors Pinacci and Annibali Pio Fabris. The former was a fiery, the latter a pleasant and brilliant singer. The strongest point of the former was his acting ability. Canfani was an agreeable violinist, and Bencini a good performer on the clavier. Palafuti, who had once accompanied the Knight Perfetti in Rome when the latter was solemnly crowned a poet, was a good *theorbist*. Ludwig Erdmann, a German, was not a bad oboist and at the same time very friendly toward his fellow countrymen.

On January 8, 1726, I went from Florence to Livorno to hear an opera, and from there to Bologna where a comic opera was being performed.

On February 4 I heard an opera at Ferarra, and thereupon went to Venice, via Padua. Here two operas were being performed during the carnival in the theatre which bore the name of St. John Chrysostomus. One was *Siface* by Porpora, the other *Siroe* by Vinci. Both composers were present, but the latter opera was acclaimed more than the former. Cavalier Nicolino, a contralto, Romanina, a low soprano, and the famous tenor Giovanni Paita added luster to the performance. Nicolino, whose real name was Grimaldi, and Romanina, whose real name was Marianna Benti Bulgarelli, were both only fair singers but excellent actors. Paita had a not very strong, but pleasant, tenor voice which would not have been as beautiful or even by nature if he had not known the art of combining the head voice with the chest voice. His way of singing was masterful in an adagio, his delivery moving, and the ornaments reasonable. He did not sing an allegro with the greatest of fire, but on the other hand, not lifelessly either. He did not use many *passagien;* his acting was fairly good. The orchestra playing these operas was not bad and was led by the Bolognese Laurenti, a good violinist.

Vivaldi had composed the operas at the *Theatro San Angelo* and was himself the leader of the orchestra. The actors were very mediocre.

I did not find many good instrumentalists in Venice besides the violinists Vivaldi and Madonis and the oboist, San Martino from Milan.

The three composers: Lotti, Benedetto Marcello, and Albinoni, all of them well-known, were studying in Venice at the time.

The best church music was heard in the orphanages, *alla Pietà alli Incurabili,* and *ai Mendicanti,* performed only by girls. The *alla Pietà* was at that time superior. Apollonia, a very strong singer, and another girl who played the violin, were very well liked here. Besides these, there was Angeletta, who had been brought up in the orphanage, but had married a banker. She had a beautiful voice and was strong in singing as well as on the clavier. She was the one who first acquainted Kapellmeister Heinchen with the Electoral Prince of Saxony, now King of Poland.

In Venice I received Royal permission through Count von Lagnasco in Rome, to go to France. My necessary expenses were to be paid, but I have never received this remuneration.

On May 11 I traveled via Modena to Reggio and Parma. In both places operas were being performed. The one in Parma was *I Fratelli riconosciuti*. The music was by the then very famous Giovanni Maria Capelli, a clergyman, who was at the same time a fiery and inventive composer. The best singers were the above mentioned Farinelli, whose real name is Carlo Broschi, Giovanni Carestini, and Paita.

Farinelli had a well-carrying, well-rounded, rich, high, and even soprano voice, the range of which extended from the "a" below middle "c" to the "d" above the staff. Many years later it increased in depth several tones without losing the high ones. For this reason, in many operas, an adagio was usually written for him in contralto range, and the others in soprano range. His intonation was pure, his *trillo* beautiful, his chest unusually strong in the long holding of tones. His throat was very flexible, so that he could produce the largest intervals quickly and with the greatest of ease and certainty. Broken passages, as well as all other runs, provided no difficulty for him, and he was very prolific in his use of the optional ornaments of an adagio. The fire of his youth, his great talent, the general acclaim, and his fluent throat, at times caused him to be wasteful of his talent. His figure was favorable for the theatre, but his acting did not particularly come from the heart. The good fortune which became his later in Spain—after visiting England and France— making him a Knight of the Order of Calatrava and Director of the Royal Music is so well known that it is not necessary to go into detail here.

Carestini also had a strong and well-rounded soprano voice, which by and by changed to one of the most beautiful, strong, and low contraltos. At that time his range extended from approximately the "b" below middle "c" to the "c" above the staff at the most. He showed great fire in *passagien* and like Farinelli, according to the good school of Bernacchi, thrust these out with the chest. He undertook many arbitrary changes, usually successfully, but sometimes to excess. His acting was very good, and his singing fiery. Later he improved very much in the singing of an adagio.

From Parma I went to Milan. Here I heard a serenata in which again, Farinelli, and Antonio Pasi were singing. Pasi had a pleasant soprano voice, the range of which was not, however, extremely high. His way of singing an adagio was masterful, and his delivery convincing. The high notes created some difficulty for him, and were not always pleasing, which detracted somewhat from the purity of his intonation. He lacked the vocal ease which is necessary for an allegro movement.

The Milan orchestra had much excellent material, especially the violinists, among whom were several skillful people. Tedeschini, a Swiss, was a good leader, but here, too, as in all of Italy, there was a lack of basses, and excepting the oboist San Martino, of wind instruments, without which an orchestra cannot be complete. The two church composers, San Martino, brother of the oboist, and Fiorini, were not bad. Among the nuns there were several singers gifted with beautiful voices, who did not lack good singing style. In fact, I found everywhere in Italy, among the feminine sex, more beautiful voices and better singers in the nunneries than in the theatres.

On May 30, I went from Milan to Turin. The Royal Orchestra there, which was led by the famous violinist Somis, was composed of good musicians, but did not excel over the Milan orchestra. Fiore was the Kapellmeister. LeClaire, now one of the foremost violinists of France, was then in Turin studying with Somis. There were no good singers, with the exception of Mlle. Somis, who had a beautiful soprano voice and a good singing style. She later married the famous painter Carlo Vanlo, and went to France with him, where she now lives.

I left Turin, and thus Italy, on the 23rd of June, 1726, and traveled over Mt. Senis through Geneva and Lyon to Paris, where I arrived on the 15th of August.

Here, due to the musical taste, I was placed from one extreme into the other, from diversity into monotony. Though the French style was not unknown to me and I did like their manner of playing very much, I liked neither the warmed-over and worn ideas of their opera composers, nor the small difference between recitative and aria, nor the exaggerated and affected howling of her male singers, and especially her female singers. Antier, Pelissier, and Le Maure were then singing in the theatre. These French singers did not lack beautiful voices, if only they had known how to use them correctly. The male voices, also, as received from nature were not bad. Besides several operas by Lully, a new one called *Pyrame e Thisbe* was performed. Its joint composers were Francoeur and Rebel. The former had been in Vienna with General Bonneval and had also heard the Prague opera of 1723. One could notice in the arias composed by him that their author had been outside the borders of France, in fact, the whole opera bored me less than the others.

The greatest splendor of their operas really consisted of their acting, at which the French nation is particularly good, the stage sets, and the dances. The orchestra was poor at that time, and played more according to ear and memory than the written music, and had to be kept in order by time beating with a big stick. However, outside of the orchestra, there was no lack of good instrumentalists. Fortcroix and Roland Marais were good gambists. The first had a great deal of skill, but the latter had more neatness and pleasantness in his playing. Guignon and Battiste were good violinists. The former played in the Italian, the latter in the French style. Blavet, Lucas, the two brothers Braun, Naudot, and several others played the transverse flute. Among them Blavet was the best. His helpfulness and good way of living caused us to become friends, and I must praise him for the many kindnesses which he showed me in various ways. Also, there was no lack of good organists, clavier players, and violoncellists.

I preferred the church music of the French to their operas.

The *Concert Spirituel* and *Concert Italien* were not to be looked down upon, but the former was visited more than the latter. The reason for this was undoubtedly a prejudice against foreign music, a disease of the French nation which will prevent her from bettering her style of music as long as she persists in this prejudice.

In Paris, for the first time I had the second key added to the transverse flute. The reason for this is found in my *Versuch einer Anweisung die Flöte zu spielen.*

In the beginning of the year 1727 I received orders from Dresden to speed up my return. Thus I did not dare to ask for new permission to go to England. However, my desire to see this country was so great that I dared to travel there without asking permission from the court. On March 10 I left Paris and arrived in London, via Calais, on March 20. Le Riche, former chamber oboist in Dresden and a friend of mine for many years, had sent me an open letter addressed to a merchant in London, on the basis of which I could draw as much money there as I needed.

The Italian operas were then in their fullest bloom in London. Among Handel's compositions, *Admetus* was the newest and had splendid music. Faustina, Cuzzoni, and Senesino—all three virtuosos of the first rank—were the main actors, the others being mediocre.

Cuzzoni had a very agreeable and clear soprano voice, a pure intonation and beautiful *trillo*. Her range extended from middle "c" to the "c" above the staff. Her ornamentation did not seem to be artificial due to her nice, pleasant, and light style of delivery, and with its tenderness she won the hearts of her listeners. The *passagien* in the allegros were not done with the greatest facility, but she sang them very fully and pleasantly. Her acting was somewhat cold, and her figure was not too favorable for the theatre.

Faustina had a not very clear, but well-carrying mezzo-soprano voice which at the time did not range much more than from the "b flat" below middle "c" to the "g" above the staff, but in time increased several tones in depth. Her way of singing was expressive and brilliant (*un cantar granito*), and she had a light tongue, being able to pronounce words rapidly but plainly in succession. She had a facile throat and a beautiful and very polished *trillo* which she could apply with the greatest of ease wherever and whenever she pleased. The *passagien* could be either running or

leaping, or could consist of many fast notes in succession on one tone. She knew how to thrust these out
skillfully, with the greatest possible rapidity, as they
can be performed only on an instrument. She is unquestionably the first who has used these *passagien* consisting of many notes on one tone in singing, and with
the best possible success. She sang an adagio with much
emotion and expression, provided no extremely sad
emotion dominated the movement, which can be expressed only by a double appagiatura (Schleifer) or a
steady flow of the voice. She had a good memory for
arbitrary changes and an excellent judgment in giving
the proper stress to the words which she delivered with
great clarity. She was especially strong in acting,
because she had such a high degree of ability in the
dramatic art (or, to use Herr Matheson's expression,
'the hypocritic') and could assume any expression she
pleased. She was equally well suited for a serious,
amorous, or tender role. In one word, she was born
for singing and acting.

The orchestra consisted mostly of Germans, a few
Italians, and some Englishmen. Castrucci, an Italian
violinist, was the leader, under Handel's direction they
made a very good impression.

The second opera I heard in London was by Bononcini, but it was not as popular as the first. Handel's
workmanship (*Grundstimme*) was better than Bononcini's melodic line (*Oberstimme*). In this opera, two
factions were heard from, one in favor of Faustina, and
the other in favor of Cuzzoni. The factions were so

incensed that one whistled when the other applauded, and vice versa, so that finally the opera had to be suspended for the time being.

Pater Attilio, an opera composer, was in London at this time, as well as the old castrato, Tosi, who has written a useful book about the art of singing.

There were only a few solo instrumentalists, for example, Handel, as is known, on the clavier and the organ; Geminiani, a great master on the violin; Debur, an Englishman, and student of Geminiani, a very pleasing violinist. The two brothers Castrucci were fair soloists. Mauro d'Alaia, who had come to England in the company of Faustina, was a good violinist and a good leader. His playing was neat and quite brilliant, although he did not go in for extraordinary difficulties. The flautists were Wiedemann, a German and Festin, an Englishman.

I had the good fortune to be made acquainted in many elegant homes. In fact, one tried to persuade me to remain in England. Handel himself suggested this, and I was not adverse to following his advice. Milady Pembrok, a connoisseur of music, wanted to give a benefit for me.*

*A benefit in England is, as understood musically, a public concert given for the sake of a virtuoso who is heard at this concert and which is sponsored by a person of high rank, in a home especially selected for this purpose. The sponsor sees to it that admission tickets are distributed, and friends of the performing musician compete in trying to sell as many tickets as possible. All the proceeds are given to the person for whom the benefit is given. However, he also bears the cost. Sometimes the proceeds of the performance of an opera go to the composer or to a popular singer, after this has been announced by proclamation, and this is also called a benefit. Faustina and Farinelli especially have experienced the generosity of the English on occasions such as these.

This provided, of course, a great temptation for me.
I believed, however, to owe the first fruits of my trip
to the King, my Lord, and thus decided to decline the
offer. However I reserved for myself the possibility of
taking advantage of this offer another time, in case I
ever returned to England, which I was really willing
to do if circumstances should allow it.

On June 1, 1727, I left England. In Holland I toured
the leading cities, such as Amsterdam, The Hague,
Leiden, Rotterdam, etc., only briefly as there was no
good music in any of them at that time. I then went
via Hannover and Braunschweig back to Dresden,
where I arrived on July 23.

Now I reflected on all the good and bad music that
I had heard on my journey. I found that I had
gathered quite a store of ideas, but that it would be
necessary to put them in proper order. In every place
in which I had stopped I had composed something, imitating the style prevalent there. But, I also thought
about the merit which the original has over the imitation. Thus I began to direct my greatest efforts toward
the goal of forming a personal style so that possibly
I too could become an originator in music. However,
it would take thought, experience, and time to achieve
this. Thus, whereas formerly a composition might be
finished in an hour, I now allowed myself a day's time,
being only too sure that the first ideas might be successful, but that they are, if not always the worst, certainly
not always the best. That, in fact, a fine sensitivity and
mature judgment are necessary to purify them and

bring them into their proper relationship to one another, so that a piece will be popular not only for a short time and fleetingly, but, if possible, always. For this good plan the constant intercourse with my dearest friend, Herr Concertmeister Pisendel, and his wholly correct and penetrating judgment, stood me in good stead. The beautiful church music, the excellent operas, and exceptionally fine vocal virtuosos whom I could hear in Dresden constantly, brought me new pleasure and set me always newly afire.

Up to this time I had been oboist and flautist in the Polish Kapelle, and my yearly salary had consisted of 216 thalers. However, during my journey, my place had been given to another, and I was transferred to the Saxon Kapelle. This happened in the month of March in the year 1728, after the death of a violinist whose salary of 250 thalers I received, but also retained my salary from the Polish Kapelle. From this time on I abandoned the oboe completely, because its embouchure is different from the flute, and remained solely with the transverse flute.

In May of this year I traveled with the Chief Steward, Baron von Seyfetiz, in the train of the Most Serene King of Poland to Berlin, where upon the demand of Her Majesty, the Queen of Prussia, and with permission of the King of Poland, I had to remain several months. Pisendel, Weiss, and Buffardi also were ordered to come here.

After I had the honor of allowing myself to be heard several times before Her Majesty, the Queen, I was offered a position by Her Highness for 800 thalers a year. I was ready to accept, but the King, my master, would not agree. However, I did receive permission to go to Berlin as often as I was asked for.

In the same year, 1728, the Crown Prince of Prussia, now His Reigning Majesty, decided to study the transverse flute and I had the honor of teaching His Highness. For this reason I had to go to Berlin, Ruppin, or Reinsberg twice every year.

After the death of the King of Poland in 1733, His Now Reigning Majesty of Poland did not want to release me from his service. Rather, he raised my salary to 800 thalers, and confirmed again the above mentioned permission which I had received for trips to Berlin. Since I had the honor of also instructing His Excellency, the Margrave of Bayreuth on the flute, which had begun in Berlin, I also had reason to be called to Bayreuth now and then.

In the year 1734 I had 6 solos for the transverse flute engraved. I do not acknowledge the edition of other sonatas which were published under my name long before in Holland.

On June 26, 1737, I married the widowed Frau Anne Rosina Caroline Schindlerin, née Hölzelin, whose deceased father had been a captain in the Bavarian service at the fortress of Braunau.

Because of the lack of good flutes, I began in the year 1739 to drill and tune some myself, which practice never did me any harm.

In November 1741, I was called by His Majesty of

Prussia to Berlin for the last time, and offered a position by His Highness with such favorable conditions that I could no longer refuse to accept: two thousand thalers a year for life, plus a special payment for my compositions, a hundred Dukaten for each flute that I would construct, the privilege of not having to play in the orchestra, but only in the Royal chamber music, and not having to take orders from anyone but the King. All this justified my giving up a service from which I could never hope for such advantages. His Majesty, the King of Poland, was too merciful to refuse me for long the release which I sought in writing, especially since I was not obliged to His Highness as a countryman, nor did the traveling money advanced me, in addition to my salary, oblige me to stay.

Thus I left Dresden in December, 1741, since I began to serve in the Royal Prussian Service at that time.

In the year 1752, I let my *Versuch einer Anweisung die Flötetraversiere zu spielen* be published. Around this time I also invented the detachable head, with which one can make a flute a half tone higher or lower, without changing the middle pieces, and without damaging its pure tone. In fact, all of the royal music here—the dominating, sensible, mixed and lovely style of theatrical composition; the various good Italian vocal virtuosos whom we have had, or still have; the good orchestra, which already in the years 1731-1740 was in such good condition that it attracted every good composer and player to Ruppin and Reinsberg, and could give complete satisfaction; and which finally was improved into becoming one of the finest orchestras in Europe after the beginning of the present reign: the various outstanding virtuosos who are in this orchestra—all this, I say, is already so well-known and famous that it would be superfluous to describe each in detail according to its merit.

This is my career, and in this way Divine Providence has guided me, and has fulfilled the desire which I had many years ago during times when it did not seem likely that I should make my fortune either in Dresden or Berlin. I am grateful to Providence and to the mercy of the King, that I find myself in a desired state of well-being.

Johann Joachim Quantz.
Potsdam, August 1754.

LIST OF ABBREVIATIONS

I. PERIODICALS

SIMG   *Sammelbände der Internationalen Musikgesellschaft* (quarterly, 1900-14).

SzMw   *Studien zur Musikwissenschaft* (Beihefte der Denkmäler der Tonkunst in Oesterreich; annual, 1913-34).

ZfMw   *Zeitschrift für Musikwissenschaft* (monthly, 1918-35).

II. BOOKS

DTB   *Denkmäler der Tonkunst in Bayern*, 65 vols., 1892-1931.

DTOe   *Denkmäler der Tonkunst in Oesterreich*, 83 vols., 1894-1938.

Quellenlexikon   *Biographisch-bibliographisches Quellenlexikon der Musiker und Musikgelehrten der Christlichen Zeitrechnung bis zur Mitte des 19. Jahrhunderts*, by Robert Eitner, 10 vols., Leipzig, 1899-1904.

Lexikon   *Neues historisch-biographisches Lexikon der Tonkünstler*, by Ernst L. Gerber, 4 vols., Leipzig, 1812-14.

NOTES TO THE AUTOBIOGRAPHICAL TEXTS

PAGE

162   "Freyung." A street in Vienna.

162   "Gsur," Tobias. Gsur was *Regens chori* at the Benedictine church on the Freyung. From 1772 until his death, bass singer in the Imperial *Hofkapelle* and choir director at the *Schotten* in Vienna. His successor was Joseph Eybler, well-known from Mozart's biography.

163   "Huber," Karl. Appointed (1772) to the *Hofkapelle;* died (1779) in Vienna at the age of sixty-four. Cf. Köchel, L. von, *Die kaiserliche Hofmusikkapelle zu Wien von 1543-1867*, Vienna, 1868.

164   "Hubaczek." One of two brothers, both horn players, in the service of Prince Hildburghausen.

164   "Prince Joseph (Maria) Friedrich (Wilhelm) von Hildburghausen." Hildburghausen, a successful Field-Marshal in the Turkish wars, resigned after the defeat of Rossbach (1757), for which he was held responsible. He lived as a *Grand Signeur* and patron of music in

NOTES

Vienna. Beginning *ca.* 1740, his orchestral *Akademien* took place on Friday evenings, if there were no theatrical performances. As an aristocratic patron of orchestral music, he was a predecessor of Prince Esterhazy.

165 "Jomelli," Nicola (1714-74). One of the most important operatic composers of the neo-Neapolitan school. Often called the "Italian Gluck."

165 "Bonno," Giuseppe (1710-88). Imperial Court Composer and later *Kapellmeister* (1774) in conjunction with Salieri. Mozart wrote to his father on Apr. 11, 1781, that "he is an old, honest, good man." Cf. Wellesz, E., *Giuseppe Bonno, SIMG* 1909/10; and Schienerl, A., *Giuseppe Bonnos Kirchenkompositionen, SzMw,* 15.

167 "Tesi." Tesi-Tramontini, Vittoria (1700 or 1706-75). Celebrated singer. Legend has it that she was in love with Handel. For a description of her voice, see Quantz' autobiography, p. 302 below.

168 "Metastasio" (r. Tiapassi), Pietro (1698-1782). Famous librettist and court poet. Cf. Nettl, P., *The Other Casanova,* New York, 1950.

168 "Farinelli" (r. Broschi), Carlo (1705-82). One of the most famous castrati of the 18th century. His Spanish sojourn lasted from 1737-59. In 1761 he settled in Bologna. Cf. Nettl, *op. cit.;* and Quantz' autobiography, p. 307 below, for a description of his voice.

172 "Trani," Joseph. Violinist in the Viennese *Hofkapelle* from 1767-88; d. 1797, at the age of 90, accord. to Köchel, *op. cit.* Because of his advanced age he functioned only as a teacher in the Hildburghausen orchestra.

172 "Schlosshof." Castle built by Lukas von Hildebrandt for Prince Eugene of Savoy (1725). Located in lower Austria, near the confluence of the March and the Danube.

172 "Pompeati," Angelo. Husband of the famous singer, Theresa Pompeati. Cf. Nettl, *op. cit.,* pps. 89ff., 92ff., 127ff.

173 "Locatelli," Pietro (1693-1764). An audacious virtuoso, renowned for his cadenzas. A pupil of Corelli.

173 "Zuccarini" (Zuccari), Carlo. Violinist; in the mid-18th century in London. Cf. Moser, A., *Geschichte des Violinspiels,* 1923, p. 285.

173 "Tartini," Giuseppe (1692-1770). Virtuoso violinist and composer. As *Maestro delle Nazioni* he had pupils from all over Europe. He wrote *ca.* 140 concertos, his *Devil's Trill Sonata* winning for him a world-wide reputation.

173 "Ferrari," Domenico (1722-80). Celebrated virtuoso, especially successful in Paris where he played in 1754. He was a master at playing harmonics.

174 "Heinisch," Teresia. Soprano, wife of Pettmann. Cf. Pohl, *Joseph Haydn,* 1875. Vol. I, p. 115.

174 "Fribert" (Frieberth), Joseph. *Ca.* 1784, *Kapellmeister* in Passau. Composer of *Singspiele.* Cf. Reichardt, *Theaterkalender in Gotha,* 1785.

175 *"Il ballo cinese."* The performance took place on Sept. 24, 1754. Cf. Schmidt, A., *Christoph Willibald Ritter von Gluck,* 1854, p. 53; Wotquenne, *Thematisches Verzeichnis der Werke Glucks,* 1904, p. 196.

175 "Starzer," Katharina. Soprano. Cf. Pohl, *op. cit.,* I, p. 115.

177 "Quaglio," Giovanni Maria. Member of a famous family of artists.

179 "Fux," Johann Joseph (1660-1741). His *Gradus ad Parnassum* was published in 1725, and translated into German by Mitzler in 1742.

NOTES

180   *"Cavaliere dello Sperone d'oro"* (Knight of the Golden Spur). Other famous musicians who were members of this order: Orlando Lasso, A. Scarlatti, Mozart, and Abbé Vogler. Not all of Gluck's contemporaries considered this an outstanding honor.

180   "Bibiena," Ferdinando (1657-1743). Famous theatrical architect and painter.

180   "Guarini," Giovanni Battista (1538-1612). Famous poet and author of the pastoral poem, *Il pastor fido.*

180   "1758" is wrong and should read "1756."

182   "Durazzo," Count Giacomo. From 1754, director of the Viennese theatres. A partisan of Gluck, he arranged Metastasio's libretto, *L'Innocenza Giustificata,* for him in 1755. Cf. Einstein, A., *DTOe,* Vol. 82 (forward); Haas, R., *Gluck und Durazzo im Burgtheater,* 1925.

184   *"Gränzinger."* Evidently, *"Grinzinger."* Dittersdorf calls it "the best Austrian wine."Today it is served mostly as *Heuriger* (young wine).

184   "Mestre." Suburb of Venice.

185   "Mazzoni," Antonio. Accord. to Fétis, he was born in Bologna, in 1718. At the time Burney met him there in 1770 he was second *maestro di capella* at the cathedral. Cf. Fétis, *Biographie universelle des musiciens,* Paris, 1837-44; Eitner, R., *Quellenlexikon.*

186   "Spagnoletti," (Paolo Diana?). Grove (*Dictionary of Music and Musicians,* 4th ed., 1940) gives his birthdate as 1768. If this date were correct, he would have had to play five years before his birth when Dittersdorf heard him. E. Heron-Allen, Esq., who wrote the article on Spagnoletti in Grove misquotes Eitner (*Quellenlexikon*), claiming that Eitner gives Spagnoletti's birthdate as 1761.

186   "Lolli," Antonio (*ca.* 1730-1802). Cf. Moser, A., *Arcangelo Corelli und Antonio Lolli, ZfMw,* III, p. 415.

187   "Archduke Joseph's coronation." Imperial coronation of Joseph II, Apr. 3, 1764, in Frankfort.

188   "Patachich," Adam, Freiherr von Zajezda (1717-84). From 1759, Bishop of Grosswardein (Hungarian Nagyvárad). His tolerance and kindness in religious affairs won over thousands to the Roman church. Cf. Wurzbach, *Biographiches Lexikon des Kaiserthums Oesterreich,* 21, p. 341f.

188   "Haydn," Michael (1737-1806). Haydn left Grosswardein in 1762, taking another position as concertmaster in Salzburg.

190   "Fuchs," Peter (1753?-1831). Cf. Pohl, *op. cit.,* II, p. 18; Eitner, *op. cit.* Eitner's reference, based on Köchel (*op. cit.*), does not agree with the time of engagement recorded by Dittersdorf. If Eitner's date is correct, Fuchs would have been a very young boy, too young to hold such an important position as concertmaster.

190   Pichel (Pichl), Wenzel (1741-1807; accord. to Gerber, *Lexikon,* died in 1805). Pichel was a violinist and a prolific composer. A. Moser (*Geschichte des Violinspiels*) says that his compositions for the violin are among the best in the literature, comparing his studies with those of Fiorillo. Cf. Dlabacz, *Kunstlerlexikon für Böhmen,* 1815.

190   "Pater Michael." Harpsichordist and organist at the monastery of the Minorites in Vienna. Cf. Eitner, *op. cit.*

190   "Himmelbauer," Wenzel. Cf. Eitner, *op. cit.*

190   "Oliva," (Giuseppe, accord. to Gerber, *op. cit.*). French hornist;

supposedly a member of the Esterhazy *Kapelle* under Haydn.

191 "Naumann," Johann Michael. Naumann built the cathedral in Grosswardein from 1762-82. Cf. Thieme-Becker, *Allgemeines Lexikon der bildenden Künstler*.

195 "Bavarian War of Succession." Lasting from 1778-9, it was terminated by the Peace of Teschen. As head magistrate of Freiwaldau, Dittersdorf founded, in 1788, the *Weiler Dittersdorf*. Cf. *Altvater* (Silesian Journal), 1900, p. 114.

198 "chastity commission." This commission was introduced by Maria Theresia. Memories of it survive in H. von Hofmannsthal's and R. Strauss's *Rosenkavalier*. Cf. Nettl, *op. cit.*, p. 146.

199 "Greybig" (Kreibich), Franz (1728-1797), Greybig was a violin virtuoso and conductor. In his capacity as a member of the house *Kapelle* of Joseph II he was the butt of many jokes. Cf. Abert, *Mozart*, I. p. 888.

FRANZ BENDA'S AUTOBIOGRAPHY

205 "Brixi" (Brixy). Family name of a number of well-known Bohemian musicians active during the 18th century. The most prominent member of the family was Franz Xavier (1732-1771), whose father, Simon (d. 1737), was *Regens chori* and organist at St. Martin in Prague. Simon is evidently the one mentioned by Benda.

205 "St. Nicolai Church." Situated in the "old city"; from 1635 in possession of the Benedictines. Cf. Schönfeld. *Vollständige Beschreibung der königlichen Haupt und Residenzstadt Prag*, Prague, 1787, I, p. 126.

205 "Czernin." Member of a well-known aristocratic Czech family.

206 "Rakonitz." A town in northwest Bohemia, not far from Pilsen.

207 "Heinichen," Johann David (1683-1729). Well-known from his *Der General-Bass in der Composition* (1728), one of the best works of its kind. From 1717, *Hofkapellmeister* in Dresden. Cf. Hiller, J. A. *Lebensbeschreibungen berühmter Musikgelehrten und Tonkünstler*, 1784; Seibel, *Joh. David Heinichen*, diss., 1913.

207 "Pyrna" (Pirna). A town on the Elbe, in the foothills of the *Sächsische Schweiz*.

208 "Counts von Kleinau" (r. Klenau). Cf., Helfert, Vladimir, *Jiri Benda*, I, 1929, p. 38.

209 "Melnicker wine." Made in a famous Bohemian wine center, Melnik, situated at the confluence of the Moldau and the Elbe.

209 "Charles VI." The coronation took place in 1723, on which occasion a number of musical works were performed. (See the footnote to page 294, below). Cf. Köchel, *J. J. Fux*, 1872; Wellesz, ed., *Costanza e Fortezza*, *DTOe*, XVII, 34 and 35; and Quantz' autobiography, pps. 294ff. below.

209 "Zelenka," Johann Dismas (born, accord. to Dlabacz, *op. cit.*, ca. 1680- d. 1745). He composed a Latin comedy, *Melodrama de Sancto Wenceslao*, for the coronation of Charles VI.

NOTES

210 "Ursini" (r. Orsini), Cajetano (Gaetano) (d. 1750, at the age of 83). Alto, member of the *Hofkapelle* in Vienna. He sang the role of *Porsenna* in Fux's *Costanza e Fortezza*, and at an operatic performance on the occasion of the Empress Elizabeth's birthday in the Bohemian town of Znaim. Cf. Nettl, *Musik-Barock in Böhmen und Mähren*, 1927, p. 16. See below, footnote to p. 294.

210 "Vivaldi," Antonio (*ca.* 1680-1743). Famous composer and violinist.

210 "*Bierfiedler.*" Literally, "beer fiddler." A derogatory expression applied to musicians of lower social and artistic classes.

211 "Konyczek." Served, *ca.* 1722, in the *Kapelle* of Prince Lobkowitz. Cf. Dlabacz, *op. cit.*

212 "Lebel." Cf. pps. 28ff. *supra.*

213 "Uhlefeld," Count Corfitz Anton (1699-1760). Ambassador to Turkey. He was the father of Maria Wilhelmine, and the father-in-law of Franz Josef Thun, the latter two being famous patrons of Mozart. *Geschichte des Oestreichischen Hofs und Adels*, 1851, 7-8, p. 235.

213 "Francischello." A famous violoncellist in the early part of the 18th century. Praised by Quantz and Geminiani, as well as Benda. Cf. Fétis, *op. cit.;* Eitner, *op. cit.*

214 "Czarth" (or Tzarth, or Zarth) (1708-1778). The name was probably originally "Cert" (devil). He was one of the most highly praised violinists and composers for the violin of his time. Cf. *DTB*, XV and XVI; Walter, *Geschichte des Theaters und der Musik am Kurpfälzischen Hofe*, 1898.

214 "Pachta," Count. Member of a famous aristocratic Bohemian family. Cf. Nettl, *Mozart in Böhmen*, 1938, p. 99.

215 "Ohlau." The "*Ohlauer Vorstadt*" in the eastern part of Breslau.

218 "Hoecks" (Höckh), Carl (1707-1772). On the recommendation of Benda he was appointed concertmaster in Zerbst in 1733. In 1759 he replaced J. F. Fasch as court *Kapellmeister*. His autobiography is in Marpurg, *Historisch-Kritische Beyträge zur Aufnahme der Musik*, 1754-58, and 1778, III. Cf. Moser, *Geschichte des Violinspiels*, p. 331.

218 "Bruehl," Count Heinrich (1700-1763). From 1733 he was *Kammerpräsident* to August II (the Strong); from 1746, Prime Minister of Saxony and Poland, and the real ruler of Saxony under August III.

218 "King August." August II, or, as the Saxon Elector, August I (1670-1733). The exact date of his death (p. 220) was Feb. 1, 1733.

222 "Pisendel," Johann Georg (1687-1755). One of the most outstanding violinists of his time. Cf. Hiller, *Lebensbeschreibungen*, 1784; Moser, *op. cit.*, p. 316.

222 "Fasch," Johann Friedrich (1688-1758). He was the founder of the famous Berlin *Singakademie*. Cf. Hiller, *op. cit.;* Engelke, B., *J. F. Fasch*, diss., 1908; and the same title in *SIMG, X*, 1909.

222 "materialist." An old (colloquial) Austrian expression denoting the owner of a combination drug-hardware store.

223 "Graun," Johann Gottlieb (1702-1771). Johann Gottlieb was the concertmaster in Berlin; his brother, Karl Heinrich (1703 or4—1759) was the *Kapellmeister*. Cf. Mennicke, *Zur Biographie der Brüder Graun*, in *Neue Zeitschrift für Musik*, XIII, 1904; Moser, *op. cit.*, p. 39.

224 "Reinsberg" (Rheinsberg). Town in the *Kreis Ruppin*, near Potsdam. It was bought by Frederick William II and given to his son,

NOTES

the Crown Prince (later, Frederick II, the Great) who rebuilt the castle and the gardens. He lived there during the last years before he became king. Cf. Fontane, F., *Wanderungen durch die Mark Brandenburg*, 1925.

224   "Quantz," Johann Joachim. See his autobiography, pps. 280-319 below.

225   "youngest brother." Benda, Joseph (b. 1725 accord. to Reichardt). He joined the Berlin *Kapelle* in 1740, substituting as concertmaster for his brother, whose position he received in 1786. He retired in 1797, and died in his 80th year on Feb. 22, 1804.

225   "the elder one." Benda, Georg (1722-1795). The most important composer of all the brothers. He composed many *Singspiele*, and was one of the creators of the *melodrama*. From 1750, *Hofkapellmeister* in Gotha. Cf. Helfert, *op. cit.*; Istel, E., *Die Entstehung des deutschen Melodrams*, 1906.

225   "Gitschin" (Jitschin). Town in N.E. Bohemia. One of the more important Bohemian towns of the 18th century, although somewhat impoverished today. Georg studied there at the Jesuit *Gymnasium*.

225   "Jung-Buntzlau" (Mladá Boleslav). Town in N. E. Bohemia, situated on the Iser.

226   "Hattasch," Dismas (*ca.* 1725-1777). Cf. Dlabacz, *op. cit.*; Forkel, J. N., *Musikalish-kritische Bibliotek*, 1778.

226   "Nowawes." A town (the name means "new village") in the *Kreis Teltow* near Potsdam. Nowawes was founded by Frederick II for the Czech Protestants.

228   "Rudolstadt" (Rudolfstadt). Formerly the capital of the Principality of Schwarzburg-Rudolstadt. Located on the Saale.

230   *"Malum Hypocondriacum."* At that time, a term used to describe various intestinal disorders. Neefe also uses the expression (p. 284 below).

230   "Kayserling," Count Hermann Carl von. From 1733-45, Russian ambassador in Dresden. It was he who ordered, through Goldberg, the famous *Goldberg Variations* from Bach. Pisendel, Weisse, Friedemann Bach, and many other musicians were his guests at one time or another. Spitta (*Bach*, II, p. 706) says he left Dresden in 1745, a date which conflicts with Benda's chronology.

231   "repeater." A watch with a striking apparatus which, upon pressure from a spring, will indicate the time.

231   "the Cardinal." Cardinal Klemens August, Prince-Archbishop of Cologne (1723-61), was the brother referred to. He was a great lover and patron of music. Cf. Thayer, A. W., *Ludwig von Beethoven*, 1917, I, p. 24.

223   *"Musikalische Lebensläuffe."* This refers to Marpurg's *Historisch-kritische Beyträge zur Aufnahme der Musik*.

235   "Arndt," Johann (1555-1621). His *Wahres Christentum* (True Christianity) shows him to be a forerunner of Pietism.

236   "Loescher," Valentin Ernst (1637-1749). Lutheran theologian, founder of the first theological journal in Germany. As one of the most important representatives of Lutheran orthodoxy, he fought against Pietism.

239   "King Stanislaus." Leszcsynski, Stanislaus (1677-1766), King of Poland.

242   "Marpurg." Benda's autobiography was evidently requested by Mar-

NOTES

purg for publication in his *Historisch-kritische Beyträge etc.*, and later used by Hiller (see below, p. 245). The manuscript was in the possession of Benda's son-in-law, J. F. Reichardt, who submitted it to Ledebur through Koepke (see below, p. 245). Ledebur was responsible for its publication in the *Berliner Musikzeitung*, where it appeared in 1856.

243 "Queen of England." The wife of George III, Charlotte of Mecklenburg-Strelitz.

244 "strong things." Translation of *"starke sachen." "Stark"* is the German equivalent of the Italian word *"grosso,"* i.e., the whole phrase means full-voiced compositions.

245 "Koepke," Rudolph (1813-1870). Literary historian. Cf. Bernhardi, W., *Rudolph Koepke*, in *Koepke's Kleinen Schriften*, 1872.

245 "Reichardt," Johann Friedrich (1752-1814). The famous composer and writer about music. He worked closely with both Goethe and Schiller.

245 "Ledebur," Carl Freiherr von. Editor of the *Tonkünstler-Lexikon Berlin's*, 1861.

THE LIFE OF CHRISTIAN GOTTLIEB NEEFE

248 "Tag," Christian Traugott. Accord. to Eitner, *op. cit.*, cantor in Glauchau *im Schönburgischen*. I am unable to determine whether he was a relative of Christian Gotthilf Tag (1735-1811), about whom Rochlitz wrote in *Für Freunde der Tonkunst*, III.

248 "Marpurg," Friedrich Wilhelm (1718-1795). *"Anleitungen"* refers to his *Anleitungen zum Klavierspielen* (1755), *Systematische Einleitung in die musikalische Setzkunst* (1757), *Kritische Einleitung in die Geschichte etc.* (1759), and *Anleitung zur Musik überhaupt und zur Singkunst besonders* (1763).

248 "Bach," Carl Philipp Emanuel (1714-1788). His *Versuch über die Wahre Art das Clavier zu spielen* (1753) has been translated into English by W. J. Mitchell, New York, 1949.

248 "Hiller," Johann Adam (1728-1804). One of the pioneers in the creation of the German *Singspiel* and an outstanding writer about music.

248 "hypochondria." See the note to *Malum Hypocondriacum*, p. 230 *supra*.

249 "Crusius," Christian August (1715-77). One of the most important philosophers of his time. He had a far-reaching influence on Lambert, M. Mendelssohn, and the young Kant. Cf. Marquardt, *Kant und Crusius*, 1885; Festner, *C. A. Crusius als Metaphysiker*, 1892.

249 "Gellert," Christian Fürchtegott (1715-69). A famous German poet, representative of the rational element in German pre-classical poetry, and an opponent of the bombastic Baroque style. Cf. May, K., *Das Weltbild in Gellert's Dichtung*, 1928.

249 "Gessner," Salomon (1730-88). Swiss poet and painter, representative

NOTES

of the idyllic and "prettified" *empfindsamer* style. Cf. Wölfflin, *Salomon Gessner*, 1889.

251 "Engel," Johann Jakob (1741-1802). Director (1787-94) of the royal theater in Berlin and the author of popular books on philosophy. His novel, *Herr Lorenz Stark* (1801), was famous in his day. Engel wrote the libretto for *Die Apotheke*.

252 "Bonnet," Charles (1720-93). French-Swiss scientist and philosopher who tried to reconcile the Christian doctrine of revelation with the requirements of reason. Cf., Bonnet, *Oeuvres completes d'histoire naturelle et de philosophie* (1779-88).

252 "Mendelssohn," Moses (1729-86). Grandfather of Felix, a famous philosopher of Jewish extraction. Mendelssohn was a propagator of rationalism and instrumental in the movement toward emancipation of the Jews. Lessing immortalized him in his play, *Nathan der Weise*.

252 "Spalding," Johann Joachim (1714-1804). Lutheran theologian. He exerted a great influence on Lavater and Schleiermacher. Cf. Nordmann, H., *Die Theologie J. J. S.*, 1929.

252 "Jerusalem," Karl Wilhelm (1747-72). His suicide over unrequited love was utilized by Goethe in his *Werther*. Cf. his *Philosophische Aufsätze*, pub. by Lessing in 1776.

254 "Home," Henry (Lord Kames) (1696-1782). English philosopher, belonging to a group of moral philosophers who assumed a "moral sense" as the basis of their ethical system, plus psychic phenomena, ideas which played an important part in their aesthetic theory. His *Elements of Criticism* were translated into German by Meinhard in 1765.

254 "Sulzer," Johann Georg (1720-79). Philosopher and aesthetician whose *Allgemeine Theorie des schönen Künste* (1771-4) exerted a great influence on his contemporaries. The musical articles in this encyclopedia were by Kirnberger and J. A. P. Schultz.

254 "Weisse," Felix Christian (1726-1804). German playwright and poet. He exerted a great influence on the development of the German *Singspiel*, modeling his libretti after English and French examples. Many of his *Singspiele* were set to music by his contemporaries. Cf. Schletterer, *Das deutsche Singspiel*, 1863; Minor, *C. F. Weisse und seine Beziehungen zur deutschen Litteratur des 18ten Jahrh.*, 1880.

254 "Garve," Christian (1742-98). Philosopher and translator of English philosophical writings. Cf. *C. Garve's Moralphilosophie und seine Stellungnahme zu Kants Ethik*, Erlanger diss., 1905, by Paul Müller.

254 "Oeser," Adam Friedrich (1717-99). Artist, pupil of Bibiena and Donner. From 1759, director of the Leipzig *Kunstakademie*. He was an opponent of the Baroque style and a defender of classicism. Goethe was a pupil of his. Cf. Dürr, *A. F. Oeser*, 1879.

254 "Bause," Johann Friedrich (1738-1814). Engraver; member of the *Kunstakademie* in Leipzig.

255 *"Woechentliche Nachrichten und Anmerkungen."* A. Einstein, in his edition of Neefe's autobiography in the series *Lebensläufe deutscher Musiker* (page 26), points to the fact that Hiller published two instrumental pieces (1767), a three-voiced sacred ode (1767), and two sonatinas (Ab and Bb, 1768), by Neefe in this publication.

NOTES

256 The "contributions to various journals" include an essay, *Ueber die musikalische Wiederholung* in *Das deutsche Museum* (1776) ; and the *Musikalische Nachrichten von Münster und Bonn* in the *Berlinische Musikalische Zeitung*, No. 38, ed. by Spazier. (See below, footnote to page 263, for the article on Beethoven which appeared in Cramer's *Magazin*.) Cf. Schiedermair, *Der junge Beethoven*.

257 "Seiler" (Seyler). Seiler's troupe played (1771-4) in Weimar at the *Wilhelmsburg* before it burned. Afterwards, the troupe played in Gotha, and in Leipzig in 1776. Seiler's *Kapellmeister*, Anton Schweitzer, composed Wieland's *Alceste* for the company.

Concerning Hiller's activities in connection with Seiler, cf. Calmus, G., *Die ersten deutschen Singspiele von Standfuss und Hiller*, 1908; and Hiller's autobiography in Einstein, A., *op. cit.*, pps. 25, 35.

258 "Demoiselle Zink." Neefe's wife; accord. to the *Theaterkalender*, played the role of mother in various plays given in 1784.

259 "Grossmann-Hellmut" and "Bondini." Two important theatrical troupes. The latter, together with the troupe of Guardasoni, played in Prague, Dresden, etc., being instrumental in the performance of Mozart's *Don Giovanni, Le Nozze di Figaro,* and *La Clemenza di Tito* in Prague. As the *Theaterkapellmeister* under Grossman, Neefe received only 700 Gulden.

262 "Max Friedrich" von Königsegg-Aulendorf (1761-84). The political affairs of the Archbishopric during his rule devolved more and more into the hands of Baron von Belderbusch.

262 "Countess von Hatzfeld." She was a patron of music and a gifted singer and performer on the *Clavier*. Cf. Schiedermair, *op. cit.*

262 As "court organist" he received a salary of 400 Gulden which was reduced by half after the beginning of the reign of Maximilian Franz, but soon thereafter reinstated after two "*Promemorias.*" He was blamed by members of the Electoral *Kapelle* for Calvinism and inadequacy as an organist.

263 This "vicar" was none other than Beethoven. Neefe wrote about him in Cramer's *Magazin*, Mar. 2, 1783:

"Louis von Beethoven, son of the tenor singer mentioned, a boy of eleven years and of most promising talent. He plays the clavier very skillfully and with power, reads at sight very well, and—to put it in a nutshell—he plays chiefly "The Well-Tempered Clavichord" of Sebastian Bach, which Herr Neefe put into his hands. Whoever knows this collection of preludes and fugues in all the keys—which might almost be called the *non plus ultra* of our art— will know what this means. So far as his duties permitted, Herr Neefe has also given him instruction in thorough-bass. He is now training him in composition and for his encouragement has had nine variations for the pianoforte, written by him on a march—by Ernst Christoph Dressler—engraved at Mannheim. This youthful genius is deserving of help to enable him to travel. He would surely become a second Wolfgang Amadeus Mozart were he to continue as he has begun." Thayer-Krehbiel, *Ludwig van Beethoven*, 1921, I, p. 69.

JOHANN BAPTIST SCHENK'S
AUTOBIOGRAPHY

PAGE

Schenk's autobiography, accord. to G. Adler, was written on 18 pps., 8vo, in a very distinctive hand. This manuscript, in the form of a letter, was sent to Aloys Fuchs (1799-1853), in whose possession it remained for a long while. Fuchs, a Viennese musician and collector of musical materials, also had a fragment concerning Beethoven in his collection which was copied by Otto Jahn and later published by Thayer in the second ed. of his Beethoven biography. After Fuchs' death his collection was scattered to the four corners of the world. The letter contains a handwritten annotation by Fuchs, saying that "the author of these lines, J. Schenk, was a friend of mine for many years, and died in Vienna, Dec. 29, 1836."

265   "November 30, 1761." Schenk is in error here. We know from biographical research that he was born sometime in 1753, and baptized on Nov. 30, 1753. Consequently, he was 77 years old at the time he wrote this sketch. He died on Dec. 29, 1836.

265   "Tomaselli." Possibly "Gioseffo" Tomaselli, a tenor and teacher in Salzburg. Cf. Eitner, *op. cit.*

266   "Stoll," Anton. A well-known friend of Mozart, for whom he wrote his *Ave Verum Corpus* (K. 618) in Baden. Stoll was often the butt of Mozart's jokes.

"Gellert." See the footnote to p. 249 *supra.*

267   "Wagenseil," Georg Christof (1715-1777). Pupil of J. J. Fux. One of the most important forerunners of the Viennese classical school.

267   "Fux," Johann Joseph. See the footnote to p. 179 *supra.*

268   "Hasse," Johann Adolf (1699-1783). One of the most prolific and influential operatic composers of the 18th century. His wife was the famous Faustina-Bordoni. See Quantz' autobiography, p. 302 below.

268   "Galuppi," Baldassare (*Il Buranello*) (1706-1785). One of the most important operatic composers of his time.

268   "Gallus" (r. Mederitsch), Johann (1755-1835).

268   "Salesian convent for women." The order of the B. M. V. Mary, founded in 1610 by Francisco de Sales.

269   "Kees," Franz Bernhardt von (d. 1795). Vice president of the Court of Appeals. He was one of the great patrons of music at that time, and the concerts which he gave twice weekly in his home in Vienna were attended by such musicians as Haydn, Mozart, Dittersdorf, Albrechtsberger, etc. Cf. Gyrowetz, *Autobiography*, 1848; Gräffer, *Kleine Wiener Memoiren und Wiener Dosenstücke*, Munich, 1918.

269   "Hofmann," (Hoffmann) Leopold (*ca.* 1730-1793). As the *Kapellmeister* of St. Stephen's he was Mozart's superior in 1791. Hoffmann was one of the most prolific church composers of his times, and also an important symphonist, a representative of the Viennese preclassical style. Haydn had a poor opinion of him.

269   "Swieten," Baron Gottfried von (1734-1803). Son of the personal physician of Maria Theresia, Gerhardt van Swieten. As director of the Imperial Library in Vienna he gave the ill-famed order to destroy a great part of the library, mostly incunabula. Musically he

NOTES

performed a very important service by introducing the works of Handel and J. S. and C. P. E. Bach in Vienna.

269   "lauretanian litany." Presumably the one preserved in manuscript at Klosterneuburg.

269   "Mariazell." Presumably "Klein Mariazell," the location of a Benedictine abbey and pilgrim's shrine in lower Austria.

270   "Blumauer," Aloys (1755-98). A prominent Free Mason, although he was originally a Jesuit father. As a poet he was a representative of the rationalist movement of the 18th century, and an imitator of Wieland and Bürger.

270   "Goethe." The *Singspiel* referred to is *Ervin und Elmire,* preserved in manuscript in the library of the *Gesellschaft der Musikfreunde,* Vienna.

270   "Michaelis," Johann Benjamin (1746-1779). Viennese poet who wrote in the style of Wieland.

270   "Muellner," (Gollenhofer) Josepha (1769- after 1823). Eitner, *op. cit.,* gives her first name erroneously as "Johanna." Accord. to Köchel, *op. cit.,* from 1811-23 she was a harpist in the Imperial *Kapelle* in Vienna. Four concertos by Schenk for the pedal harp are preserved in the library of the *Gesellschaft der Musikfreunde* in Vienna, dated 1784-8. Cf. Wurzbach, *op. cit.*

272   "Gellinek," Abbé Joseph (1758-1825). Gellinek was on friendly terms with Mozart, who got him a position as court chaplain and musician with Count Kinsky. In 1795 he entered the service of Prince Esterhazy, in Eisenstadt, and remained there until his death.

275   "Beethoven and Gellinek had some kind of quarrel." In Carl Czerny's *Autobiography* we read that Gellinek told Czerny's father that he was once invited to compete in improvisation with a "strange newcomer" (Beethoven), whereupon he failed miserably. What the later quarrel between Beethoven and Gellinek was about we do not know.

275   "Albrechtsberger," Johann Georg (1736-1809). Famous theoretician, composer, and teacher.

276   "Salieri," Antonio (1750-1825). Famous operatic composer. His animosity toward Mozart became proverbial.

277   *"Der Dorfbarbier."* The autograph is dated 1796. Published in *DTOe,* by Robert Haas. It is the one operetta by Schenk still performed today.

277   "Weidmann," Joseph. He was also the librettist of the *Dorfbarbier.*

278   *"Der Fassbinder"* was performed in 1802. The aria, *Ich war auch ein Bürschl* is printed in Haas, *Wiener Cömodienlieder aus drei Jahrhunderten,* 1924.

279   *"Die Huldigung."* The text is by Hölty.

279   *"Der Mai."* A cantata for soli, chorus, and orchestra. Both these cantatas, together with *Die Schäferstunde* (1779) and *Das traute Stündchen der Liebe* (1779) are found in the library of the *Gesellschaft der Musikfreunde.*

THE LIFE OF JOHANN JOACHIM QUANTZ, AS SKETCHED BY HIMSELF

PAGE

280   Quantz was baptized on Feb. 6, 1697. Concerning biographical details, cf. Nagel, W., *Miscellanea, Monatshefte für Musikgeschichte,* 29, 1897; Raskin, A., *J. J. Quantz, sein Leben und seine Kompositionen,* diss., Cologne, 1923; and Schäfke, K., *Quantz als Aesthetiker,* in the *Archiv für Musikwissenschaft,* 6, 1924, pps. 213ff.

281   "German bass violin." An instrument combining features of both the bass violin and the 'cello, with 5 or 6 strings. It is now obsolete.

281   "Quantz," Justus. He became, in 1689 or 1690, a municipal musician in Merseburg.

282   *"flute à bec"*—recorder.

282   "Kiesewetter," (Johann Friedrich?). Accord. to Kahl, W., *Selbstbiographien deutscher Musiker,* 1948, *musicus instrumentalis* among the town musicians of Merseburg. From 1707 until his death in 1712, organist at St. Maximi in Merseburg.

283   "Telemann," Georg Philipp (1681-1767). Famous composer, contemporary of Bach and Handel.

283   "Hofmann," Melchior (d. 1715). Successor of Telemann at the New Church in Leipzig and as director of the *collegium musicum.* Cf. Gerber, *op. cit.;* Mattheson, J., *Grundlage einer Ehrenpforte,* new ed., 1910, pps. 117ff.

283   "Heinchen" (Heinichen). See the footnote to p. 207 *supra.*

283   "Biber," Heinrich Franz. See pps. 17ff. *supra.*

283   "Walter," Johann Jakob (b. 1650). Chamber musician at the Saxon Electoral court, and later (1688) Italian secretary at the Electoral court in Mainz. Together with Biber and Westhoff, representative of a school of violin composition that demanded great virtuosity, with double stops, high positions, etc.

283   "Albicastro" (Italianized name of Heinrich Weissenburg). A military officer during the War of the Spanish Succession, he published a number of trios and violin sonatas. Concerning Biber, Walter, and Albicastro, cf. Moser, A., *op. cit.;* Beckmann, G., *Das Violinspiel in Deutschland vor 1700,* 1918.

284   "Bischofswerde." Near Bautzen in Lusatia.

284   "Radeberg." Also near Bautzen, on the edge of the Dresden Heath. Concerning the fire, cf. Mörtzsch, O., *Kleine Chronik von Radeberg,* 1912.

285   "Schalle," Georg (1679-1729). Cf., Eitner, R., *Monatshefte für Musikgeschichte,* 10, p. 128.

286   "Heine" (Heyne), Gottfried (d. 1738). Municipal musician in Dresden. Cf. Nagel, *Miscellanea, Monatshefte für Musikgeschichte,* 29, p. 73ff.

287   *"Kunstpfeifer."* The *Kunstpfeifer* was a municipal musician, but in contrast to the *Bierfiedler,* one of a higher social rank. Cf. Haas, R., *Aufführungspraxis der Musik,* 1931, pps. 208ff.

287   "Volumier," Jean-Baptiste (1677-1728). In 1706, Volumier entered the service of the Saxon Elector in Dresden as concertmaster. He was credited with the introduction of Lully's "orchestral discipline" in Dresden. Cf. Terry, C. S., *J. S. Bach,* 1929.

NOTES

287   "Pisendel." See the footnote to p. 222 *supra*.

287   "Veracini," Francesco Maria (1684-1750). Veracini achieved a great reputation as a violinist and composer of sonatas for this instrument.

287   "Hebenstreit," Pantaleon (1669-1750). Violinist and dancing teacher. He was also the inventor of the "Pantalon," the name being given to the instrument—after Hebenstreit's own first name—by Louis XIV. In 1705 he made a tremendous sensation playing this instrument in Paris. In 1714 he was appointed as chamber musician and "pantalonist" in the *Kapelle* of August the Strong at an unusually high salary. He was also the director of Lutheran church music in the court chapel. His instrument was somewhat like a dulcimer, and played by means of two small hammers. Only two parts could be played at one time.

287   "Weiss, Sylvius Leopold" (*ca.* 1684-1750). He was the last great lutenist, celebrated as an unsurpassed master on this instrument. Cf. Volkmann, *S. L. Weiss,* 1907.

287   "Richter," Johann Christian (1689-1744).

287   "Buffardi" (Buffardin), Pierre Gabriel (1690-1768). From 1715-49, first flautist in the Dresden *Kapelle.* Later, he became Quantz' teacher on the flute. For a while he was in Constantinople, where he met and taught Johann Jakob Bach, the brother of Johann Sebastian. Cf. Spitta, *op. cit.,* I. p. 217.

288   "Vienna." While in Vienna Quantz studied counterpoint with Zelenka.

288   "Schmidt," Johann Christoph (1664-1728). Bach thought enough of him to copy his motet, *Auf Gott hoffe ich.* Cf. Mattheson, J., *Critica Musica,* 1722, p. 266.

288   "Polish Kapelle," identical with the so-called *Kleine Kammermusik,* was established in 1717. Its director was Giovanni Alberto Ristori (1692-1753).

291   "Pistocchi," Francesco Antonio (1659-1726). *Ca.* 1696, said to have been the *Kapellmeister* of Margrave Friedrich III of Anspach. From there he went to Vienna. Cf. Busi, *G. B. Martini,* 1891, p. 183.

291   "Torelli," Giuseppe (1660-1708). Composer of violin concertos and *concerti grossi.* From 1698-99, *Kapellmeister* in Anspach, which position he left to travel—evidently in the company of Pistocchi—to Vienna.

291   The operas, *Ascanio overo gli odi delusi dal sangue,* and *Teofane,* were given in Dresden in 1718 and 1719 respectively.

291   "Lotti," Antonio (1667-1740). From 1717-19 in Dresden. One of the outstanding composers of the Venetian school. Cf. Spitz, C., *A. Lotti,* diss., Munich, 1918; Fürstenau, M., *Zur Geschichte der Musik und des Theaters am Hofe zu Dresden,* 1861, pps. 106ff.

291   "Bernardi," Francesco (*ca.* 1695-1740). Famous castrato, known as Senesino, a name likewise applied to Tenducci, who was born in the same city (Siena). He began his career as a mezzo-soprano, his voice later shifting to the alto range. Later, he went to London, where he worked with Handel.

291   "Berselli, Matteo." Soprano, who also went to London, where he was called "Bercelli."

291   "Lotti," Santa Stella. She came to Dresden from Mantua.

NOTES

292 "Tesi." See the footnote to p. 167 *supra;* and Dittersdorf's *Life,* pps. 167ff. *supra.*

292 "Durestanti," Margherita. In 1709 she sang the title role in Handel's *Agrippina.* She, together with Senesino, was later called by Handel to London.

292 "Hesse," Johanna Elizabeth (neé Döbricht). She and her two sisters were singers at the Leipzig opera. She and her husband, Ernst Christian Hesse, were both invited to participate in the Dresden festivities. Cf. Gerber, *op. cit.*

292 "tempo rubato." The term was first established by P. F. Tosi in his *Opinioni de' cantori antichi e moderni,* 1723. This method of singing was little understood by the Germans at the time. Cf. Kamienski, L., *Zum Tempo Rubato* in *Archiv für Musikwissenschaft,* I, 1918, p. 115f.

294 "*Costanza e Fortezza.*" See the footnote to p. 209 *supra.* (The author has in his possession a list of the performers who traveled with the *Hofkapelle,* and where they were quartered in Prague, which he intends to publish at a future date.)

295 "Caldara," Antonio (1670-1736). Famous 'cello virtuoso and composer.

295 "Ambreville," Rosa, the wife of the 'cellist Giovanni Peroni; and Eleonora Borosini, the wife of Francesco Borosini. Cf. Nettl, *Musik-Barock in Böhmen und Mähren,* p. 16.

295 "Orsini." See the footnote to p. 210 *supra.*

295 "Carestini," Giovanni (1705-1760). Also called "Cusanino." One of the great castrati, a pupil of Bernacchi. He was particularly appreciated by Hasse. Cf. Burney, *A General History of Music,* 1776. p. 307.

295 "Braun" (Praun), Christoph (d. 1772).

296 "Piani, Giovanni Antonio (ca. 1685-1760). From 1721-40, first violinist in the Imperial *Kapelle.*

296 "Conti," Francesco (1682-1732). Whether Ignazio Conti (1699-1759) was his son or not cannot be determined. Mattheson, in the same article cited by Quantz, refers to the highly descriptive style of Francesco, a style which evidently displeased him.

297 "Hartig," Ludwig Joseph Freiherr von. From 1715-17, director of the Prague Music Academy. Cf. Nettl, *Musik-Barock in Böhmen und Mähren,* 1927; Mattheson, *op. cit.,* p. 102f.

297 "Tartini." Concerning his stay in Prague, cf. Dounias, M., *Die Violinkonzerte Giuseppe Tartini's,* 1935.

298 "Locatelli." See the footnote to p. 173 *supra.*

298 "Piantanida," Giovanni (1705-ca. 1782). Cf. Burney, C., *The Present State of Music in France and Italy etc.,* 1771.

298 "Schönborn," Prince-Bishop Johann Philipp Franz von (1719-24). (After Kahl, W., *op. cit.*) His brother was Lothar Franz von Schönborn (1695-1729). Concerning musical conditions in Würzburg, cf. Kaul, O., *Geschichte der Würzburger Hofmusik im 18. Jhr.,* 1924, pps. 11ff.

298 "Chelleri" (Keller, Cheler, or Kellery), Fortunato. Born 1668 (after Eitner, *Quellenlexikon),* or 1686 (after Kahl, *op. cit.*). He died in 1757.

298 "Count von Lagnasco." Peter Robert Taparelli, Count Lagnasco, was

NOTES

the Saxon ambassador in Rome. In 1721 he married Countess Josepha Thun, neé Waldstein, his second wife.

300 "Gasparini," Francesco (1668-1727). The work cited by Quantz is the *L'armonico pratico al cimbalo*, Venice, 1708. It is one of the most important manuals on accompaniment. (Cf. Haas, *op. cit.*, p. 200.) Quantz is in error, of course, if he believed that Gasparini invented the *recitativo accompagnato*. He is also in error concerning the age of Gasparini, who was much younger than Quantz indicates.

300 "Polignac," Cardinal Melchior de. Archbishop of Auch from 1661-1741. From 1725, in Rome, where he proved to be a great patron and lover of the arts.

301 "Pittoni," Ottavio (1657-1743). A prolific church composer who combined the strict "Palestrina style" with homophonic and even operatic elements. His tremendous output was the result of his opinion that his works should be performed at no other church. Some of his psalms and motets are written for 36 voices. Cf. Fellerer, *Der Palestrina Stil und seine Bedeutung in der vokalen Kirchenmusik des 18. Jhr.*, 1929.

301 "Bencini," Pietro Paolo (d. 1755). Cf. Fellerer, *op. cit.*, p. 199.

302 "Montanari," Francesco (d. 1730). Schering, in his *Geschichte des Instrumentalkonzerts*, 1927, 102f., defends him against Wasielewski, pointing to the finesse of his minuet-allegros.

302 "Scarlatti," (Domenico). Called "Mimo" by Quantz.

302 "Sarri" (Sarro), Domenico (1678-?). Representative of the first Neapolitan school.

302 "Vinci," Leonardo (1690-1730). Representative of the first Neapolitan school. Composer of both *opere serie* and *buffe*.

302 "Farinelli." See the footnote to p. 168 *supra*.

302 "Strada," Anna Maria. Famous as one of Handel's singers.

302 "Tesi." The performance of male roles by women was very frequent in the Baroque era. Others who did the same thing were Durestanti and Cuzzoni. These same anti-naturalistic ideas of the late Baroque were responsible for the importance of the castrato.

302 "Scarlatti," Alessandro (1659-1725). The most famous and chief representative of the first Neapolitan school. In previously discovered records he is frequently called "Barone." Cf. Benedikt, *Das Königreich Neapel*, 1927.

302 "Hasse," Johann Adolph (1699-1783). Representative of the late Neapolitan school, and the husband of Faustina-Bordoni. Accord. to Benedetto Croce, *I teatri di Napoli* (1891), a *favola boschereccia* "*Florinda*" by Hasse was performed in 1725, with Tesi, Farinelli, Vico, and Guglielmini.

303 "Mancini," Francesco (1679-1739). Member of the first Neapolitan school.

303 "Leo," Leonardo (1694-1744). Member of the first Neapolitan school.

303 "Feo," Francesco (1685-1745). Member of the first Neapolitan school.

303 "Franchischello." See the footnote to p. 213 *supra*.

304 Accord. to an anecdote told by Marpurg and repeated by Gerber, Quantz had to leave Naples as the result of a jealous quarrel with the Spanish ambassador. It seems that they both courted a certain *marchesa*, a pupil of Quantz, and that the ambassador threatened to

NOTES

shoot Quantz as they drove in his coach through the city. This anecdote has not been verified.

304 "Allegri," Gregorio (1582-1652). His *Miserere* was still performed, at that time, in its original version, i.e., in the so-called *falso bordone* style. It was rearranged in 1738 and 1770. Mozart, Mendelssohn, and others heard this famous piece, but not in its original version. Evidently, Quantz was not too impressed with what he heard.

304 "Dornick," Count Franz Ernst von Salm-Reifferscheid (1698-1770). A patron of music who gathered together a huge collection of scores and instruments.

305 "Pinacci," Giovanni Battista (*ca.* 1720-1760). He came to London with Strada in 1730, where he worked with Handel.

305 "Perfetti," Bernardino (1681-1747). Celebrated improviser, crowned poet laureate on May 13, 1725. Cf. Nettl, *The Other Casanova*, p. 13.

305 "Erdmann," Ludwig. *Ca.* 1730, oboist in Lucca. Cf. Nerici, *Storia della musica in Lucca*, 1879.

305 "Porpora," Nicola Antonio (1686-1766). One of the late composers of the Neapolitan school. Spectacular virtuosity is the main distinguishing feature of his operas.

305 "Nicolino" (Grimaldi). From 1708 in London, where he was a great success in Handel's *Rinaldo*. He had a beautiful voice, and he was acclaimed as an excellent actor. Addison, in his *Spectator*, recommends him as a model for tragedians. Cf. Chrysander, *G. F. Handel*, I, p. 272f.

305 "Romanina," Marianna Benti-Bulgarelli Garberini, called "Romanina." (d. *ca.* 1734). In 1725 she came to Prague with the impressario, Denzio, probably from Dresden. In Prague she performed the main role in Bioni-Fioré's *L'Innocenza giustificata*. Cf. Teuber, *Geschichte des Prager Theaters*, 1883, I, p. 119.

306 "Laurenti," Girolamo Nicolo (d. 1752). His father, Bartolomeo, was said to have been the teacher of Corelli. Cf. Wasielewski, *Die Violine und ihre Meister*, 1883; Moser, A. *op. cit.*

306 Accord. to Wiel, T. A., *I teatri musicali di Venezia nel settecento* (1897), the following operas by Vivaldi were performed at that time: *Cunegonda, La fede tradita e vindicata*, and *Farnace*. Eitner (*op. cit.*) also mentions *Dorilla in Tempe*.

306 "Madonis," Ludovico. In 1726, orchestral conductor in Breslau. In 1729, member of the *Violons du Roi* in Paris. Later, he went to Russia, where he became concertmaster in St. Petersburg (1731 or 33). Cf. Mooser, *Les annals de la musique en Russie à 18 Siècle*, 1948; Nettl, *op. cit.*, p. 140; Wasielewski, *op. cit.*, p. 188.

306 "San Martino," Giuseppe (1693-1770). Brother of Giovanni Battista Sammartini, one of the earliest Italian symphonists. At the time of his death he was director of chamber music to the Prince of Wales.

306 "Marcello," Benedetto (1668-1739). Famous composer of the *Estro poetico-armonico* (1724), an archaic setting of the psalms. Also, world-famous author of the polemic against the abuses of opera, *Il teatro alla moda* (1722).

306 "Albinoni," Tommaso (1674-1745). At that time, a famous operatic composer, although now he is known more for his solo concertos and his *concerti grossi*. He had some influence on Bach and Handel.

336

306 "Apollonia," Anna Maria. She appears in Pöllnitz (*Lettres*, 1747) as *la première chanteuse*. She was a pupil of Tartini.

307 "Angeletta" (Angioletta). She was an acquaintance of Heinichen, whom she introduced to the Saxon Elector during his stay in Vienna in 1717.

308 "Pasi," Antonio. Born (accord. to Fétis, *op. cit.*) in 1696, or (accord. to Gerber, *op. cit.*) in 1710. Gerber praises his ability to sing an adagio, and says that he was particularly good at singing small ornaments and *tempo rubato*.

309 "San Martino" (Sammartini), Giovanni Battista (1701-1775). One of the pioneer composers in the field of the symphony. Cf.Torrefranca, *Le origini de la sinfonia*, 1913; Sondheimer, R., *G. B. Sammartini*, in the *ZfMw*, 3, 1920, pps. 83ff.

309 "Le Claire," Jean Marie (1697-1764). One of the outstanding violinists of the French school of the 18th century. He was murdered in Paris.

309 "Somis," Giovanni Battista (called "Ardy") (1686-1763). A pupil of Corelli and Vivaldi, and the founder of the Piedmontese school of violinists which developed violinists like Le Claire, Pugnani, etc. Cf. Wasielewski, *op. cit.*, pps. 97ff.; Moser, A., *op. cit.*, pps. 242ff.

309 "Somis," Antonia Christiana. Daughter of Giovanni Battista Somis. After marrying "van Loo," she went to Paris, where she became an outstanding teacher.

310 "musical taste." Quantz conforms, in this respect, with the opinions of the Italian and German observers. His objections are practically the same as those propounded later by the encyclopedists.

310 "Antier," Marie (1687-1747); "Pelissier," Madame (1707-1749); and "Le Maure," Catherine Nicole (b. 1704). All were famous in classical roles, excelling in operas by Lully, Cambert, Colasse, Campra, Destouches, Rameau, etc.

310 "Franceour," Francois (1698-1787). Operatic and instrumental composer.

310 "Rebel," Francois (1701-75). These intimate friends wrote 10 operas together.

310 "Bonneval," Count Claude Alexandre (d. 1747). Fought with Prince Eugene against the Turks, but later joined their forces in 1729. Known as "Achmet Pascha." Concerning his musical adventures with Casanova, Cf. Nettl, *op. cit.*, p. 190.

310 Concerning "the beating of time with a big stick," cf. Schünemann, G., *Geschichte des Dirigirens*, 1914; Haas, *op. cit.*; Nettl, *op. cit.* Both Casanova and Baron Grimm criticize the bad methods of French conducting.

310 "Fortcroix," Antoine (1672-1745). A member of a distinguished family of gambists.

310 "Marais," Roland. Son of the famous gambist, Marin Marais (1656-1728).

311 "Guignon," Giovanni Pietro (1702-1774). He was one of the last of the *Rois de ménetriers* (fiddler kings). Cf. Schletterer, *Geschichte des Spielmannszunft in Frankreich und der Pariser Geigen Könige*, 1884.

311 "Battiste," Anet Jean-Baptiste, generally known as "Battiste." To-

gether with Le Claire and Guignon, founders of the French violin school.

311   "Blavet," Michel (1700-1768). For a time, also in the service of Frederick II in Rheinsberg. One of the greatest flautists of his time, and composer of the comic opera *Le jaloux corrigé* (1752).

311   "Lucas." Performed in 1726, at the *Concerts Spirituels*. Concerning musicians of the time, cf. De la Laurencie, L., *La musique de Lulli à Gluck*.

311   There are a number of works by Quantz, some of which possibly appeared in Paris, published under the name of "Quouance." Cf. Brenet, *La librairie musicale en France de 1653 à 1796*, SIMG, 1907, pps. 423ff.

311   "Le Riche," Francois (b. 1662). Well-known oboist. Telemann dedicated his *Kleine Kammermusik* (1716) to him.

312   *"Admetus."* Handel's *Admeto* played in London from Jan. 31-Apr. 18, 1727. Cf. Chrysander, *op. cit.*, pps. 697ff.

312   "Faustina." Faustina Hasse-Bordoni (1700-1781). World-famous operatic virtuoso. Cf. Niggli, *F. Bordoni-Hasse*, 1880; Högg, M., *Die Gesangkunst der Faustina Hasse*, Diss., Berlin, 1932.

312   "Cuzzoni," Francesca (1700-1770). She sang for Handel from 1722-26, at which time she was succeeded by Faustina, after their famous quarrel. In 1727 she married the composer Sandoni. Cf. Rochlitz, *op. cit.*, pps. 243ff. The famous scandal took place on June 6, 1727, during a performance of Bononcini's *Astyanax*.

313   "Castrucci," Pietro (1679-1752). He died of insanity in Dublin. He came to London with Lord Burlington, replacing Michael Christian Festing as concertmaster in Handel's orchestra. Handel had a good opinion of his abilities. He invented the *violetta marina*.

313   "Bononcini," Giovanni Battista (1665-1750). A famous operatic composer whose compositions show remarkable melodic power. Rival of Handel. Because of a famous affair, involving plagiarism of a work by Lotti, Bononcini was forced to leave London. After 1732 he lived in Paris, Vienna, and Venice.

314   "Attilio" (Ottavio Ariosti). Italian court musician in Mantua and Florence. Also, for a while, in the diplomatic service of Joseph I.

314   "Tosi," Pietro Francesco (1646-1727). A famous castrato whose vocal treatise, *Opinioni de' cantori antichi e moderni* (1723), was translated into English (Galliard, 1742) and German (Agricola, 1757).

314   "Debur" (Dubourg), Matthew (1703-1767). Famous English violinist, pupil of Geminiani. He was the successor of Kusser as master of *Her Majesty's Band of Music in Ireland*.

314   "Geminiani," Francesco (1674-1762). Famous violinist and composer of *concerti grossi*, whose treatise, *The Art of Playing on the Violin* (1731), founded a new school of violin playing. In 1725 he established in London the first masonic lodge created specifically for musicians, the *Philo-Musicae et Architecture Societas*.

314   "Festing," John (d. 1772). Flautist and oboist, performing (1727) in Handel's operas.

314   "Pembrok" (Pembroke). She was the leader of the "Cuzzonites." A letter of hers, containing references to Cuzzoni, can be found in Chrysander, *op. cit.*, II, p. 160.

BIBLIOGRAPHY

PAGE

317 "Margrave (Friedrich) of Bayreuth." The correspondence of the Margravine with her brother, Frederick II, was published by Oppeln-Bronikowski (1924). She wrote on Oct. 18, 1732, that "He (Quantz) is the God of music."

317 Many anecdotes about this marriage were told by Reichardt, Gerber, and Zelter. Cf. Nettl, *The Book of Musical Documents*, 1948, p. 78.

BIBLIOGRAPHY TO PART I

CHAPTER I
[Fuhrmann, P.], *Alt- und Neues Wien*, Wien, 1739.
Nettl, Paul, *Die Wiener Tanzkomposition in der zweiten Häfte des 17. Jahrhunderts*, in *Studien zur Musikwissenschaft*, 8.
Schwerdfeger, Josef, *Vienna Gloriosa*, Wien, 1923.

CHAPTER II
Nettl, Paul, *Heinrich Franz von Biber*, in *Sudetendeutsche Lebensbilder* Reichenberg, 1926.
———— *Zur Geschichte der Musikkapelle des Furstbischofs Karl Liechtenstein-Kastelkorn von Olmütz*, in *Musik-Barock in Böhmen und Mähren*, 1927.

CHAPTER III
Nettl, Paul, *Alte jüdische Spielleute und Musiker*, Prag, 1923.
———— *Die Prager Juden-Spielleutezunft*, in *Musik-Barock in Böhmen und Mähren*, 1927.

CHAPTER IV
Rochlitz, Friedrich, *Scheller, Eine Scene*, in *Für Freunde der Tonkunst*, II, Leipzig, 1825, pps. 356ff.

CHAPTER V
Rost, B., *Vom Meister des volkstumlichen deutschen Liedes, Franz Abt*, 1924.

CHAPTER VI
Gradenwitz, Peter, *Johann Stamitz*, Wien, 1936.
Haas, Robert, *Johann Stamitz*, in *Sudetendeutsche Lebensbilder*, Reichenberg, 1926.
Riemann, Hugo, in *Denkmäler der Tonkunst in Bayern*, III, 1; VII, 2.

CHAPTER VII
Kelly, Michael, *Reminiscences*, 1826.
Abert, Hermann, *W. A. Mozart; neubearbeitete und erweiterte Ausgabe von Otto Jahns Mozart*, Leipzig, 1923-4, 2 vols.

BIBLIOGRAPHY

CHAPTER VIII

Kahl, Willi, *Das lyrische Klavierstück Schuberts und seiner Vorgänger seit 1810*, in *Archiv für Musikwissenschaft*, III.

Nettl, Paul, *Schubert's Czech Predecessors*, in *Music and Letters*, 1941.

Tomaschek, Johann Wenzel, *Autobiography*, in *Libussa*, IV, Prag, 1845, ed. by Paul Alois Klar.

CHAPTER IX

Adler, Guido, *Musikalische Werke der Kaiser Ferdinand III, Leopold I, und Joseph I*, Wien, 1892, 2 vols.

Burney, Charles, *A General History of Music from the Earliest Ages to the Present Period*, London, 1776.

Nettl, Paul, *Das Wiener Barocklied*, Wien, 1934.

———, *Giovanni Battista Buonamente*, in *Zeitschrift für Musikwissenschaft*, IX.

———, *Zur Geschichte der kaiserlichen Hofmusik-kapelle von 1636-1680*, in *Studien zur Musikwissenschaft*, 16-19.

Smijers, Albert, *Die kaiserliche Hofmusik-kapelle von 1543-1619*, in *Studien zur Musikwissenschaft*, 6-9.

INDEX

341

INDEX

INDEX

345

INDEX

INDEX